YACHTING
MONTHLY

NORTH WEST SPAIN

CRUISING COMPANION

A yachtsman's pilot and cruising guide
to ports and harbours from
Hondarribia to Bayona

DETLEF JENS

NAUTICAL DATA LIMITED

Cover picture: Hondarribia by Andrey Urcelayeta

Photographs by Mikel Arrazola, Michael Balmforth, Anke Brodmerkel,
Detlef Jens, Juanma - Tapia, Turespaña, Turgalacia, Andrey Urcelayeta

Aerial photography by Patrick Roach

Art direction: Chris Stevens

Cruising Companion series editor: Mike Balmforth

Consultant editors: Lucinda Roch, Edward Lee-Elliott

Published by Nautical Data Ltd,

The Book Barn, Westbourne, Hampshire, PO10 8RS

First Edition

Copyright © Nautical Data Limited 2002

ISBN 1-904358-10-1

IMPORTANT NOTE
This Companion is intended as an aid to navigation only. The information contained within should not solely
be relied on for navigational use, rather it should be used in conjunction with official hydrographic data.
Whilst every care has been taken in compiling the information contained in this Companion, the publishers,
author, editors and their agents accept no responsibility for any errors or omissions, or for any accidents
or mishaps which may arise from its use.

Neither the publisher nor the author can accept responsibility for errors, omissions or alterations in this book.
They will be grateful for any information from readers to assist in the update and accuracy of the publication.

Readers are advised at all times to refer to official charts, publications and notices. The charts
contained in this book are sketch plans and are not to be used for navigation.
Some details are omitted for the sake of clarity and the scales have been chosen to allow best
coverage in relation to page size.

Correctional supplements are available upon request from the publishers whose address may be found on this page

Printed in Italy

PREFACE

I first visited Spain's Costa Verde (Green Coast) many years ago now, in winter, when we involuntarily spent far more time here than originally planned. This was due to the minor calamity of dismasting outside Bilbao in a typical Galerna, a short but vicious storm that occurs occasionally off this coast. Needless-to-say, our engine

wasn't working that day, so we were towed into the Abra de Bilbao by a friendly fisherman, who fortunately motored past; otherwise we might have been washed up against the very scenic, but in this case rather uninviting, cliffs below Cabo Villano. We were even more fortunate in that he dropped us off at the Las Arenas Yacht Club and in fact the whole incident turned out to be a blessing in disguise. While waiting for a smart new rig to arrive from the UK, we had a highly enjoyable two-month break. During that time, we not only benefited enormously from the tremendous hospitality of the yacht club, often making ourselves shamelessly at home in its opulent, almost palatial clubhouse, but we were also able to explore Bilbao itself and the wonderful Basque Hinterland as far as the wide plains of the Rioja region, most of which is described in this book.

We fell in love with this wild and, in many respects, still remote and exotic part of the world. Finally, when our new mast had at last been stepped, we cruised leisurely westwards along this coastline, marvelling at how different it was to anywhere else we would expect to find in Europe. During that unforgettable winter, we must have been the only cruising yacht for many miles around, spending virtually every night at anchor in beautiful but often shallow and treacherous river mouths or alongside old fishing boats and rustic stone piers. This is a far cry from the conditions encountered today and, during our various return visits, we have of course noticed the gradual change in the marine infrastructure. Several modern marinas have now opened up and, conveniently placed at regular intervals along the coast, all provide good facilities for yachts.

I sincerely hope that this book will help to make your cruise along this wonderful coast a truly memorable experience, both on the water and ashore.

Fair winds and happy cruising.

Detlef Jens, October 2002

ACKNOWLEDGEMENTS

Detlef Jens would like to thank the harbour masters of all those marinas referred to in the book, the boatmen of several yacht clubs and the Spanish Tourist Authority in Frankfurt for their help and support while researching this book. Special thanks go, as mentioned in the preface, to the Las Arenas Yacht Club and of course, to all fellow cruising folk, in particular to Thierry and Jean-Carl from France as well as Geraldine and Steven from the UK.

ABOUT THE AUTHOR

Detlef Jens is a yachting writer and travel journalist who has, for many years, been a regular contributor to yachting magazines in the UK and elsewhere. He has also written and translated various yachting books.

Detlef has lived in England, Germany and France as well as on his 35-foot cruising yacht, *Enterprise*, aboard which he has predominantly explored European waters while writing about his experiences along the way. Designed and built by Van Dam in Aalsmeer, Holland, *Enterprise* is a one-off, medium displacement cruising yacht with a round-bilge steel hull and wooden decks and coachroof. Detlef describes her as 'strong, simple comfortable and reliable, although not particularly fast' – in other words a near-perfect voyaging home.

CONTENTS

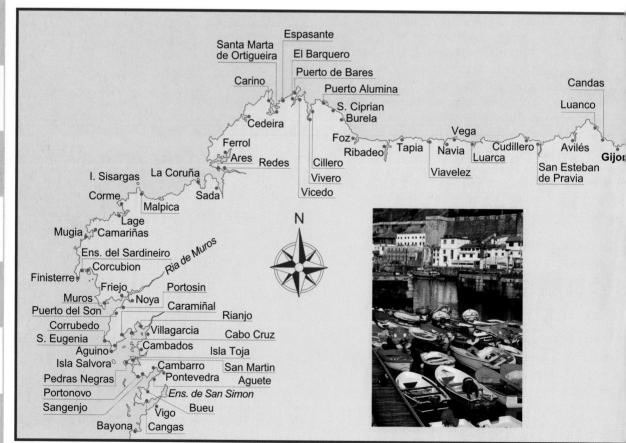

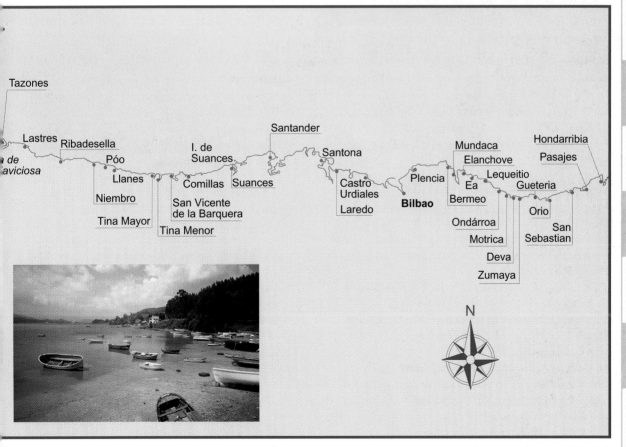

Moored in the peaceful surroundings of the Ria de Cedeira, where densely-wooded hills surround the clear, deep bay

INTRODUCTION

Costa Verde (Green Coast) is the name aptly given to the entire North Coast of the Iberian peninsula, where the land and even the sea come in endless different shades of green. All around, the hills, meadows and mountains tumble down to the water, hiding little sandy beaches in their crevices.

This is a fascinating coast: wild, rugged and romantic, and one best visited by boat.

Inland mountain ranges, most notably the Picos de Europa, isolate the northern coastal regions from other parts of Iberia. Thus, the Celts of Galicia, the Asturians, Cantabrians and Basques have preserved their particular cultures. In the Basque country, the oldest language of the western world, known as Euskara, is still widely spoken today, while the Reconquista, the fight against the Arabs who had invaded almost the whole of Iberia, began in Asturias.

This coast is steeped in history, rich in culture, scenically beautiful and has a colourful hinterland, so it is difficult to understand why this part of the world is still being ignored by so many cruising yachtsmen. It is in fact relatively easy cruising ground, as there are no off-lying dangers, the coast is normally steep-to, the tidal range is small, there are numerous harbours and anchorages and the water is clear. Of course, the usual care is needed for inshore pilotage,

and some entrances and approaches are more difficult than others, but overall this coast is not a complicated one to navigate.

It is less than 500 miles from Falmouth to any of the ports in northern Spain. Although you will have to cross the Bay of Biscay, with today's sea-going yachts and reliable weather forecasts, this passage has lost the threat which it so often held for our forebears. Reasonably accurate forecasts for three to five days, which is all it takes for a modern yacht to cover this distance, allows us to pick and choose a suitable weather window. Obviously, the crossing of Biscay still remains a serious offshore voyage with all its implications, but you shouldn't be overawed by what, in the vast majority of cases, will prove to be a very pleasant summer passage.

For the increasing number of long-term cruising folk migrating south for the winter, or may be even longer, northern Spain lies directly *en route*. Many will make a landfall in La Coruña or one of the other Galician ports around Finisterre, but most will sail past those provinces further east, missing out on some spectacular places. Cruising along the Costa Verde is among the most fascinating and exotic experiences you can have in European waters, and I would unhesitatingly recommend any yacht heading south to spend a few extra weeks doing just this.

A good look-out is required for the large number of fishing boats along the north coast of Spain

To sail there and back, as well as enjoy some time in the area, would take six weeks or more, so unless you are fortunate enough to have an extended summer holiday, you will need to consider alternative options. A change of crew is one possibility, or even leaving the boat in Spain for the winter is well worth contemplating. However, not everyone will want to go as far as the Dutch singlehander, who came into San Sebastian one fine morning to stay for a few nights, but didn't actually leave until well over two years later.

CRUISING STRATEGIES

The north coast of Spain stretches over a distance of about 350 miles or so from Hendaye, on the French border, to Finisterre. If heading further south for a long-term cruise and wanting to take in the north coast of Spain *en route*, the natural choice will be to aim for the Basque country in the east and then make your way westward along the coast.

When sailing to the Basque country, the Biscay crossing can be broken up into shorter hops, or even day trips along the French coast. Once south of La Rochelle, however, a long and inhospitable stretch of coast follows – from the mouth of the Gironde (which can be quite hair-raising in strong onshore winds against an out-flowing ebb tide) 150 miles south to Hendaye. Arcachon is about half way in between, but has a difficult entrance that might not be possible to negotiate under certain conditions, namely in strong winds from the west. If crossing Biscay in one hop from the UK or from anywhere in Brittany, you should of course pick a suitable weather window and make sure you leave the continental shelf swiftly. In heavy weather, the seas get very much steeper

along the edge of the shelf, where the ocean shallows suddenly from 4,000-plus metres to around 100 metres. This is roughly parallel to the Breton coastline and is about 80 to 100 miles offshore. If the weather threatens to deteriorate, head out past this zone as quickly as possible. Many yachts (and their crews) have suffered serious damage simply by staying in this area of shallowing water in vicious seas and heavy weather, while others, further out in the deeper ocean water, have sailed through the same conditions completely unscathed.

Crossing the Bay of Biscay should only be attempted in summer, aiming to arrive in Spain no later than August. An autumn or winter crossing is possibly foolhardy and simply asking for trouble.

As far as the landfall is concerned, nearly all of the larger harbours in northern Spain are perfectly suitable, with straightforward and well-lit approaches. One major hazard is the heavy shipping off the north-western tip of Galicia, between Finisterre and La Coruña. Further east,

Ideal cruising conditions off the Costa Verde

Settled weather near the Rio de Deva off the Basque coast

shipping is much less, although some coastal traffic will be encountered.

Fishing craft is also hazardous at times, as the modern boats tend to be quite quick and are not always noted for the quality of their look-out. Large offshore trawlers can be met virtually anywhere in Biscay, while small, often poorly-lit fishing boats are ever present along the coast.

The planning of a round trip to Biscay – one long passage there and port-hopping back or

Gijon marina is a secure place to winter your boat

vice-versa – largely depends on the time of year and the actual weather when under way. Winds can be light and variable along the coast in summer and are sometimes affected by local influences such as gusts coming down from the mountain ranges. The prevailing winds in this part of the world are westerly but, due to a low pressure area which often develops over the Iberian peninsular in summer, there is a good chance of easterly or north-easterly winds.

Coastal fog is an important factor to take into account during the summer months. Galicia, in particular, is notorious for fog, which is so thick at times that you can't even see your own bow, let alone other vessels. It consistently lingers each day until mid-afternoon, when it is dispersed by a brisk 20-25 knot wind. In these conditions it goes without saying that a radar reflector is essential, however, it is highly advisable to have either an active radar responder and/or radar installed as well; indeed, many port authorities are even considering making radar mandatory.

Crew changes can be arranged most conveniently in Bilbao (Getxo marina) or Santander, which have direct ferry (and, in the case of Bilbao, flight) connections to and from the UK, while La Coruña can be reached by air via Madrid. The timing of a possible crew change will also influence the general planning of a Biscay round trip.

If you plan to leave your boat in Spain during the winter, either ashore or in the water, there are several good options: Hendaye (France), Getxo, Zumaya, Santander, Gijon, Sada, La Coruña, Vigo and Bayona all have good, sheltered and secure marinas, most with lifting out and hard-standing facilities as well as local service companies and chandlers on hand for any maintenance and repair work.

An added incentive to leave the boat in Spain is the fact that marina charges are generally much lower than in the UK.

Rafted up at San Sebastian

FLIGHTS TO AND FROM SPAIN

Almost 30% of all international travellers to Spain arrive by air. Once in Spain, the number to call for flight information (domestic and international) is *Infor Iberia*, Tel: 913 29 57 67

For further information, you can also check the following websites:

AENA	www.aena.es
IBERIA	www.iberia.es
AVIACO	www.aviaco.es
SPANAIR	www.spanair.com
EASYJET	www.easyjet.com

DISTANCES

From Falmouth to:

Getxo	470 miles
Santander	460 miles
Gijon	440 miles
La Coruña	455 miles
Bayona	550 miles

From La Rochelle to:

Getxo	190 miles
Santander	200 miles
Gijon	250 miles

PRACTICALITIES

There is virtually no trouble with authorities and clearance procedures or other formalities, so long as you are a European citizen sailing a European registered yacht. The issue of VAT on board can be a painful one if your vessel is not registered in the EU. Indeed cruising folk from

The bustling fishing port at San Martin del Grove offers no facilities to yachts

outside the EU have had problems in this respect when staying for more than six months.

For a European yacht arriving from a member state, no formalities are necessary on entering Spain. As far as documentation is concerned, marina offices will normally require to see the ship's registration documents, the insurance policy number (only third-party insurance is mandatory in Spanish marinas, but you must carry a Spanish translation of your insurance certificate, which your insurer will provide on request), and the passport of the owner or captain. Generally speaking, Spanish officials nowadays have a rather relaxed attitude towards yachts. The bottom line is that they tend to leave you alone as long as all is well, but beware of legal and other hassle if any incident should occur, especially if involving local vessels.

Until fairly recently, a yacht cruising along the Spanish north coast would have had to be quite self-sufficient, as there were only a few harbours with any proper yacht facilities. This situation has changed quite dramatically over the past five years or so and there are now a number of modern, convenient and sheltered marinas. However, if you want to explore the many beautiful anchorages along this coast, you should have some decent ground tackle on board. Usually, a fair-sized CQR or Bruce type anchor, with plenty of chain, will do the trick, but ideally a variety of two or, better still, three different hooks should be carried, as some anchorages have thick weed. A heavy fisherman or similar type might be needed here to provide adequate holding.

Despite the increasing number of marinas along this coast, quite a few ports are still rather rustic fishing harbours, where yachts lie alongside fishing vessels or stone walls. Long warps, good fenders and a fender-board are necessary in this situation.

To cross the Bay of Biscay safely, your yacht should be well-equipped for long offshore passages, although the voyage could be broken down into day-to-day port hops, a route manageable by any yacht fit for coastal cruising in UK waters.

When sailing south after September, both boat and crew must be prepared for some gruelling conditions. Excellent books have been written about this subject, among which are *Heavy Weather Sailing* by Peter Bruce and *How to Cope with Storms* by Dietrich von Haeften. Sailing can be very tough along the northern Spanish coast in autumn and winter, with westerly gales pounding against the Galician harbours and anchorages. A heavy swell from the north-west is more or less a constant feature of this entire coastline, especially in winter, when some harbours can become impossible to enter.

Another local meteorological characteristic is the dreaded Galerna, a miniature depression that is sometimes created in the wake of a passing cold front along the north coast. A Galerna can bring wind up to gale force within minutes, creating rough seas, but seldom lasts longer than a few hours.

Provisioning is no problem at all in Spain, which offers the best of both worlds – large supermarkets for easy and convenient stocking up of the basics, as well as delightful small local shops and markets for fun-filled exploration of regional produce and specialities. The mainstream European supermarkets can be found in or close to the more significant places and all stock the sort of international food that we

Local specialities on display at Ribadeo market

The Rio Sella exemplifies the spectacular, unspoilt cruising grounds of the Costa Verde

have become so accustomed to. Needless-to-say the larger supermarkets accept credit cards, although usually a bottom spending limit is set. The big department store, El Corte Ingles, which is in every major Spanish town, also has a very good food section.

Food prices are set at the general European level, although on the whole alcohol is still very much cheaper than in the UK and the local produce is inexpensive.

Spares for yachts are harder to come by. Although several new marinas have been built, well stocked chandleries with knowledgeable staff are few and far between. Moreover most chandlers cater for the needs of the anglers and fishing boats. Also bear in mind that ordering parts from the UK can be a long and time-consuming exercise in Spain. However, most items are found in the larger cities of Santander, Gijon and La Coruña as well as in the marinas of Getxo and Zumaya. Due to the vast number of fishing boats, spares and repairs for diesel engines are relatively easy to organise in almost all ports.

Which brings me to the question of the on board energy-source for cooking. Without going in to detail on the pros and cons of various fuels, I only have two remarks to make – paraffin is getting harder to find both in the UK and in the rest of Europe, and gas is convenient if you use

the right bottles. Camping Gaz is now available virtually throughout Europe and, although slightly more expensive than other forms of bottled gas, it is simply unbeatable for convenience. Refilling strange bottles of gas requires a great amount of research, time and nerves in a foreign country (if it's possible at all) but, at least in continental Europe, an empty cylinder of Camping Gaz can be readily exchanged for a full one almost everywhere.

Language, of course, is another vital matter.

A travelift is among the facilities at the Las Arenas yacht club

Although the Spaniards are almost as chauvinistic about their language as the French, far fewer of them understand English, so a basic grasp of Spanish helps enormously. French is fairly widely spoken in most of northern Spain, particularly towards the eastern part of the north coast. A problem that can perhaps confuse the visitor is local dialects. In Galicia, Asturia, Cantabria and notably Eskadi, the inhabitants prefer their own patois, so even if you have tried to learn some basic Spanish, you may find it difficult to communicate with the people you meet there.

YACHT CLUBS

Yacht clubs in Spain, especially in the north, are somewhat different to what most sailors from other countries expect. The majority of them are based in rather palatial buildings, more akin to luxury hotels of a bygone age than to a yacht club. This is because first and foremost they are social clubs for the rich and influential, which explains why many of them are not very hospitable to foreign cruising folk in dripping oilskins and mouldy pullovers. Having said this, there are several yacht clubs which, besides their social function, are also quite active in sailing and are therefore more welcoming to yachtsmen. These include Las Arenas (Abra de Bilbao), Castro Urdiales, Bayona or La Coruña.

MARINAS

Although still comparatively undeveloped, new marinas with dedicated facilities are springing up all along the north-west coast of Spain. When I first sailed here, seven or eight years ago, we regarded the almost complete absence of any yachting infrastructure more as an attraction than a disadvantage. We didn't expect anything other than to anchor in shallow, tricky river mouths, tranquil bays or try our luck in scruffy little fishing-basins, always with the possibility of being woken up at three o'clock in the morning by the crew of a fishing boat either coming home or wanting to leave.

Of course, there is much to be said for dedicated yacht moorings and marinas, especially with the growing number of cruising boats now moving around the coast. Some of the new commercial marinas, such as Getxo, Zumaya and Hondarribia, are certainly up to northern European standards, and there are generally now enough places with modern yachting facilities along this coast to enable you to alternate these with visits to more undeveloped harbours.

Sunset at Cudillero

WEATHER, TIDES AND CHARTS

The weather along Spain's northern coast is mainly governed by the North Atlantic weather systems, thus being quite similar to conditions on the British and French Atlantic coasts. The summers are dry and warm, but not too hot, while the winters are mild and very wet.

The yearly medium temperatures for the four provinces are:

	Jan	Apr	Jul	Oct
The Basque country	4.3°C	9.3°C	18.7°C	12.9°C
Cantabria	9.7°C	11.9°C	19.3°C	16.1°C
Asturias	7.7°C	10.4°C	18.1°C	14.1°C
Galicia	10.2°C	12.1°C	18.4°C	15.7°C

It rains quite frequently, even in summer, which is why this coast is so lush and green. During the summer the showers tend to be short and sharp, while in winter, prolonged periods of grey, overcast and rainy weather will almost certainly be encountered. Coastal fog can occur during the summer (see under 'Cruising Strategies' page 7 for more information).

Winds are predominantly from the west. Inshore

while on passage. During the rainy seasons of autumn, winter and spring, some rivers can have quite forceful outflows, often overriding the tidal effects. Also, masses of flotsam will drift off the coast and river mouths in these months, including a large amount of plastic debris. In some areas fishing floats are frequently spotted, and surface drift nets can also be a hazard when motoring, so a sharp look-out is essential.

The west going current along the north coast of Spain is created by the North Atlantic current, which flows into the Bay of Biscay in its northern part and then curves south and eventually west. This can be overturned by strong prevailing westerly winds, which will create an east flowing current along the coast, mainly in winter. When crossing the Bay of Biscay, allowance should be made for the east setting current.

Most charts for this area are referenced to European Datum 1950 and our chartlets are drawn from these. The adjustment to change to WGS 84 Datum is given on all charts/chartlets. New charts, however, are now being referenced to WGS 84 Datum, so check datums carefully before plotting on or reading off a chart.

MAJOR ATTRACTIONS

With an abundance of breathtaking landscapes, Northern Spain has no shortage of culturally and historically significant places. It is less visited and less well-known than Andalucia, which is popularly thought of as being typically Spanish, although in reality its culture was largely shaped during the period of Moorish domination.

along the north coast, the winds tend to be variable, with lulls and sudden squalls descending from the mountains. Gales are frequent in winter, especially in Galicia around Finisterre. In autumn, winter and spring, beware also of the Galernas, mini-lows that quickly build in the wake of a cold front passing along the mountainous north coast of Spain and which can bring squalls of up to force eight or more within minutes. During the height of the summer, you can experience north-easterly winds, but these will be mostly light and variable.

An impressive overview of the historical Pamplona

There are three major attractions in the northern provinces, each a few miles inland from the coast: Pamplona, the Picos de Europa and Santiago de Compostela.

Pamplona is the capital of Navarre and the setting for the fiesta made famous by Ernest Hemingway.

The Picos de Europa stretch across Cantabria and Asturias and, apart from their scenic assets, offer exceptional walking, mountaineering and downhill skiing in the appropriate season.

Tidal ranges are particularly significant when entering and leaving many of the harbours and rivers along this coast. Tidal streams, however, are generally not strong, so can normally be ignored

The pilgrim city of Santiago de Compostela is famed even amongst circles normally not closely associated with the Catholic Church.

Enjoying traditional tapas at a bar in San Sebastian

For a change from scenery and culture, a visit to Spain's well-established wine growing area – La Rioja – is a must for all but the most determined abstainer.

Scattered along this beautiful coastline are some notable historic cities, where the traveller can enjoy himself and absorb the ambience. Drinking in the cool tabernas of the old quarters of San Sebastian (Donostia) or Bilbao (Bilbo), for example, helps you tune in to Iberian heritage and culture. Both these cities are vibrant with events during the summer, among which are music festivals, exhibitions and theatre performances. Bilbao also has the Guggenheim museum, which is well worth a visit if you are interested in architecture and the arts.

La Coruña is an impressive city, again exuding the history and culture of Iberia, although one of the greatest contemporary travel writers has a different view of the Galician commercial capital: 'First I must go to La Coruña which marches on the ocean like a balcony, a city of light and wind and large windows where it feels so very different from the rest of Spain, as if she belongs more to the sea than to the vast, stony mass of mainland behind her.' (Cees Noteboom).

GETTING TO PAMPLONA AND LA RIOJA

Although there's an adequate transport system from the coast to the inland areas, it takes a bit of working out and is not nearly as convenient as hiring a car (particularly as car hire in Spain is probably the cheapest in Europe). As always, its

The vibrant streets of Pamplona during the Fiesta de San Fermin

The castle at Pamplona, the capital of the ancient kingdom of Navarre

worth shopping around – tourist offices will usually furnish a list of hire companies. For more details please refer to the section on travel.

Yachtsmen can venture inland from a safe haven such as the marinas of Hendaye (for Pamplona) or Getxo (for La Rioja). Hire cars are conveniently available in both marinas. From Hendaye, the distance to Pamplona is less than 60 miles, while the Rioja plain is slightly over 60 miles from Getxo, but is still a leisurely drive away.

PAMPLONA AND THE FIESTA

Pamplona, also called Iruña, is worth visiting, whether it is fiesta time or not. Many travellers are deterred by the surroundings of this city which, despite being the industrial centre of the region, has a compact old quarter with a fun and vibrant atmosphere.

The centre of urban life here is the Plaza del Castillo, surrounded by cafés such as the Café Iruña, which was Hemingway's favourite. Sitting in the shade of one of these cafés, while the sun glares down on the square, is a particularly pleasant way to pass the time. However, more active visitors might want to wander around, looking at the sights of the city, which include the Cathedral Metropolitana, built in different stages from 1397 to the 18th century, when the finishing touches were completed.

Bang in the centre of the old quarter is the Casa Consistorial – the town hall, built here because the three different parts of the old town were continuously at war with each other from the 13th

to the 15th century. Political and ethical differences, most probably combined with sheer bloody-mindedness, were the cause of this remarkable state of affairs, so the town hall was built in 'no man's land', right in the middle of it all.

The Museo de Navarra (by the town wall near the river) has a collection of archaeological

*The **Los Encierros** is the highlight of the fiesta*

findings, as well as paintings and frescoes. A stroll along the town walls, from where you can indulge in wonderful views across the valley of the Rio Arga and the old town itself, is very enjoyable.

And then there is the fiesta: 'At noon of Sunday, the 6th of July, the fiesta exploded. There is no other way to describe it', wrote Hemingway in his novel *Fiesta – The Sun Also Rises*. The Fiesta de San Fermin, as it is called, takes place each year from the 6 – 14 July, and Hemingway's tale is the perfect way to convey the atmosphere: 'The fiesta was really started. It kept up day and night for seven days. The dancing kept up, the drinking kept up, the noise went on. Everything that happened could only have happened during a fiesta. All during the fiesta you had the feeling, even when it was quiet, that you had to shout any remark to make it heard. It was the same feeling about any action. It was a fiesta and it went on for seven days.'

The party has been going for more than 400 years and initially served to honour the patron saint of the town. Since then, much has changed. The population of Pamplona quadruples for the fiesta and excessive drinking is the norm. Be prepared to be showered in liberal quantities of wine and also beware of an alarmingly high rate of petty theft. The highlight of the fiesta however is *Los Encierros* – the running with the bulls. Every morning at eight o'clock the bulls run along a barred-off route through the old quarter chasing a mad crowd of drunken, crazy or brave (or possibly all three) people. It is seen as a test of courage to run before these aggressive animals and it is, indeed, an extremely dangerous and sometimes lethal pastime. Every year there are many victims, some of whom are seriously injured, and every once in a while someone is killed. It is probably wiser to stay behind the barriers and watch the spectacle, rather than be part of it.

Similar *Los Encierros* takes place in other fiestas: Tudela (24 – 28 July), Puente la Reina (25 – 31 July), Tafalla (15 – 20 August), Estella (beginning the Friday before the first Sunday in August), and Sanguesa (11 – 17 September).

To secure a good vantage point you have to get there at about six o'clock in the morning. However, as sleeping is out of the question during the average fiesta night anyway, this is not such a daunting prospect.

Later, inside the Plaza de Toros, amateurs can try their luck against 'fighting cows' with bandaged horns (known as *Vaquillas*), which is fun to watch. The proper bull fights start in the afternoons, for which tickets are sold out early

and then traded for excessive prices on the black market. But the fiesta is also about bands playing all night, partying in the streets and noisy fireworks – in short, the whole crazy atmosphere of the town.

The place to be is the Hotel Yoldi (Avenida Ignacio 11), where the bullfighters stay during the fiesta and where the true aficionados meet in the bar to discuss the fighting.

It is essential to book accommodation really early for the fiesta. Among the better hotels are:
Tres Reyes (Jardines de Taconera),
Tel: 948 17 32 00; Fax: 948 17 23 87

Maisonnave (Nueva 20),
Tel: 948 22 26 00; Fax: 948 22 01 66

Europa (Espoz y Mina 11),
Tel: 948 22 18 00; Fax: 948 22 92 35

Avenida (Av. De Zaragoza 5),
Tel: 948 24 54 54; Fax: 948 23 23 23

Yoldi (San Ignacio 11),
Tel: 948 22 48 00; Fax: 948 21 20 45

Leyre (Leyre 7),
Tel: 948 22 85 00; Fax: 948 22 83 18

Pamplona also boasts three restaurants awarded with a Michelin-star:

The sheltered Rioja plain is ideal for viniculture

Josetxo (Place Principe de Viana 1),
Tel: 948 22 20 97 (closed Sundays and August)

Rodero (Arrieta 3), Tel: 948 22 80 35,
(closed Sundays and 15 days in August)

Europa (in the Hotel Europa),
Tel: 948 22 18 00 (closed Sundays)

LA RIOJA

Famous for its wines, La Rioja is, after the
Balearics, the second-smallest autonomous
community (Comunidad Autonoma) of Spain. It
is made up of two distinctly different regions,
the plain of the Rio Ebro in the north and the
mountain range of the Sierra to the south, which
rises to just over 2,000 metres.

Although the capital of the province, Logrono,
is not really worth a visit, the wide plain and
vineyards certainly are. So too are the several
ancient, romantic villages, such as Laguardia,
Navarrete and Najera, which are on the way to
the pilgrim city of Santiago.

Laguardia was re-conquered from the Moors
in 923, becoming the residence of the kings of
Navarre and the capital of La Rioja in the 10th
and 11th centuries. The main attraction here is the
church of Santa Maria la Real, initially built by
King Sanchez of Navarre in 1052, although the

Sampling Rioja wines in one of the many wine centres

building we see today dates back to only 1422.
The Pantheon Real contains the graves of the
kings of Navarre and León.

This old town, the capital of the Rioja Alavesa
region, is an ancient, walled village exuding
charm and character. Just walking through the
narrow alleyways is quite an experience, as is
a visit to one of the underground wine cellars.
Assuming that an interest in wine has brought
you to this area in the first place, a visit to the
Villa Lucia Wine Centre, with its wine cellar,
museum and an interactive show explaining
important aspects of the local wine culture,
should not be missed.

This is an ideal area for cultivating vines, as
the wide plain is sheltered in the north by the
Cantabrian mountain range and by the Sierra de
la Demanda in the south. Today, the region has
just under 200 bodegas (wine producing
companies), which produce an average of nearly
200 million litres of Rioja wines each year, three
quarters of which are the celebrated reds. Less
popular but equally good in quality are the golden
Blancos (whites) and the young, fresh Claretes or
Rosados, the light and crisp rosé wines.

As far as the quality is concerned, the wines are
classified using the following system: Joven are
young, fresh wines, which probably have not seen
the insides of a wooden cask but are excellent
value as an everyday drinking wine. These are
seldom exported.

Crianza is a red wine that has to be matured in
the cask for at least a year, plus several months in
the bottle. White and rosé Crianzas, however, only

Over 200 million litres of Rioja wines are bottled each year

have to ripen in the cask for six months.

Reserva are selected wines that should mature for at least three years, one of which must be spent in the characteristic oak casks. For white and rosés, the minimum is two years of storage, with at least six months being spent in oak.

Gran Reserva is selected from the best vintages. The red will have matured for at least five years, with two years spent inside the cask, while whites and rosés will have been stored for at least four years, again with a minimum of six months in the cask.

Another hint at the quality of the wine is the origin: the Rioja region is divided into three main areas of origin (DOC). These are the DOC Rioja Baja, which produces strong but simple reds, the DOC Rioja Alavesa, the home of strong but fresh, young wines, and finally the DOC Rioja Alta, producing the majority of Reserva and Gran Reserva wines.

VITORIA-GASTEIZ

The capital of the Basque country looks rather uninspiring when approached from afar by car, as its outskirts are dominated by rather bland industrial architecture and huge blocks of flats. However, once in the heart of the city, the picture could not be more different. The historic centre of this old university town has narrow alleys and buildings dating back more than 800 years, when the King of Navarre,

Sancho The Wise, founded the city.

This centre is located slightly above the two main squares, the Plaza Virgen de la Blanca and the Plaza España. The latter, built in the late 18th century, is considered the social centre of the town and is enclosed by beautiful neo-classical buildings. The mediaeval quarter, located between here and the old cathedral, attracts most visitors to Vitoria. It is also called the Campillo and features many mediaeval houses and small palaces. Also worth a visit is the unusual Fournier, the museum of Playing Cards, which has an extensive collection. Further museums are situated in the new town, on Paseo de Fray Francisco de Vitoria, among them the Museu de Bellas Artes (Arts) in the Palacio de Agusti, which is a museum of arms and coins.

If you want to spend a night in pleasant surroundings after visiting Vitoria, then drive on towards San Sebastian (Donostia) for about nine miles, where you will find the Parador de Argomañiz. This is a wonderfully quiet and luxurious hotel in a restored Renaissance palace (Carretera N1, km 363, Tel: 945 29 32 00). Vitoria itself has numerous hotels, guesthouses and hostels, all at varying prices.

THE PRE-HISTORIC CAVES OF ALTAMIRA AND RIBADESELLA

The Cuevas de Altamira – often referred to as the Sistine Chapel of Caves – has been closed to the

The cathedral of Maria Inmaculada at Vitoria-Gasteiz

The church of San Miguel is among many historic buildings at Vitoria-Gasteiz

general public for some time now. Instead, there is a remarkable museum near the site of the original cave, which houses a replica of the real thing. Visits to the actual cave can be arranged for special groups on request, although apparently you have to apply years in advance. Those who do gain access enter through an air lock positioned in the cave entrance, which protects it from daylight and maintains a consistently low temperature and high humidity level – climatic conditions that have successfully preserved the ancient paintings up to now. Formerly, visitors who wanted to see the original cave brought with them their warmth, bacteria and curiosity, all of which gravely endangered the paintings.

The museum is located a mile or so from Santillana del Mar, which is approximately half way between San Vicente de le Barquera and Santander, making the latter's marina the best base from which to plan a visit. (See below for opening times).

The first cave with Stone Age paintings was discovered at Altamira in 1879. At the time, it almost defied belief that they were nearly 15,000 years old, for Darwin's influence had led scientists to believe that early man was ape-like and therefore incapable of mentally challenging or artistically creative acts. Thus the Altamira

paintings were immediately declared to be fakes. Only after the discovery of other Stone Age caves, whose paintings could be dated on the basis of their relationship to archaeological finds, were they finally confirmed as originals.

These cave paintings, drawn in the late Palaeolithic period, depict animals living during the last Ice Age, among which are a horse, several deer, bison and a number of abstract figures. The paintings were made using natural pigments such as yellow, red and brownish ochres as well as black manganese earth and charcoal. In places, they are engraved into the rock. For the bison in particular, the colours are graduated into such a vast array of shades that the creatures appear three-dimensional and amazingly realistic.

At the entrance to the museum is a general introduction to the various epochs of the Stone Age, its art and particularly its cave paintings.

The museum is open from June to September, Tuesday to Saturday from 0930 to 1930; Sunday 0930 to 1700. From October to May, Tuesday to Sunday from 0930 to1700. Closed Monday, as well as 1 May, 28 June, 16 August and 24, 25, 31 December. (Museo Nacional y Centro de Investigacion de Altamira. 39330 – Santillana del Mar, Cantabria, Tel: 942 81 88 15; Fax: 942 84 01 57). The museum can be best reached from

Santander by bus (direction Santillana del Mar) or by hire-car.

The caves at Ribadesella are even older than those of Altamira, although the paintings are not quite as stunning. The entrance to the Cueva de Tito Baustillo was probably closed by a landslide during the Stone Age and the cave was not rediscovered until 1968. Cut off from all outer influences, the paintings in one of the cave chambers remained virtually intact for thousands of years. They are believed to be 15,000 to 20,000 years old and depict stags, goats, deer and, above all, horses.

The caves lie on the river's west bank, a little way upstream of the harbour and town of Ribadesella, past the road-bridge. They are open from May to September, Wednesday to Sunday: 0930 – 1200 and 1500 – 1700. Entry is restricted to 375 people per day and, as this limit is quickly reached during the busy summer season, it is highly advisable to be there well before the official opening hour.

THE PICOS DE EUROPA

These mountains, rising to near alpine heights (the peaks are mostly over 2,500m), are only a few minutes drive from the coast. They stretch from east to west over a distance of about 25 miles and roughly 12 miles north to south, and form part of the Cordillera Cantabrica chain, extending all the way from the Basque country to Galicia. Be warned – the Picos generate cloud and sometimes rain, so as with the rest of the Costa Verde, dull, damp weather is not unknown. In fact, you may well not even see those lofty mountain tops.

The Picos de Europa is noted for its authentic villages

The National Park of the Picos de Europa is the largest in Europe and stretches over part of three provinces: Asturias, Cantabria and Castile-León. The Cantabrian sector is extremely popular with tourists, which means that the choice of accommodation is wider than in other, more remote parts of the mountains. Even so, during the summer it would be wise to book accommodation in advance or find a place to stay early on in the day.

The main features of this mountain area are its spectacular gorges, fast running salmon rivers and unspoiled upland villages, all interlinked by roads and footpaths offering walks of varying difficulty. Eagles can be seen soaring above this wild terrain, but you are less likely to spot the wolves, bears, wild boar and deer, which are also resident here.

The best places to leave the boat unattended for a few days if you are planning a trip to the mountains are the marinas at Santander and Gijon. These are well sheltered and offer fairly good security, unlike the two harbours closer to the mountains – Ribadesella and San Vicente de la Barquera – where leaving a boat unwatched would be imprudent, as both are busy fishing ports with no dedicated berths for yachts.

Potes is the main gateway into the mountains on the Cantabrian side. This picturesque village of ancient houses is less than 30 miles south of San Vicente de la Barquera. It can be reached by bus from Santander, as can the wonderful route from Potes to Fuente De, which winds itself upwards along the Rio Deva, rising more than 800 metres in a length of only 13 miles. Drivers should be warned that cows and horses love to linger behind the sharp corners or simply wander along the road. Two remote and romantic villages can be found along the way, Cosgaya (with several hotels and restaurants) and, even more isolated, Espinama, with only three simple but pleasant hostels.

Fuente De is busy in summer, full of activity such as riding excursions and paragliding courses, and from where a dramatic trip by cable car to El Cable (1,834 metres) is a wonderful experience for those not afraid of heights. From the top, enthusiastic hill walkers can, if suitably equipped, climb the Pena Vieja (2,618 metres). Allow roughly four hours for the round trip.

At the foot of the mountain is the Parador Rio Deva (Tel: 942 73 66 51; Fax: 942 73 66 54, closed November to Mid-March). Cees Noteboom stayed here once and wrote the following lines in *Roads to Santiago*: 'The wall facing me is as white as paper, or as white as snow. It is a Spanish wall: this is the Picos de Europa. It is May, and snow is still falling. The Parador I'm staying at lies at the foot of a steep cliff, but that sounds too cosy. Teeth of a dragon, mandibles of a god, a crest with jagged, frayed edges, scars from old wounds. These are the mountain passes and valleys of the Kings of Asturias, who changed the course of European

The mountains of Picos de Europa, only a few minutes drive from the coast

with cliffs of several hundred metres high on either side. The hiking trail leads across rickety bridges and along cliff faces above the deep gorge, so is definitely not for the faint-hearted. Sturdy and comfortable boots are a must (don't even think about wearing deck shoes on this terrain), and a torch is useful for negotiating the rather dark, wet tunnels that you will come across. Having said this, the walk is very popular in summer, when parts of it are even serviced by Land Rover taxis. The gorge emerges at the hamlet of Poncebos in Asturias, about four miles south of the village of Arenas de Cabrales.

This walk undoubtedly requires forward planning and probably a full day to achieve. It is therefore more realistic on a brief visit to tackle one of the short circular walks that are waymarked and promoted by the National Park Authority, and about which they publish excellent leaflets. (Parque Nacional de los Picos de Europa, C/Architecto Reguera 13-1°, 33004 Orviedo/www.mma.es)

Cangas de Onis is situated at the north-west corner of the Picos and is a good centre for trips into the mountains and to Covadonga. Besides being a pleasant town with a variety of hotels and restaurants, it is also strategically situated at the northern end of the Desfiladero de Beyos, another spectacular gorge that leads into the heart of the mountains and through which the headwaters of the Rio Sella begin their journey to the sea at Ribadesella. Cangas has dozens of hotels, guest-

Breathtaking views of the Picos de Europa

history and consequently of the world. That sounds intriguing, if also like an overstatement, but he who writes such things is in harmony with his surroundings. Nature in these parts plays on an immense pipe organ. The sea is 30 kilometres away to the north, the mountain soars to 3,000 metres, the granite decor of a theatre without performances, a semicircular backdrop of gaunt, rocky bluffs that make a nonsense of all else. The road ends here, and behind the unassailable walls live the eagle, the brown bear, the cock-of-the-wood (*capercailze*). The Parador is called Fuente De after the Rio Deva, which rises in the mountains above; the river has to fight its way to the sea, carving the gorges I drove through yesterday.'

The Posada de Valdeon is a small village in a similarly fantastic location, at the foot of another jagged massif, reminiscent of the Dolomites. The village is very close to the southern end of the famous gorge of Garganta de Cares, through which a spectacular five-mile rail track to Poncebos follows the Rio Cares. The road ends and the trail begins at the tiny hamlet of Cain, and accommodation is available both here and in Valdeon.

The canyon separates the Macizo Central (central massif) from the Macizo Occidental (western massif) of the Picos de Europa, houses and restaurants, as well as a helpful tourist office which publishes some useful brochures in English (Tel: 985 84 80 05/www.cangasdeonis.com).

Arenas de Cabrales is about 20 miles east of Cangas de Onis on the north flank of the central massif. It is known as the 'cheese-town', since the local speciality, *Queso de Cabrales*, is rather a special cheese made from a blend of cow, sheep and goat's milk. It is stowed away in natural caves at temperatures of around 10°C and a humidity of 90% in order to mature properly. Arenas de Cabrales has a rural air about it and offers a variety of accommodation (Tourist office: Tel: 985 84 64 84).

Not far south of Cangas de Onis is the famous canyon of Covadonga, where Don Pelayo and his men slaughtered a few Moors in 722 and was subsequently recognised by the Asturians as their king. This beautiful area is one of the most popular in the Picos de Europa, as Covadonga is where the Reconquista began and is something of a national shrine for Spaniards. The focal point is the Cueva Santa (the holy cave), which is the place where Pelayo and his people are alleged to have retired after the battle.

The two mountain lakes, Lago Enol and Lago Ercina, are about eight miles further on from here, along a winding road (served by buses). The shores of these lakes can even more easily be reached by car and get very crowded at the height of the summer season. However, a short walk along one of the many trails will soon lead to a more secluded spot. An excellent information centre gives visitors an insight into the ecology of the mountains, and nearby old mines have been preserved to show how lead, tin and other minerals were extracted.

SANTIAGO DE COMPOSTELA

The name Santiago (meaning Saint James) is derived from the town's connection with the Apostle James, who around the time of 44 BC went to north-west Spain to convert people to christianity. After returning to Palestine, he was murdered by Herodes Agrippa, who prohibited any burial. His body was therefore smuggled on to a small ship, which was driven by the currents to the Spanish coast. Here, covered in an armour of scallop shells, he was finally buried in a secret place.

It wasn't until many centuries later, in 813 AD, that a shepherd stumbled upon the grave, and on discovery of the apostle's tomb, the king had a church built in honour of Saint James. Reputedly, from then on Saint James' spirit performed many miracles and fought as Santiago Matamoros (Moor-killer) on the battlefield. Not surprisingly, his fame spread rapidly and pilgrims started to come from far and wide to pay homage, adopting the tradition of wearing a scallop shell in remembrance of him.

Thus Santiago de Compostela, grave of the apostle, became, after Jerusalem and Rome, the most important destination for Christian pilgrims. The constant seething presence of Christians in what is now the northern part of Spain, but was once formerly the kingdoms of Navarre, Aragon, León and later Castile, eventually forced Islam to retreat to the pillars of Hercules and then to Africa.

Santiago de Compostela is not the largest town in Galicia, nor the most prosperous, but it is the most impressive of the region, for it is filled with more ancient, awe-inspiring and mysterious buildings than any other city within this part of Spain. It is not surprising therefore that it, and the Pilgrim's Way, has been granted World Heritage Status by UNESCO.

Today, an old and influential university, which has a substantial student population, helps to keep the town alive, with numerous cafés and bars and many cultural events such as concerts, exhibitions and theatre. Once more I would like to quote Cees Noteboom: 'I stand and look, but the eyes that see are not mine, they belong to the

St James on the Portico of Glory, Santiago de Compostela

The town hall at Santiago de Compostela, which boasts a greater number of significant buildings than any other town in this part of northern Spain

others, to those of the past. It is their gaze, the view is their reward for walking, for risking their lives, believing, they had given all they had just to be with the saint for once in their lives, with his relics, and now they sighted the city, the towers of the cathedral, later the same day they would enter the Puerta Francigena, they would climb the steps to the cathedral, rest their hands in the hand-shaped hollow in the central column of the Portico de la Gloria which they had heard so much about, they would pray at the Apostle's grave and receive full absolution. They were different people, with the same brains thinking different thoughts.' And again: 'In old Spanish cities you are woken by church bells. Santiago is not a big city, but there are forty churches, and now and then each of them has a request or an announcement to make which reverberates between the stone walls. Walls are usually made of stone, you might protest, and yet it is as if the core of this place is stonier than elsewhere, you walk on great blocks of granite, and granite is also the material of the houses and churches. When it rains, like yesterday, it gleams and comes alive. I walked among black umbrellas and they were like a colony of migrating bats. Narrow streets, spacious squares where the fine drizzle shrouded the looming shapes of the buildings. No cars, so that the human measure prevailed, voices and footsteps, and once, from an alley, a strain of sorrowful music, *la gaita*, the Galician bagpipe. It was coming from a tavern where I had eaten a meal and drunk deep purple wine from a white bowl.'

Churches and cloisters, ancient monuments and buildings come in their dozens, so the answer is to simply wander around and absorb the atmosphere. A good place to start is the Plaza del Obradorio in front of the incredible, impressive cathedral, the ultimate goal for the pilgrims and one, as Somerset Maugham once wrote, 'that takes you by storm'. The square is surrounded by buildings of various epochs and styles, among them the Hospital Real, the pilgrim's hostel built by the Reyes Catolicos Isabella and Ferdinand in 1492. Today, this magnificent structure houses the best hotel in town, the Hotel Los Reyes Catolicos, which is in fact one of the most stylish in all Spain (Tel: 981 58 22 00; Fax: 981 56 30 94).

The Colegio de San Jeronimo, dating back to the 1500s

Other notable buildings are the 18th century Palacio de Rajoy, now home to the Galician regional government, the Colegio de San Jeronimo, part of the university and dating back to the 16th and 17th centuries, and the Palacio de Gelmirez, the 13th century Bishop's Palace. The cathedral itself is surrounded by more squares – Plaza de las Platerias, Plaza de la Immaculada and the Plaza de la Quintana, which is especially lively in the evenings, being a popular meeting place for students.

In addition to many good restaurants, Santiago has one with a Michelin star: Toñi Vincente (Rosalia de Castro 24, Tel: 981 59 41 00, closed Sunday and 1 – 15 August, credit cards accepted). This superb restaurant is every bit as good as its reputation suggests.

THE COASTAL REGIONS OF NORTHERN SPAIN

Northern Spain's major attractions and the Pilgrim's routes traverse all four of the coastal regions of Northern Spain. The following takes a look at each:

THE BASQUE COUNTRY

The Basques call their country Euskadi and have their own language, culture and history. It is a land of dramatic contrasts. High mountain ranges west of the Pyrenees are divided by fertile, lush valleys, which in turn reach down to a rugged coast with many small fishing

The dramatic mountain ranges of the Basque Country

harbours. On the one hand, the Basque country is one of the most industrialised regions of Spain, on the other, they still have ancient forms of agriculture and many rural traditions in secluded mountain communities.

The Basques regard the territory on both sides of the frontier as their home. This comprises the French region of Pyrenées-Atlantiques and the Spanish areas of Navarre, Guipúzcoa (in the mountains), Vizcaya (along the coast) and Alava (the high inland plain). The latter three, since 1980, have been the autonomous region of Euskadi.

The language is called *Euskara*, the only living European language that doesn't belong to the Indo-Germanic family. Linguists have long since tried to fathom out its roots – some have traced it back as far as the times of Noah, others believe it to be even more ancient, coming from the age when tools and weapons were still made from stone – an indication for this theory being the linguistic closeness of the terms *aitzor* (axe) and *aitz* (stone).

Under Franco's regime, *Euskara* was outlawed,

Preserving the original architecture of a Basque town

the Civil War, and when Franco's regime finally came into power, harsh repression was his punishment for one of the strongest opposition provinces. Although largely autonomous today, the terrorist attacks of the extremist wing of ETA, the movement formed in 1968 to gain complete independence for the Basque country, have never entirely ceased. There have been many initiatives to stop the violence, but a small cell of ultra-extremists have carried on the bloodshed regardless. During the 1970s, the Basque country was avoided by most tourists for fear of terrorist bombs, but now, sadly, ETA is concentrating its lethal activities in other areas of Spain. The terrorist hard-liners have also been isolated from their former supporters, and their activity has been dramatically reduced to such an extent that Spain, and the Basque country itself, is as safe – or unsafe – as any other part of the western world.

CANTABRIA

Westward of the Basque country is the autonomous region of Cantabria, where Santander is its capital. Still further west is Asturias, with the inland capital of Oviedo. Both areas share the mountain range of the Cordillera Cantabrica, of which the Picos de Europa is one part, and possibly form the most scenic coastline of all Spain. Between Castro Urdiales in the east and San Vicente de la Barquera in the west, Cantabria has more than 70 beaches, tucked away between the rocks. The Montaña, or mountainous inland area, with a less numerous population spread

spoken only in rural communities or in secret. Today, it is an official language in the Basque country and is also taught and used in the schools. Indeed many lessons are actually given in *Euskara,* along with others in modern Spanish. Adults wishing to learn the language can do so in evening classes, although it's worth knowing that at least 500 lessons are considered necessary before you can even attempt to have a conversation.

The Basques are proud people, never tired of pointing out that they neither bowed to Moorish nor Roman invaders in the past. Thus it comes as no surprise that there are no Roman or early Christian buildings here, although some pre-historic caves in Guipúzcoa and Vizcaya do exist.

However, they were on the side of the Republic during

The headland at Santander, the capital of Cantabria

across small rural and urban enclaves, is one of the areas which best characterises the region. Many of its highest peaks reach sub-zero temperatures and are covered by snow from December to May. Here, the density of the population is less than 10 people per square kilometre.

All in all, Cantabria currently has around half a million inhabitants, the majority of whom live in towns along the coast. The local economy is based on service industries, agriculture and fishing. Commercial fishing is centred around the harbours of Santander and Santoña, followed by Suances, Comillas, Castro Urdiales, Colindres, Laredo and San Vicente de la Barquera, while the canning industry is significant in Santoña, Castro Urdiales and Laredo. Fish and shellfish farming is now growing in Pesués, in the Tina Menor estuary.

In a locality as mountainous as Cantabria, forest resources are always of great importance. Besides native trees such as walnut, oak or beech, several species of eucalyptus were introduced in the nineteenth century and again in the 1940s. Because of its rapid growth and easy transformation into timber at the factory in Torrelavega, eucalyptus has been a real boon to the area.

The first inhabitants of this region were small groups of nomads: pre-historic cave-dwellers of the early Stone Age, who have left some remarkable paintings in caves at Altamira and Ribadesella, as already mentioned previously.

ASTURIAS

The Principality of Asturias lies sandwiched between the sea and the soaring peaks of the Cordillera Cantabrica. The population of over one million is spread throughout the main cities of Oviedo, Gijon and Avilés, as well as many smaller towns such as Llanes, Cangas de Narcea, Ribadasella, Cangas de Onis and Luarca.

The economy is based on much the same activities as in neighbouring Cantabria, and Avilés is an important industrial and trading centre. For the visitor, the most appealing side of Asturias is nature, with pride of place going to the Picos de Europa National Park and the leafy woods and forests of Muniellos, Redes and Peloño. Other attractions include pre-Romanesque art, dating back to the dynasty of the Asturian monarchs, and a wide choice of museums and art galleries.

The Ria de Pontevedra forms one of the rias characterising Galicia

GALICIA

Galicia is almost a world of its own at the end of the peninsula. Bordering the Atlantic in the north and west, and separated from the Spanish mainland by mountain ranges in the south and east, Galicia has a culture which is more Celtic than Iberian.

The landscape is wild and impressive, characterised by mountains, winding rivers and the long rias, which are river valleys that were flooded following changes in sea level. With their wooded coasts reminiscent of south-west Ireland or western Scotland, these are called Rias Altas to the north and Rias Bajas to the west.

The name Galicia is derived from the Roman *Gallaeci*, meaning Celtic Tribes. These folk arrived here around 1,000 BC, followed by the Romans in 137 BC.

Galician culture has common roots with that of the Irish, Welsh, Scots and Bretons, as demonstrated by its music (bag pipes are popular here) and a strong tendency towards melancholic poetry and literature. This is also evident in the Galician language, which can be traced back to the early 11th century and from which Portuguese is believed to have developed. Galicia has always had a strong affinity with Portugal, at least until its southern neighbour was finally separated from Spain in 1668.

The Roman era in Galicia ended in the 5th century, after which a kingdom of the Suebes was established. Like the Basque country in the east, Galicia remained relatively free of Moorish influence during the seven centuries in which the rest of Spain was dominated by them. Later, Galicia fell under the sovereignty first of the monarchs of Asturias, then of León.

Even today Galicia has a distinctly different feel from other Spanish regions, which may be due to the fact that it looks out towards and largely survives off the sea. Trade, shipping and fishing are the main economic factors, together with, more recently, tourism and a new service industry of trade fair and conference activities at the La Coruña and Santiago conference centres and the Vigo, Silleda, Ferrol and Ourense showgrounds.

THE PILGRIM'S WAY TO SANTIAGO

'The only pilgrim is he that travels to or from the house of Santiago', is what Dante Alighieri is reputed to have said. In fact, there is more than just one way to Santiago; indeed a whole network of routes lead here from all over Europe. For more than eight centuries now, the cult engendered by the figure of the Apostle James has generated an endless flow of people.

The best known, maintained and served route is the Camino de Santiago – the French Pilgrims' Way. It enters Spain by two routes, the passes of Somport and Orreaga-Roncesvalles in the Pyrenees, which merge together at Puente la Reina. Traversing Navarre and La Rioja, the journey takes in the interesting and historic villages of San Millan de la Cogolla and Santo Domingo de la Calzada before reaching Burgos, with its monumental Gothic cathedral and Las Huelgas Reales Convent.

Thereafter the trail – the Camino de Santiago – meanders through the Palencian countryside, with its treasure-trove of Romanesque remains (Frómista, Villalcázar de Sirga, Carrión de los Condes), past Sahagún and San Pedro de las Dueñas, and on to León with its cathedral suffused with the radiance of its majestic stained-glass windows, and the churches of St Isidore and St Mark, splendid examples of Romanesque and Plateresque respectively.

Onwards now, through Astorga and the El Bierzo hill country, the trail winds into Galicia via O Cebreiro and the monastery church of Santa Maria del Cebreiro, site of a popular pilgrimage commemorating the miracle of the Holy Eucharist.

The path then takes the traveller to Santiago, past a number of gorgeous abbeys (San Xulián de Samos, Vilar de Donas, Sobrado dos Monxes), pre-Romanesque and Romanesque churches and chapels (San Antolín de Yoques, San Pedro de Melide, Santiago de Barbadelo) and ancient

roadside hostels where the original wayfarers once lodged (Palas de Rei, Leboreiro, Castaleda), finally reaching Lavacolla and Monte del Gozo on the city outskirts.

Santiago is a city of sights, and it's probably best to explore its streets, squares and hidden corners before succumbing to the delights of Galician cuisine or purchasing a piece of the renowned local gold or silver work as a memento of your stay. The main feast days are 24 and 25 July in honour of the city's patron saint, Santiago (Saint James).

The Northern (or Asturian) way is probably the more accessible route for visiting yachtsmen, traversing, as it does, the Basque Country, Cantabria and Asturias. This northerly coastal trail was in fact the original one, in the times when the Moors were still very much a threat just a little further south. It was not until towards the end of the 11th century, when the Christian army drove the Moors further and further south, that the now classic route, as described above, was introduced. The original way was called the Jacobean route, and the pilgrims who followed this would wander along much of the coastline that we today visit by yacht.

From Hondarribia to Balmaseda: the Jacobean route in the Basque Country

Central and northern European pilgrims converged on Hendaye and, after crossing the Bidasoa River, entered the Basque territory via lrun. From here they went on to Hondarribia, where its mediaeval urban centre and remains of walls have warranted it recognition as a Historic-Artistic Monument. They then proceeded on their journey towards San Sebastian (Donostia), a city that according to some historians was erected as a sanctuary and hospice for pilgrims. It conserves several of its old buildings, such as the parish church of San Vicente, built in the Gothic style in the 15th century, and the Basilica of Santa Maria, built in the 18th century and featuring a fine baroque portico.

The pilgrims continued their journey to Mount Igueldo and then on to Orio and Zarauz. In Zarauz, just east of Guetaria, the parish church of Nuestra Señora la Real conserves a pilgrim's tomb and a baroque altarpiece. The towers of Luzea and Motza are good examples of Basque defensive architecture.

Nearby, in Guetaria, you can visit the magnificent Gothic cathedral of San Salvador, from the 15th century. On the way from Guetaria to Zumaya, in Azpiazu, is one of the most beautiful rural temples in the province of

Guipúzcoa, which harbours magnificent flamboyant Gothic carvings.

Zumaya boasts the imposing parish church of San Pedro, with a precious 15th century altarpiece by the Basque sculptor Juan de Anxieta. The road went inland momentarily after Zumaya towards Itziar, the last milestone in Guipúzcoa, with its Plateresque church from the 16th century. The Virgin of Itziar is a 13th century wooden carving.

Leaving Guipúzcoa and entering adjacent Vizcaya, pilgrims crossed the valley of Artibai and Markina-Xemein, immediately coming to a new milestone: the collegiate church of Cenarrazu-Ziortza. Built in the 14th century, it is the only collegiate church in Vizcaya and was declared a national monument in 1948.

Gernika, with the church of Santa Maria and its splendid Gothic portico, was the place where pilgrims disembarking in nearby Bermeo joined the coastal route. Before entering Bilbao, you will find the old church of Nuestra Señora de Begoña, erected in the Gothic style in the 15th century and enlarged later in the 17th century. It contains a precious image of the Virgin Mary in the Romanesque to Gothic transition style (13th-14th century).

Bilbao was entered by the Paseo de Los Caños and, after crossing over the Castle Bridge (nowadays called the Bridge of San Antón), travellers came to the Church of San Antón, erected in the late Gothic style. In the centre of the old city, enclosed by walls, stands the cathedral of Señor Santiago, a magnificent example of the Basque Gothic style, built in the 16th century. Its ornate Gothic cloister is especially interesting and it also has an old Gate of the Pilgrims, nowadays known as the Gate of the Angel. The old quarter of Bilbao was declared a Historic-Artistic monument in 1972.

The last milestone in the pilgrims' route along the Basque coast is Balmaseda, a town overlooked by the ruins of a castle on a knoll. Visitors often stop to see the church of San Severino, built in the late Gothic style (14th-15th centuries) and subsequently rebuilt in the baroque style, and the Romanesque Old Bridge or Bridge of Muza, with its impressive tower and three mismatching arches. Located upon the old Roman road joining Castille and Vizcaya, it has been declared a national monument.

From Balmaseda, pilgrims had a choice between two possible routes: one of them crosses the Valley of Mena and leads to Burgos, the junction with the inland way to Santiago; the other route entails leaving Bilbao to enter Cantabria by the road along the coast through Castro Urdiales.

From Castro Urdiales to San Vicente de la Barquera: the Jacobean route in Cantabria.

From Ria Bilbao, the estuary of the Rio Nervión, the old Jacobean road entered the province of Cantabria via Castro Urdiales, once the Roman town of Flavióbriga. Dominated by a castle, the old quarter of the town also boasts the 13th century church of Santa Maria de la Asunción, one of the Gothic masterpieces in Cantabria.

The castle, towering majestically by the sea next to the church, is a fine example of mediaeval military architecture. It is built on a pentagonal plan, with defensive towers at each corner. Today the castle continues to be useful, as the port lighthouse is built upon it.

The pilgrim city of Santiago de Compostela

After crossing the Aguera river, pilgrims arrived at Laredo, a town located to the east of the estuary at the mouth of the Asón river. A seaside atmosphere pervades the old town, where the most important artistic feature is the church of Nuestra Señora de la Asunción, commenced in the 13th century and completed in the 18th century.

On traversing the Asón river, travellers came to Santoña, one of the safest harbours in Cantabria thanks to its sheltered location. The church of Santa María del Puerto, constructed in the Gothic style during the 13th and 14th centuries, was a mandatory visit for pilgrims. In Bareyo, following what is known as the Route of the Seven Towns, lies one of the most representative works of the Cantabric Romanesque, the precious 12th century church of Santa Maria.

Santander was reached by crossing the bay. Its recorded history starts in the 11th century, when a village originated around the Abbey of San Emeterio, although the church of Santismo Cristo is undisputedly the most interesting archaeological monument in the city. Pilgrims would leave the rich merchants' town by the Gate of San Pedro and cross the estuaries of the Pas and San Martin de la Arena rivers, which took them to Santillana. From here, after encountering Cobreces and Comillas, pilgrims entered San

Vicente de la Barquera via the famous Bridge of la Maza, with its 32 impressive arches. Remains of its mediaeval splendour, which peaked between the 13th and 15th centuries, may still be seen in the ruins of the castle, the walls and, in particular, its parish church. The 13th century Gothic church of Santa Maria de los Angeles reflects through its vigorous style all of the features of the Cantabric Gothic; in its interior, which was renovated in the 16th century, a small chapel harbours the statue of the Inquisitor Antonio Corro, considered the most beautiful funereal sculpture in the region. The town has been declared a Historic-Artistic monument.

From Llanes to Castropol: the coastal route in Asturias.

Llanes is the first point of interest along the Jacobean route in the province of Asturias. Among the remains of its mediaeval past are the church of Santa Maria (which was probably built in the 12th century), portions of the wall erected under Alfonso IX in the 13th century, as well as the fortified tower which stands amidst the ruins of the castle from the same period.

After leaving Ribadesella, a town featuring a picturesque old quarter, and Villaviciosa, with its Gothic church of Santa María de la Oliva, the Asturian way splits in two. One of the branches, following the coast, leads to Gijon, and along this route rises the church of San Salvador de Deva. Gijon has no remains from the mediaeval period, although its newly excavated and preserved Roman thermal baths and walls are of great interest.

The other branch made its way towards Valdediós, the greatest mediaeval monastery in Asturias, built by order of Alfonso III alongside the pre-Romanesque church of San Salvador (9th century). Continuing towards Oviedo, the route goes by Argelles and Colloto, with a Romanesque church in each of these towns and a mediaeval bridge in the latter one.

The rest of the coastal road went by the Cabo de Peñas, with the Romanesque churches of Piedeloro and Logerezana, both in Carreño, before reaching the city of Avilés, the most important mediaeval port on the Cantabric sea (Bay of Biscay) and the landing spot for many pilgrims sailing from France and the British Isles. From its mediaeval past, Avilés conserves the Romanesque church of San Nicolás de Bari, the church of San Francisco, a Gothic construction from the 13th and 14th century which includes Romanesque elements, and the church of Santo Tomás de Sabugo, built in the 13th century in the Romanesque to Gothic transition style.

Crossing the mouth of the Nalón river, which is overlooked by a mediaeval tower, the traveller reaches Cudillera, a typical seaside village where you can visit the church of San Pedro. Nearby, in Soto de Luiña, there is one of the best Asturian baroque collections, consisting of the parish church of Santa Maria and the 18th century rectory. The Asturian coastal route enters Castropol, which is a town on the estuary of the Eo river that forms the natural border with Galicia. From here it leads on, via Ribadeo, to Lugo and then eventually to Santiago de Compostela.

TRAVEL

Car-hire

For venturing inland on more extensive excursions, car-hire is undoubtedly the easiest and most convenient form of transport, particularly as Spain is one of the cheapest places in Europe to hire a car.

Although readily available in the larger towns, they are harder to come by in the smaller places. The procedure is exactly the same as anywhere else in Europe. An EU-recognised driving licence is necessary and, in most cases, the driver will have to be over 23 years of age.

Trains

There are two different types of rail organisation. The state train system – RENFE – mainly links the coastal cities with the larger inland cities of northern Spain, with the exception of the short route between San Sebastian (Donastia) and Irun (near Hondarribia). The narrow gauge system runs along the coast between San Sebastian in the east and El Ferrol in the west and is operated by various private companies (RENFE tickets are not valid).

Tariffs and train times vary confusingly, to such an extent that even RENFE personnel don't always seem to have a full grasp of the system. As far as time-tables are concerned, it is important to note that the frequency of trains is drastically reduced on Sundays and public holidays, as well as sometimes on Saturdays. On the positive side, train fares are generally much cheaper than in the UK.

Along the coast, only the following cities are connected to the RENFE network: Irun, San Sebastian, Bilbao, Santander, Gijon, El Ferrol, La Coruña, Santiago, Pontevedra and Vigo. Even here, most of these are not directly inter-connected, as the lines run straight inland. As in the case of the road grid, the rail network takes the shape of a spider's web centred on Madrid, with the main lines radiating out to cover the country. For further information on fares and time-tables go to: www.renfe.es or telephone 913 28 90 20.

The narrow-gauge trains, which operate along

Making gentle headway off San Sebastian

the coast, are rather slow and infrequent, and unless you are a real fan of rail transport, the better option here is to travel by bus. A possible exception is the coastal service between Bilbao and Irun – the Eusko Trenbideak – which seems to run much more regularly than the FEVE service further west, going from Bilbao to Oviedo via Santander.

A special train laid on in summer is the so-called *Transcantabrico*, a hotel-train that runs between San Sebastian and El Ferrol, taking an entire week for one trip – an 'Occidental Express' perhaps. This service is far from cheap, and bus excursions and parties on board serve to entertain the travellers. Information about the *Transcantabrico* can be obtained from RENFE.

Finally, for extensive train travel information, get hold of a copy of the Guia RENFE, which is widely available in Spain and possibly also from Spanish tourist offices.

Buses

Buses here are efficient, reasonably comfortable and even cheaper than the modest train fares, so are by far the most popular means of transport along the coast. They run between virtually all cities and stop in even the smallest village. Just as in the UK, there are inter-city services which go both day and night, making a trip from, say Vigo to Bilbao, relatively straightforward. As with the trains, the buses are less frequent during week-ends and public holidays. Services are operated by numerous local companies.

In larger towns there is usually a central bus station, where timetables can be obtained from the various operators. In small villages, however, you will probably only find one stop, so the nearest bar will be the best place to find out about the running times. If you are making an excursion to a small inland village, first establish that there is a service later in the day to take you back to the boat.

Air Travel

Whether you are changing crew or leaving your yacht in Spain for a period of time, air travel is an essential matter to get to grips with.

The advent of budget airlines has transformed travel throughout Europe, including to Northern

Spain, where low-cost flights through EasyJet go from Stansted to Bilbao. Alternatively (in 2002), there were various British Airways and/or Iberia direct services to Bilbao, Oviedo and Santiago de Compostela from Heathrow, Manchester and Gatwick. There are also no-frills flights to south-west France, in particular to Biarritz, which is only a short distance from the excellent new marina at Hondarribia.

However, as air travel is a fast changing scene and new services and routes are constantly evolving, it's a good idea to invest some time in researching and shopping around for the best possible flights and connections.

There are airports at all the major coastal cities, including Hondarribia (to the east and west), Bilbao, Santander (beside the marina), Gijon (near Avilés), La Coruña, Santiago de Compostela and Vigo.

Prices are reported to be reasonable compared to other European services.

Ferries

Finally, ferry services run to and from the UK which, although slow, are relatively inexpensive, particularly if you are travelling without a vehicle.

Brittany Ferries operates between Plymouth and Santander, while P&O plies between Portsmouth and Bilbao, so you can take your pick.

ABBREVIATIONS AND SYMBOLS

The following abbreviations and symbols may be encountered in this book; others may be found which are self-explanatory

	Boatyard	⚓	Holding tank pumpout	⇌	Railway Station
	Boathoist/travel lift	✚	Hospital	M	Sea mile(s)
Ca	Cable(s)	Ⓗ	Harbour Master		Showers
	Chandlery	ℹ	Information Bureau		Slip for launching, scrubbing
✚	Chemist	Ldg	Leading	Sp	Spring Tides
⊹	Church	◆	Lifeboat	SS	Traffic Signals
	Diesel by cans	Np	Neap Tides	Ⓥ Ⓥ	Visitors Berth/Buoy
	Fuel Berth	✉	Post Office	⊕	Waypoint
	Fish Harbour/Quay	✗	Restaurant		*All courses are true*

DISTANCE TABLE: BAY OF BISCAY AND N/NW COASTS OF SPAIN

Approximate distances in nautical miles are by the most direct route, whilst avoiding dangers and allowing for Traffic Separation Schemes. Places in italics are in Ireland, England and the west coast of France.

	1	2	3	4	5	6	7	8	9	10	11	12	13	14	15	16	17	18	19	20
Crosshaven (Cork)	**1**																			
Tuskar Rk	85	**2**																		
Longships	144	130	**3**																	
Ushant (Créac'h)	235	230	100	**4**																
Bénodet	303	298	168	68	**5**															
Belle Ile	409	336	206	106	52	**6**														
Ile d'Yeu	460	387	257	157	102	51	**7**													
La Rochelle	526	453	323	223	168	117	66	**8**												
Arcachon	515	510	380	280	227	187	138	98	**9**											
San Sebastian	572	567	437	337	290	246	203	177	87	**10**										
Cabo Machichaco	550	549	419	319	272	233	195	177	101	34	**11**									
Bilbao (ent)	549	550	420	320	273	238	201	187	116	50	16	**12**								
Santander	534	541	411	311	266	236	206	198	133	82	48	36	**13**							
Gijon	508	528	391	298	267	254	237	248	205	162	128	116	90	**14**						
Cabo Peñas	500	523	385	293	264	252	237	249	211	170	136	126	96	10	**15**					
Ría de Ribadeo	499	520	391	308	308	279	271	288	252	223	189	179	149	63	53	**16**				
Cabo Ortegal	484	510	388	307	307	290	289	313	285	258	224	214	184	98	88	40	**17**			
La Coruña	508	538	418	338	327	326	326	351	323	296	262	252	222	136	126	78	38	**18**		
Cabo Villano	523	556	439	365	356	358	359	383	355	328	294	284	254	168	158	110	70	43	**19**	
Bayona	594	627	510	436	427	429	430	454	426	399	365	355	325	239	229	181	141	114	71	**20**

THE BASQUE COAST

The Abra de Bilbao at sunset

This chapter deals with the Spanish half of the Basque coast, which also extends north from Hondarribia (Fuentarrabia) into France. The Spanish part is the more attractive area and, despite its rugged coastline, has some very accessible harbours, so navigation and pilotage is fairly straightforward.

The Spanish Basque coast stretches just over 70 miles from Hondarribia, east of Cabo Higuer, to the Abra de Bilbao, a large bay with two outer breakwaters – both pier-heads are lit – although the eastern breakwater is still awaiting completion. Coastal waters are deep and free of serious off-lying dangers. But, as with everywhere along the northern coast, squalls can descend from the mountains or, conversely, you can be becalmed close inshore.

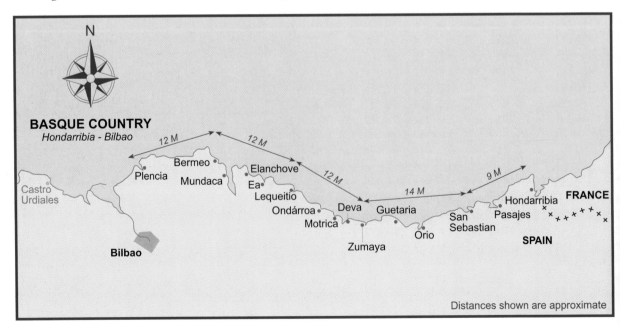

BASQUE COUNTRY
Hondarribia - Bilbao

12 M   12 M   12 M   14 M   9 M

Castro Urdiales

Plencia   Bermeo   Elanchove
Mundaca   Ea
Lequeitio
Ondárroa   Deva   Guetaria
Motrica
Zumaya   Orio
San Sebastian   Pasajes   Hondarribia   **FRANCE**

Bilbao

SPAIN

Distances shown are approximate

A village in the Rioja

San Sebastian has virtually no facilities for yachts, so plan to visit by land from one of the nearby marinas

The Basque coast has high mountains close to the sea. In heavy weather, the seas off the headlands at times become steep and confused, due to the uneven, shoaling bottom. The current can run quite strongly towards the east in periods of westerly winds, but is not pronounced otherwise. Two conspicuous capes lie on this stretch, Cabo Higuer to the east and Cabo Villano further west, near the eastern approach to Abra de Bilbao. There are several good harbours along the way, first in Hondarribia, then in Guetaria and nearby Zumaya, all of which have modern marinas while, in Abra de Bilbao lies the convenient, comfortable marina of Getxo (with a metro connection to Bilbao). The Basque country offers cruising yachtsmen the fascinating San Sebastian and Bilbao and, deeper in the hinterland, Pamplona, with its splendid fiesta that takes place each year from 6 to 14 July, as well as the Rioja plain, famous for its wines.

The Basque coast has bold headlands and few off-lying dangers. This point, near Deva (Deba) is typical

Rio Bidasoa is the frontier, and Hondarribia is the first town and port in Spain

HONDARRIBIA

Hondarribia river entrance – 43°22′.89N / 01°47′.15W

Hondarribia (Fuenterrabia) is a tidy, picturesque seaside resort on the France-Spain border, directly opposite the French town of Hendaye (Hendaya). Dominated by the typically Basque houses, which are reminiscent of Swiss mountain chalets, the old part of Hondarribia is one of the best

The shops are a few minutes walk from the marina

preserved old quarters in the Basque country.

Hendaye marina is a good, secure base to leave your boat and explore the Basque hinterland, the Rioja plain or for a visit to San Sebastian, either by car (about a 20-minute drive) or by train. The train departs from Irun station, which is best reached by bus from Hondarribia.

From Hendaye, you can easily reach Biarritz, an elegant, historic seaside resort, by bus or by car. Moreover, the airport nearby has cheap flights to and from the UK.

APPROACH AND ENTRANCE

Approach waypoint: 43°24′.02N / 01°46′.27W; 210°; 1.3M to river entrance.

Cabo Higuer, with its conspicuous lighthouse, is easily identified from the sea. Hendaye bay is immediately east of this. Entry into the bay from the north or west is straightforward. Coming from the east along the French coast, do take care not to come too close to Les Briquets, the often invisible rocks off Pointe Sainte Anne, which extend almost a mile to seaward. Stay north of 43°24′N until the entrance bears about 220°. By night the powerful

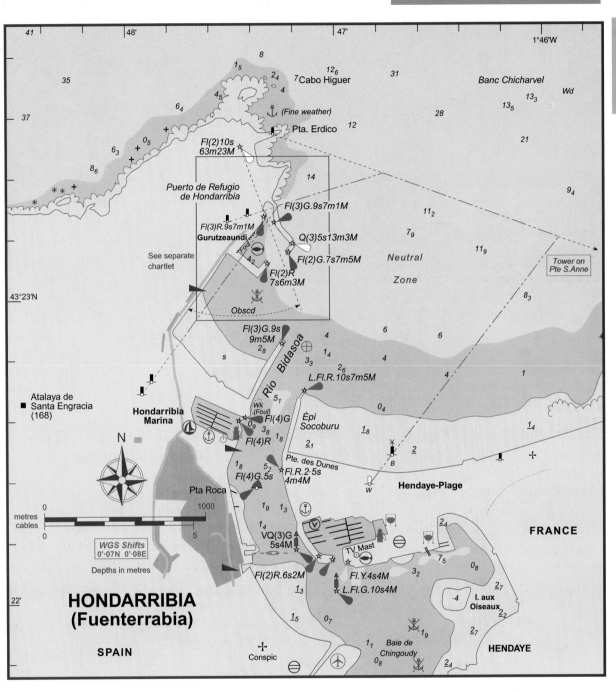

HONDARRIBIA
(Fuenterrabia)

SPAIN

light on Cabo Higuer (Fl(2) 10s 63m 23 miles), and the harbour lights of the nearby refuge harbour (Gurutzeaundi) under the headland will guide you to the entrance to the inner bay, located between two training walls, both of which are lit.

BERTHING

The new 685-berth marina, on the Spanish side to the west, is about half a mile south of the channel entrance, is dredged to approximately three metres and can be entered at any time. After the marina opened last year, there were no specific

visitor or reception berths, a situation that may change. If not, a turn to port after entering takes you past the fuel berth, where you could moor temporarily whilst awaiting a berth allocation.

An equally large, modern and comfortable marina exists on the French side, inside the inner bay at Hendaye-Plage (with a frequent passenger ferry service to Hondarribia), where berthing is on floating pontoons with fingers. Hondarribia marina is about a third of a mile from the town; that at Hendaye-Plage is perhaps twice as far from Hendaye. Anchoring is possible in fair

Facilities at Hondarribia Marina include a travel hoist and repair services

Hendaye marina is situated just across the estuary

weather outside, south-east of Cabo Higuer. The inner bay – Baie de Chingoudy – is crowded with moorings, so finding space to drop anchor can, at times, be difficult.

MARINA FACILITIES

Hondarribia pontoons are equipped with water and power. Shore services include fuel, crane, travel hoist, repairs and storage. The smart new marina building has toilets, showers and telephones together with helpful staff, who are

The marina at Hondarribia lies just inside the entrance

Hondarribia has a well-preserved mediaeval quarter

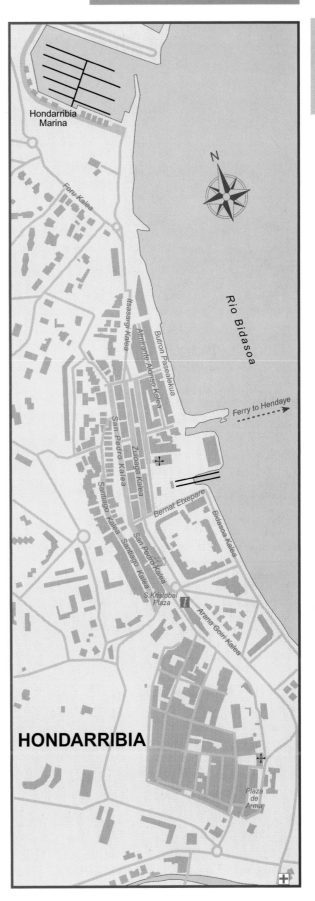

justly proud of their new yacht harbour. Facilities in Hendaye marina include electricity and water on the pontoons, diesel and petrol, a 30-ton travelift, repairs, shops and restaurants.

TRANSPORT

Links include an airport at Hondarribia, a train station at Irun, a French airport in Biarritz/Bayonne and a train station in Hendaye.

PROVISIONING

Hondarribia has a good selection of restaurants, cafés and shops, which are more than adequate for any stores that you may require. There is a small supermarket in Hendaye marina for day-to-day needs, but this is not convenient for major provisioning.

A RUN ASHORE

Founded by a Gothic King, Recaredo, in the sixth century, Hondarribia is a fortified town with a well-preserved, mediaeval centre, which is simply

La Hermanadad de Pescadores

A striking church presides over the old town

magnificent. The old town is up a hill just south of the modern town centre, and can be identified by a church surrounded by narrow cobbled streets and carefully restored buildings of the renaissance and baroque eras.

The Parador (Plaza de Armas 14, Tel: 943 64 55 00) dominates the town from its highest point, on Plaza de Armas in the old quarter. It is located in a castle that was built by the Navarese King Sancho Abarca in the 10th century, the structure of which is still very much in evidence today. The courtyard is impressive, as are the views from the terrace, but unless you are staying there, or patronising the restaurant, no admittance is permitted beyond the reception lobby.

The pretty new town lies along the river front, and numerous bars, restaurants and shops make it well worth exploring. Climbing up the hill behind the town will reward you with splendid views over the bay and Hendaye beyond, while long walks along the cliffs towards Cabo Higuer and the coast west of that are extremely pleasant. Wonderful views can also be enjoyed from the castle of San Telmo, on Cabo Higuer.

The fiesta of the Virgin of Guadeloupe on 8 September includes a procession known as the

Alarde, commemorating a victory over the French in 1638. Hendaye has a long, sandy and popular beach on the other side of the marina, which seems to be the main attraction. The passenger ferry from Hondarribia to Hendaye marina runs every 15 to 20 minutes from 1000 to 2200.

EATING OUT

Hondarribia has two gourmet restaurants, each featuring a Michelin Star. The Ramon Roteta (Irun Kalea 1, Tel: 943 64 16 93, credit cards accepted) serves superb food in a particularly elegant setting. Irun Kalea, a small road below the old town, runs towards the river. Reservation is necessary. The other restaurant is the Alameda (Minasoroeta 1, Tel: 943 64 27 89, credit cards accepted, but closed Sunday evenings and Mondays), with equally excellent cooking. Booking strongly recommended. This restaurant is on the town outskirts, south of the old quarter.

Apart from these two, there are many good restaurants and tapas bars long the San Pedro Kalea, a road running parallel to the river, inland from the waterfront. One of the more noteworthy is the restaurant Zeria (San Pedro 23, Tel: 943 64 27 80, credit cards accepted, closed Sunday nights), with seafood a speciality.

For local flavour, including fresh fish, try

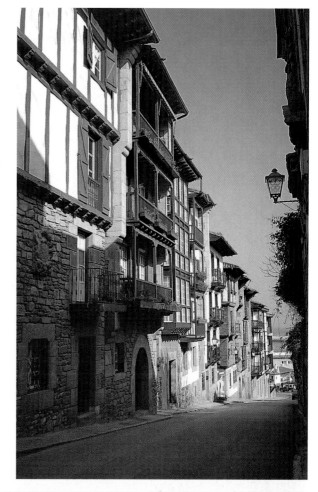

The fuel berth is to the right of this picture of the marina

A typical streetscape in the area close to the marina

La Hermanadad de Pescadores (the Brotherhood of Fishermen), an unassuming restaurant in the Calle Zuloaga. Run by the fishermen's wives, it is packed with locals every lunchtime. Ask for the catch of the day and you won't be disappointed. There are numerous bars and restaurants in the marina area of Hendaye, including Asian La Voile d'Hatien and several good ones for oysters and other *fruits de mer*.

DAYTIME ANCHORAGES NEARBY

Anchoring off Hendaye beach is recommended only in fine weather and is unsuitable for overnight stays. Another anchorage is south of the fishing harbour, tucked away under Cabo Higuer; but take care not to foul any moorings. The same goes for the inner bay, which is similarly crowded.

USEFUL INFORMATION
Hondarribia marina Tel: 943 64 27 88
Hondarribia tourist office Tel: 943 64 54 58
Hondarribia airport
Tel: 943 64 34 64 / 902 400 500
Capitainerie of Hendaye marina
Tel: (+33) 05 59 48 06 00; Fax (+33) 05 59 48 06 01

PASAJES (Pasaia)

The entrance to Pasajes can be negotiated in any weather, but the port offers few facilities for yachts

Pasajes harbour entrance – 43°20'.20N / 01°55'.68W

Pasajes, once a beautiful natural harbour, is now a major commercial fishing port. The original town, Pasajes de San Juan, is on the east side of the rio, where part of Philip's 1488 armada was built. Later, Victor Hugo and the Marquis de Lafayette were temporary residents.

The dramatic harbour entrance, which is negotiable in any weather, can easily be identified by the steep cliffs east of San Sebastian. A night entry is possible.

BERTHING

You can berth in the fishing harbour alongside the quay at Pasajes Ancho, but it is advisable to have long warps and a fender-board to hand. Also bear in mind that there is normally a constant movement of fishing and commercial craft.

The entrance to the port of Pasajes is dramatic, to say the least

There are no dedicated facilities for yachts, which are not particularly encouraged to come here. Despite its beautiful setting, Pasajes should only really be used as a port of refuge, where a berth might be found in the fishing harbour at San Pedro.

Although there are plans to build a marina, no further information was available at the time we went to press.

LOCATION/POSITION

Pasajes lies between Hondarribia to the east and San Sebastian (Donostia) to the west. It is eight miles from Hondarribia and only three from San Sebastian.

APPROACH AND ENTRANCE

Approach waypoint: 43°20'.65N / 01°55'.97W; 155°; 0.5M to the harbour entrance.

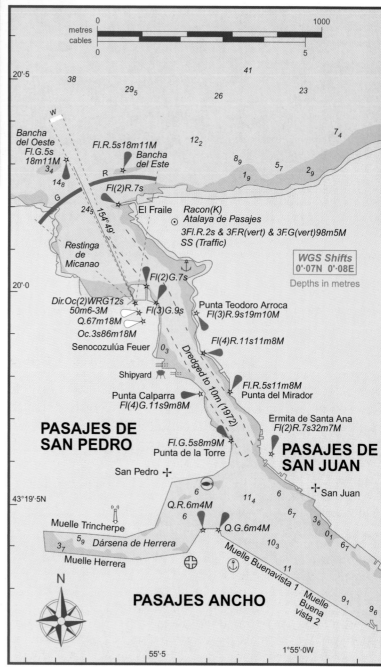

Bahia de la Concha is backed by the city, and guarded by Monte Igueldo (foreground) and Monte Urgull

SAN SEBASTIAN (DONOSTIA)

San Sebastian harbour entrance – 43°19'.51N / 01°59'.70W

San Sebastian is an attractive summer resort just 12 miles from the French border.
San Sebastian, or Donostia as it is called in the local Basque language,
is a lively city of about 170,000 inhabitants, which lies in the
sea-shell shaped bay called La Concha.

The modern part of the town, distinctly cosmopolitan, has broad avenues and tree-lined boulevards. Adjoining the picturesque, busy fishing harbour are shops, restaurants and many typical tapas bars. An elegant yacht club, with its clubhouse overlooking La Concha, welcomes visiting yachtsmen.

San Sebastian probably gives the best impression of modern and traditional Basque life of anywhere along this stretch of the coast. It gained some literary fame when Ernest Hemingway wrote about it in *Fiesta*, and has been a fashionable seaside resort since the 1850s, when Queen Isabel II came here in the summer, bringing both court and government with her.

If the mooring situation (see over) and lack of facilities do not appeal, consider mooring in the nearby marinas of Hondarribia or Zumaya, rather than miss this fascinating place. San Sebastian can be easily reached by train or bus from either town, although Zumaya's marina is more conveniently placed for public transport than the new yacht harbour at Hondarribia. However, don't be put off, transport services are fast and frequent, the distance small, and in summer at weekends, the buses run virtually all night.

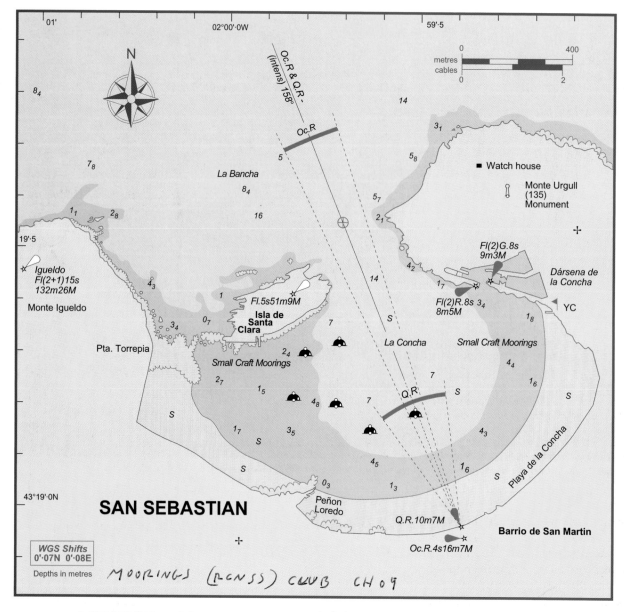

Depths in metres

MOORINGS (RCNSS) CLUB CH 09

LOCATION/POSITION

San Sebastian lies on the north coast between Cabo Higuer and Cabo Mayor, about 11 miles west of Hondarribia and 60 miles east of the Abra de Bilbao.

APPROACH

Approach waypoint: 43°19'.98N/01°59'.96W; 158°; 0.5M to harbour entrance.

The approach from seaward is straightforward – there are no off-lying dangers until close inshore, when nearing the coast from all directions. Monte Urgull, with its prominent statue, is immediately east of the entrance, and the small, high island of Isla de Santa Clara is to the west. Monte Igueldo, west of Isla de Santa Clara, has a conspicuous

lighthouse, tower and large buildings. Identify these three landmarks correctly to avoid entering the shallow Rio Urumea, which lies between Monte Urgull and the beach to its east.

ENTRANCE

The entrance to La Concha is about 200 metres wide, between Isla de Santa Clara and Monte Urgull. There are leading marks and lights (Oc R & Q R, intensified on 158°) to help entry at night or in bad weather, although they may be difficult to identify against a backdrop of city lights. In settled daylight conditions, the approach is not critical if both shores are given normal offing. In heavy seaways or big onshore swells, the seas can break inside La Concha entrance and on the bank of La Bancha, north of the Isla de Santa Clara.

San Sebastian harbour nestles beneath Monte Urgull

If entering under sail, prepare to be becalmed in the lee of Monte Urgull. Sudden gusts of wind from various directions may also occur close under the mountain and in La Concha itself. You may well be puzzled by the strange metal structures on the terraces below Monte Igueldo. These are *The Comb of the Winds*, controversial modern sculptures by Eduardo Chillida, which look more like giant, broken mooring chains than combs. Sculptures like this are *de rigueur*, it would seem, along this stretch of the coastline.

BERTHING

San Sebastian has two tidal basins. The picturesque fishing harbour is unsuitable for yachts, while the small boat basin immediately to starboard inside the harbour is tiny and crowded with local boats. With luck, it might be possible to moor alongside the pontoon in the outer part of the harbour or, in settled weather, at the pier using long mooring lines to allow for a tidal range of up to 3.5 metres at springs. In certain conditions (with strong swell outside) there is considerable surge inside the harbour, which makes it, like the bay, almost untenable.

There are two small pontoons in the outer part of the harbour, one reserved for the passenger ferries from Isla de Santa Clara, while the other is

for boats from the yacht club, which you may go alongside briefly. Whether you could lie to the latter is a matter for investigation on arrival or by contacting the club beforehand. (See details below). Usually, it is easier and more convenient to pick up a vacant mooring in front of the yacht club, which is the large building on the water's edge south-east of the harbour entrance. If you prefer to use your own ground tackle, use a trip-line, taking care not to foul any moorings. A club launch will usually pick up crews and ferry them ashore and back during the summer months.

Alternatively, you can anchor south of the Isla de Santa Clara, where a regular ferry runs to the town, again during the summer months only. This anchorage might be better sheltered than the moorings in front of the yacht club if there is any swell running into La Concha, although both locations are generally quite rolly, even in settled conditions.

HARBOUR FACILITIES

San Sebastian, like most along this coast, is purely a fishing harbour. Apart from the yacht club itself, there are no dedicated facilities for yachts, although it is possible to take on water inside the harbour, but diesel - Gasoleo A is not available alongside. Mechanics might be on hand around the fishing harbour, but any other repairs will be difficult or even impossible to carry out.

The yacht club has a pleasant bar and restaurant, along with good showers. For provisions, the old part of the city is the area nearest the harbour and has enough food shops to cater for everyday needs. A fine selection of seafood is also on sale in the harbour precincts. Supermarkets are a little further away, but there are many to choose from. The superb fish-market (Pescaderia) is located near the Plaza de la Constitution, in the old town, while other markets for vegetables and exotic cheeses are close by.

A RUN ASHORE

The half-moon shaped Playa de la Concha is famous for its sandy beach, no doubt popular with the crew's junior members. The modern part of the town is ideal for shopping in elegant stores and boutiques, while the old quarter, the Parte Vieja, is noteworthy for its architecture, atmosphere and pleasantly stuffy, old-fashioned shops as well as some remarkable churches. The Gothic church of San Vicente and the baroque church of Santa Maria, as well as the 16th century Convent of San Telmo – now a museum – are all

Looking into the inner harbour

worth a visit. The museum has a cloister and houses a collection of old and contemporary paintings as well as an interesting section on ancient Basque seafarers and shipbuilders. Basques claim that Spain could not have colonised the Americas without their navigators.

To see the city use the Bus Touristico, which goes on the Donostia Tour. Tickets are sold on the bus itself and you can get a pass that is valid for 24 hours. The service, on two different circular routes around the city, will take you to all the places that are out of walking distance. Ruta 1, quaintly called Donostia Clasica, links the Parte Vieja with Monte Igueldo, and operates from 1000 to 2100. Ruta 2, more prosaically called Donostia Technologica, links the Gros area east of the river with the inland parts of the city, and operates from 1030 to 1930. As a bonus, with your bus ticket you get discount vouchers for about 20

Wall to wall boats

Customers order from the barman or eat directly from the platters, paying afterwards. In the early evening, which in Spain is between 2000 and 2200, these bars get very crowded and noisy. You will probably find that the tapas are so good that by the time you have tasted half of them, you no longer need a proper evening meal.

Eating well is a passion in this (and perhaps in every) part of Spain. In the 19th century, gourmet clubs called *Txokes* were founded, mainly in San Sebastian. These clubs, loosely described as cooking and drinking clubs, are open

San Sebastian has a wealth of tapas bars

attractions, including the cable-car to the top of Monte Igueldo, where you can enjoy a spectacular view over La Concha and the city.

EATING OUT AND NIGHT-LIFE

San Sebastian is surely the best place to enjoy the delights of Basque cuisine, although prices here are perhaps the highest on the whole coast – in fact the Spanish say that it is not ETA that you should fear in San Sebastian, but the restaurant prices. One thing is certain, this city has wonderful regional products and traditions and believes that it has the best cuisine in Spain, with many Michelin stars to prove it.

It is more economical to indulge in one particular Basque custom: to drift from tapas bar to tapas bar through the narrow streets of the Parte Vieja, knocking back small glasses of red wine or local beer and sampling the food on offer. These small appetisers are usually laid out on the bar on huge platters of stunning variety.

The author's yacht lying at the short stay pontoon

only to men, and are just one expression of the sophisticated Basque cuisine, a style of cooking noted for its ingenious sauces and main dishes, using only fresh, local produce and fish from the Bay of Biscay. Here are a few of the good restaurants in town, any of which I would recommend you try: Urepel (Paseo Salamanca 3, Tel: 42 40 40). Quite elegant with a high standard of cooking, the classic here is the superb *sopa de*

A street in La Parte Vieja

pescado (fish soup). Prices range from €30 to €40, major credit cards accepted. The Paseo Salamanca runs along the bank of the river at the eastern end of the Parte Vieja. Close by is another favourite: Panier Fleuri (Paseo Salamanca 1, Tel: 42 42 05). It's of a similarly high standard and is not cheap. A speciality is the *ensalada de pulpo*, also known as beef with truffles. Prices are from €35 to €45. Cards accepted. Juanita Kojua (Portu 14, Tel: 42 01 80) is one of the numerous inviting eating-places in the Parte Vieja, although it is closed Sunday night. Prices are around €30 and cards are accepted. For an economical meal in traditional surroundings, try Ttun Ttun Taberna in Calle san Jeronimo (two streets from the harbour), where the menu is less than €10.

As in every major city in Spain, San Sebastian's night-life usually starts around midnight when the night-crowd drifts from the bars to the discotheques, where dancing carries on until well into the morning. Zorongo (San Martin 66)

Useful Information

Local telephone code: 943

Réal Club Nautico de San Sebastian,
Muelle Concha Tel: 42 35 74; Fax: 43 13 65

Local tourist information office
Reina Regente 3. Tel: 48 11 66; Fax: 48 11 72
E-mail: cat@donostia.org
Web: www.sansebastiantourismo.com

Looking to seaward between Monte Igueldo and Isla de Santa Clara.
This channel is not navigable

is the disco to be seen in and is open from 2330 until the morning. Bataplan (Paseo de La Concha) has an attractive terrace on which to enjoy hot summer nights; open also from 2330 onwards.

FIESTAS

Guipúzcoa, like all regions in Spain, has numerous fiestas and events. In summer these include Gastronomy Week and a Beerfest (June);

San Sebastian Jazz Festival and the Theatre Festival (July); Musical Fortnight (August); and an international film festival (September). Besides these, there are numerous fiestas and folklore festivals. Dates and details can be obtained from the local tourist office (whose telephone number is listed under Useful Information). Also, of course, there is the Semana Grande, which is the main festival week of San Sebastian and is held in mid-August.

RIO DE ORIO

Rio de Orio entrance – 43°17'.66N / 02°07'.85W

Rio de Orio is a rather shallow river leading to a small fishing village. Yacht access is limited due to draught restrictions and a low road bridge (clearance less than 18 metres) downstream of the town. The village of Orio is well-known for the races held in rowing boats (known locally as *traineras*) on the river, and has a pleasant beach near the river mouth. Unfortunately, however, the Rio Orio is reputed to be one of the most polluted rivers in Spain.

LOCATION/POSITION

Rio de Orio is half way between San Sebastian and Zumaya, each of which is situated about seven miles away.

APPROACH AND ENTRANCE

Approach waypoint: 43°18'.16N / 02°07'.85W; 180°; 0.5M to harbour entrance.

The river mouth has a training wall on the east side and a curved protective breakwater on the west side, the head of each being lit. Despite the lights, a first-time night entrance is not recommended because of limited depth and lack of clear leading marks. It is preferable to enter during the last two hours of the flood tide on a course of 145°, which is a heading well to port of the road bridge. When entering this river, I would recommend that you keep more towards the east side (near the training wall), but then change to the west side as it bends just before the bridge. You should pass the bridge underneath the western arch, where the next light is located, and continue from there along the west bank, which is marked by posts (lit), before approaching the little town in mid-stream.

BERTHING

This is a challenge when the fishing fleet is in port. The pier on the north side of the river is normally fully occupied by fishing boats, but you might, with luck or negotiation, find a berth alongside in about two metres, taking into account the tidal range when mooring. Anchoring in mid-stream could be another option, but you should take care not to block the fairway, and check soundings to establish depths. The rio may become slightly deeper near the town bridge, but precise information is unavailable.

HARBOUR FACILITIES

Facilities, which include a slipway, crane, workshop and mechanics, are geared towards the fishing fleet, although repairs may be possible.

PROVISIONING

Small shops and grocery stores in the village are perfectly adequate for day-to-day needs.

A RUN ASHORE

Orio has an attractive, historic centre around the church of San Nicolas de Bari, itself noteworthy, having originally been built in the 13th century, but then changed and rebuilt in the 16th century. The place has a mediaeval air about it, especially in the Kalle Nagusia. The beach is located by the river mouth. At high water, you can take the dinghy further upstream into some attractively rural landscape.

EATING OUT

A strong point in Orio's favour is the large number of quite good fish restaurants and grills, most of them in the village but a few near the beach.

GUETARIA

Guetaria is an interesting town with a good harbour, sheltered from the west by Isla de San Anton

Guetaria harbour entrance – 43°18'.30N / 02°11'.80W

Guetaria (Getaria) is a beautiful, small village, which has a surprisingly large fishing port and marina situated between the rocky Isla de San Antón and the mainland. This is one of the easiest and most pleasant stop-overs along the Spanish north coast. However, the number of berths that are suitable for yachts of over 12 metres in length is rather restricted, so, if you are planning to visit with a large yacht, it would be a good idea to first call the marina office by VHF or telephone (see numbers under Useful Information). Although Guetaria is slightly nearer San Sebastian than Zumaya, it is not on the railway line and the marina isn't as peaceful as Zumaya's for leaving a yacht unattended whilst visiting the city.

LOCATION/POSITION

Guetaria is situated approximately 11 miles west of San Sebastian (Donostia).

APPROACH AND ENTRANCE

Approach waypoint: 43°18'.88N/02°11'.25W; 215°; 0.7M to harbour entrance.

When sailing along the coast, Guetaria can easily be identified by the rocky Isla de San Antón, otherwise known as El Ratón because of its mouse-like silhouette. The lighthouse, a white octagonal tower beside a white, red-roofed building, is on its outer summit: Fl(4) 15s 21 miles. It is no longer an island but a peninsula and the harbour lies to the south-east of it. The approach and entry are straightforward day or night, and the *puerto deportivo* is to port immediately after entering .

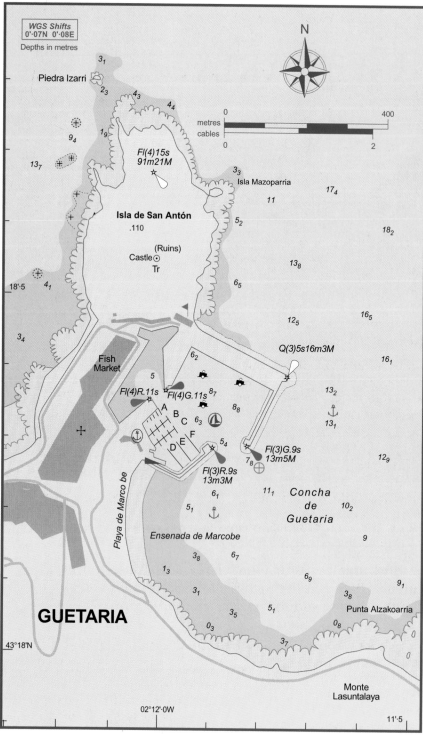

telephone and ice. Diesel - Gasoleo A is available, together with a slipway, crane and a 32-ton travelift. Workshops include diesel mechanics, electronic repairs and a small chandlery.

PROVISIONING

Small grocery shops exist in the village, which straggles uphill behind the church. A local white wine, *txakoli* (pronounced *chakoli*) is produced, which can be bought in Guetaria's shops.

A RUN ASHORE

Two small beaches lie adjacent to the marina. The narrow streets of the old village are worth wandering through, and an unusual 15th century church of San Salvador sits above the harbour. It was established in the 13th century, but was rebuilt in 1429. From the outside it looks unremarkable – a solid romanesque building, while inside, the wooden floor tilts like the deck of a ship at sea. Other parts are also off plumb and it's as if the interior were fitted out by boatbuilders who decided to follow the slope of the ground rather than the horizontal, thinking nothing of a sloping deck.

This little seafaring town is the birthplace of the first circumnavigator. Juan Sebastian Elcano set out with Magellan on their epic voyage in 1519. Magellan was killed in the Philippines and of the original fleet of five, only Elcano's ship, the *Vitoria*, which was built in the next village of Zarauz, made it back to Sanlucar de Barrameda (near Cadiz) in south-west Spain. There is a statue of Elcano in the centre of old Guetaria and his grave can be found inside the church door. One

BERTHING

On floating pontoons with finger berths. Berths for larger yachts are limited.

FACILITIES IN THE MARINA

Water and electricity are available on pontoons, while shore facilities include toilets, showers,

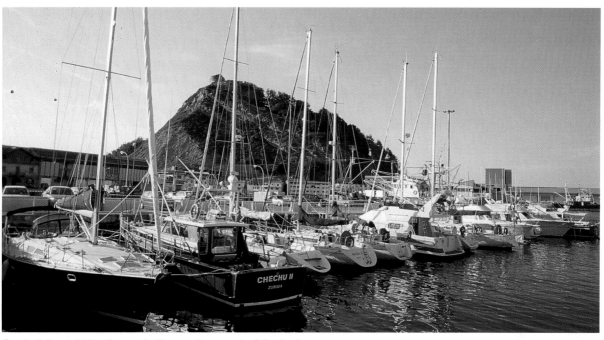

Gueteria's yacht berths are in the southern part of the harbour

special fiesta is devoted to his return: Desembarco d'Elcano takes place on 7 August every four years. People don historic costumes and re-stage Elcano's return after his circumnavigation.

EATING OUT

A cheerful and easy-going bar/restaurant lies next to the marina, with a terrace overlooking the beach and the bay beyond (Restaurant Balearri). The elegant restaurant Kaia (General Arnao 10,

Tel: 943 14 05 00), with a splendid view over the harbour and bay, serves high quality Basque dishes, with shellfish specialities. Also well situated above the harbour is the Mayflower (Katrapona 4, Tel: 943 14 06 58).

DAYTIME ANCHORAGES NEARBY

The bay south of the harbour is taken over by moorings, so there is little, if any, space to anchor.

Guetaria is one of Euskadi's prettiest villages

USEFUL INFORMATION

Marina office Tel/fax: 943 58 09 59, VHF 09
E-mail: thage@infinego-cio.com
Tourist office Tel: 943 14 09 57

The speciality here is fish grilled on an open fire

ZUMAYA

Zumaya harbour entrance – 43°18'.51N / 02°14'.55W

Zumaya (Zumaia) is a peaceful, unassuming, little seaside town with a few attractions. These are a quiet beach (by Spanish standards), a new marina offering very good facilities for yachts and a small historical town centre with a fortified church (San Pedro).

Visitors interested in arts and culture will find another gem here – the Museo Zuloaga (see over for more information).

Thanks to the new marina, you can leave your boat safely to go off exploring in land or to visit Iruña/Pamplona, La Rioja and nearby San Sebastian. The latter is served by frequent buses and hourly trains and is only a few kilometres away. The coastal cliffs for some miles west of Zumaya are striking in appearance, formed of near vertical strata that have eroded into fantastic slabs, ridges and caves backing miles of sandy beach.

LOCATION/POSITION

The town lies on the Rio Urola, only three miles west of Guetaria.

APPROACH AND ENTRANCE

Approach waypoint: 43°19'.01N/02°14'.55W; 180°; 0.5M to harbour entrance.

From the east, you can't fail to spot Guetaria, with Zumaya being only three miles further along the coast. Coming from the west, Zumaya lighthouse (Oc(1+3) 12s 12 miles), near the root of the substantial breakwater, is easily identified

The new marina at Zumaya is sheltered, peaceful and well placed for transport connections

before Isla de San Antón. The river mouth is protected by two long breakwaters and has been dredged to a minimum depth of two metres, according to the harbour master. In 2001, the depth was in excess of four metres until level with the Zumaya lighthouse, where the minimum was 2.5 metres. This entrance should be safe in all but north-north-easterly gales, when Guetaria will be a less risky approach. After entering, keep more towards the starboard breakwater where the water is deepest. The marina is on the east side going upriver towards the town and its entrance is lit. Depths inside are from 2.5 to 3.5 metres.

FIRST PONTOON FOR VISITOR **BERTHING**

When the marina is finished there will be 500 berths on pontoons with fingers. In 2001, only the berths linked to the north-east jetty had been installed. The reception pontoon and the fuel berth are directly below the marina building, opposite the entrance.

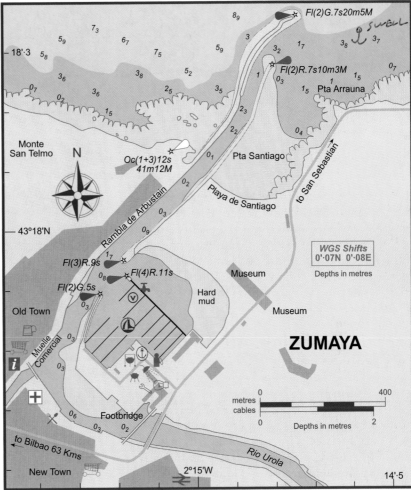

MARINA FACILITIES

The marina has all the usual facilities as well as TV-plugs on the pontoons and, as there is 24-hour security, showers and toilets are open round the clock. A slipway, chandlery, 35-ton travelift and a fuel berth with diesel - Gasoleo A complete the picture. Repairs can also be carried out here.

PROVISIONING

Shop in the small town of Zumaya, on the opposite side of the river. Taking the dinghy across might be an easier option than walking round. There is a small, but well-stocked, supermarket almost opposite the town end of the footbridge, in the new-ish residential area. Water-taxi times are available from the marina office.

A RUN ASHORE

The beach beside the entrance is wide, sandy and not too far from the marina, (also accessible by

The breakwaters have been extended, and the entrance is dredged to approximately three metres

dinghy or water-taxi). The new town, which is closest to the marina, across the river and about a 10-minute walk, looks rather provincial but is well known for two museums close by, the Museo Producto Artesanal del Pais Vasco and the Museo Zuloaga, both on the east side of the town not far from the marina.

Zuloaga (1870 – 1945) was a well respected Basque painter whose house, where he both lived and worked, has now been turned into a museum. Apart from his own works, the exhibition has some paintings from El Greco, Zurbaran and Goya and a display of the artist's own bullfighting costumes, his other passion. The museum is only open from March to September.

The Museo Producto Artesanal del Pais Vasco is a small museum showing the rural culture of the Basque country. Local cheeses, honey and desserts are on sale here as well as liqueurs, cider and the local white wine, *txakoli*.

The old town is not much further to walk to than the new town, just across another bridge, but can also be reached by water-taxi. The tourist office is beside the bridge and is a useful source of information. The old town centre, around the impressive, fortified church of San Pedro, is pleasantly relaxed compared to some of the coast's more frantic resorts. The town's fiesta takes place at the end of June.

EATING OUT

Zumaya is not a place for extravagant eating out, however the marina area is beginning to develop, and in 2001 there was already a good restaurant, café and bar overlooking the plaza. These are the Restaurante Berri, Sideria Algorri and the Bar Nao Victoria respectively. There are a few restaurants and bars in town, none of which are particularly outstanding. Tapas can be had in many of them, together with a glass of *txakoli*.

DAYTIME ANCHORAGES NEARBY

About five miles west of Zumaya is another river, the Rio de Deva (Deba). The river is canalised by training walls, but is shallow and subject to silting, with a tiny boat harbour immediately before the road bridge in the village. It is possible to anchor in the bay off the river mouth, where a small jetty north of the entrance gives minimal protection against the prevailing north-westerly

Every port has its rowing crew

The town quay is linked to the marina and the beach by water taxi. The tourist office and shopping area are nearby

swell. Beware – the head of the jetty has crumbled away and forms an underwater obstruction. Deva is not wildly exciting, but has two fine beaches and a good seafood restaurant, Restaurant Urain, near the Hotel Miramar. It is easier to visit Deva by car, as suggested in the tour itinerary (see below), unless the weather is calm and settled.

There are plenty of places you can visit nearby, leaving the yacht securely at Zumaya marina. Although as yet you can't hire a car here, you can take the bus or train to San Sebastian where all main car hire companies have offices. Alternatively, enquire at the marina office – they may have an arrangement with a company. Phoning around the following numbers (San Sebastian code 943) will quickly establish the best value: Atesa, Tel: 46 30 13; Avis, Tel: 46 15 27; Budget, Tel: 39 29 45; Europcar, Tel: 32 23 04; Hertz, Tel: 46 10 84; Sixt, Tel: 44 43 29.

PLACES TO VISIT

The following spots, all within approximately 25 miles of Zumaya, and in no particular order, are worth including in your itinerary: Deva (Deba), Motrico (Mutriku), Elgoibar, Vergara (Bergara), Oñate (Oñati), Aránzazu (Arantzazu), Beasain, Tolosa, Orio, Zarauz (Zarautz), Zestoa (Cestona) and Loyola. The Basque tourist office publishes some excellent free guides, specialising in the environment as well as cultural and general interest locations. Ask for Deva, at the mouth of

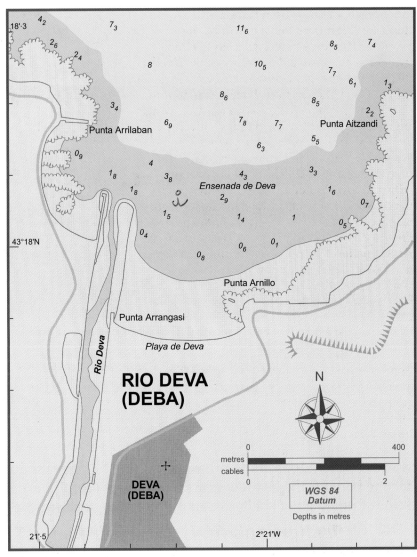

RIO DEVA (DEBA)

Punta Arrilaban

Punta Aitzandi

Ensenada de Deva

Punta Arnillo

Punta Arrangasi

Playa de Deva

Rio Deva

DEVA (DEBA)

N

metres	0 ... 400
cables	0 ... 2

WGS 84 Datum

Depths in metres

the river Deva, which has a beautiful beach and a gothic parish church. It is possible, although not easy, to take the boat into Deva, but only in calm and settled weather, as berthing or anchoring in the river is tricky.

Motrico, about four miles away, has a picturesque port that again is not particularly suitable for visiting by boat. The town is pretty, as is its neoclassical church, where some works of art, one of which is *Christ* attributed to El Greco, are kept.

Vergara is a noble and elegant town, with interesting historic and artistic connections. Here, during the 1839 civil war, Generals Espartero and Maroto signed a peace treaty, and *A beautiful Christ*, attributed to Juan de Mesa, dominates the church of San Pedro de Ariznoa. Oñate's former university building contains objects of historic and artistic interest. Also worth mentioning are the baroque Casa Consistorial (town hall) and the convents of Bidaurreta and Santa Ana.

Aránzazu lies in the mountains at 900 metres, with the shrine of the Virgin of Aránzazu, the patron saint of Guipúzcoa. Close by is the Pico Aitzgorri, the highest mountain of the province, from where you can admire the immense landscape that covers six Spanish provinces and one of France. Orio offers a delightful beach and prehistoric caves, with the nearby Parque de

Pagoeta just a few miles inland. Zarauz is an elegant town and a famous summer resort, with places of architectural interest such as the Torre Lucea, the palace of Narros.

Zestoa is an old spa town with medicinal waters and beautiful countryside. Loyola, a little further inland, is also well worth visiting. Here Ignatius Loyola, founder of the Society of Jes's (the Jesuits) was born, and the baroque basilica contains some of his relics.

USEFUL INFORMATION

Zumaya marina office Tel: 943 86 09 38;
Fax: 943 14 32 99; VHF 09
Local tourist office Tel: 943 14 33 96

Regional tourist office (San Sebastian)
Tel: 943 02 31 50. www.euskadi.net/tourismo or
www.basquecountrytourism.net

Motrico harbour has no facilities for yachts, but is worth a visit in quiet weather

MOTRICO (MUTRIKU)

Motrico harbour entrance – 43°18'.58N / 02°22'.79W

Motrico (Mutriku) is another Basque fishing village, although fishing has been in decline here for the last few years. A small, peaceful place, its picturesque harbour offers good shelter in all but north to north-easterly winds.

LOCATION/POSITION

Motrico is situated roughly half way between Zumaya and Lequeitio and is well protected.

APPROACH AND ENTRANCE

Approach waypoint: 43°18'.86N/02°22'.10W; 236°; 0.5M to harbour entrance.

Motrico is a quiet village in pleasant rural surroundings

The harbour lies between the Punta Alcolea (to the east) and Punta de Cardal (to the west). Rocky shoals extend off Punta de Cardal, where the seas break heavily in strong winds. Enter the harbour on the leading marks and lights on 236.5°.

BERTHING

In the inner harbour alongside the rather rough pier on the east side, if space permits. Depth here is around four metres. Don't go too far in, as the water shallows considerably towards the inner end. You may need a ladder to get ashore at low tide. The basin on the west side nearly dries out and is for small craft only. Also bear in mind that strong winds from the north-east make the berth alongside the pier most uncomfortable for a yacht.

FACILITIES

A chandlery is located by the small boat basin on the harbour's west side.

PROVISIONING

Shops and supermarkets are located in the town, a little way inland from the end of the inner harbour.

A RUN ASHORE

The only attraction is the working fishing harbour.

EATING OUT

It is not a place for gourmet feasts, but there is a rather pleasant restaurant called Kofradi on the short pier, mid-harbour. Easy to find, it has good all-round views of the action, if there is any, in the harbour.

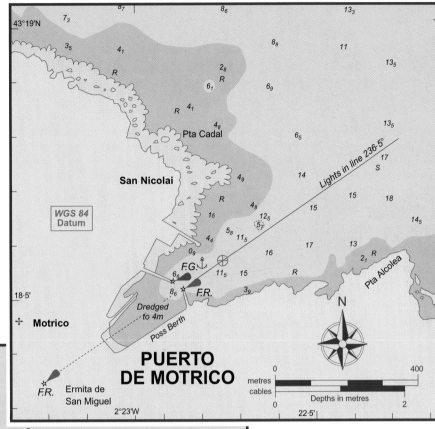

PUERTO DE MOTRICO

ONDÁRROA

ALTERNATIVE PORT OF REFUGE

Ondárroa (Ondarea) is a large and busy fishing port, located two miles west of Motrico, and could be used as a last resort if conditions won't allow you to put in to Motrico. However, it normally doesn't have space for visiting yachts, which are not really welcome here anyway. Plans do exist for a large harbour extension to be built outside the fishing harbour.

You should be able to access Ondárroa in almost all conditions, except for when the wind is blowing hard from the north-east, in which case an approach should not be contemplated. There is plenty of depth at the entrance and throughout the harbour, which is reputed to be about four metres.

Lequeitio has a relatively sheltered harbour, but is usually much busier than seen here

LEQUEITIO (LEKEITIO)

Lequeitio (off Punta Amandarri) – 43°22'.06N / 02°29'.83W

Lequeitio (Lekeitio) is a friendly, vibrant town, with an attractive old quarter near the harbour, many bars and restaurants and two good beaches. There are no dedicated facilities for yachts, but mooring alongside the pier is possible, although space is restricted and depends on how much of the fishing fleet is in port. Yachts often have to raft up alongside each other.

At one time Lequeitio rivalled San Sebastian for summer patronage by the Spanish royal family, but presumably lost out when the 1868 rebellion broke out while Queen Isabel was staying here, forcing her to flee into exile in France.

LOCATION/POSITION

You will find Lequeitio situated roughly half way between San Sebastian (Donostia) and the Abra de Bilbao: approximately 29 miles from the former and just over 30 miles from the latter.

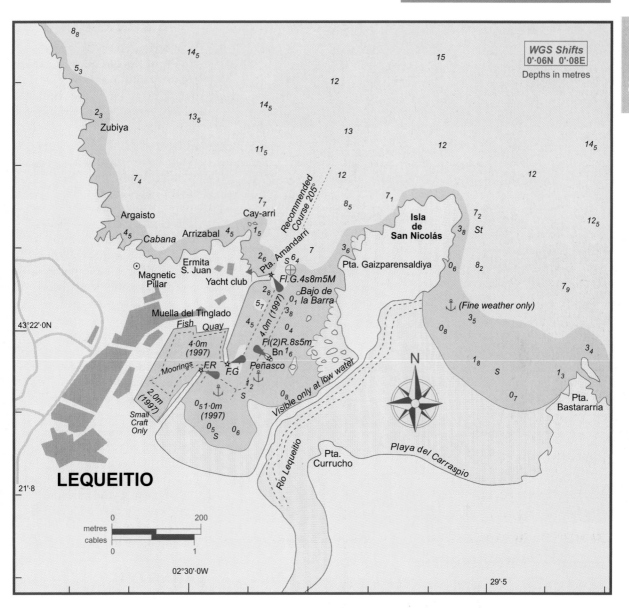

WGS Shifts
0'·06N 0'·08E

Depths in metres

8₈

14₅   15

5₃   12

2₃   13₅   14₅
Zubiya

14₅   12
13₅   12

11₅   13

7₄   12   12   14₅

7₇   Cay-arri   8₅   7₁   Isla   7₂   12₅
Argaisto   de
                                            San Nicolás   3₈ St

4₅ Cabana Arrizabal 4₅ 1₅   3₆
        Ermita   2₆ Pta. Amandarri 7   Pta. Gaizparensaldiya 0₆ 8₂
Magnetic S. Juan   S 6 4   7₉
Pillar   Yacht club   Fl.G.4s8m5M
                        2₈   Bajo de   ⚓ (Fine weather only)
                        5₇ 0₁ la Barra   3₅

Muella del Tinglado   4₅   3₈
    Fish Quay   4₅   0₄   0₈   3₄
43°22'·0N   S   1₃
            4·0m   Fl(2)R.8s5m
            (1997)   Bn 1₆   N
    Moorings FR   Peñasco   0₇   Pta.
                F.G   1 2   Bastararria
        2·0m   S   0₈
        (1997)   0₅1·0m
    Small   (1997)
    Craft   0₅   0₆
    Only   S

LEQUEITIO

21'·8

            0   200
    metres
    cables
            0   1
        02°30'·0W   29'·5

APPROACH AND ENTRANCE

Approach waypoint: 43°22'.53N / 02°29'.60W; 200°;
0.5M to waypoint off Punta Amandarri.

The harbour is tucked behind the Isla de San
Nicolas, which is conspicuous and easily
identifiable from the sea. Approach and entrance
are well marked and present no difficulties,
although drying rocks near the Isla de San Nicolas
are marked by a beacon at their south-westerly
end. When approaching, keep more to the west
side, closer to the moles than to the island.

BERTHING

There are no dedicated berths for yachts in
this fishing harbour, although you may moor
alongside the piers as and where space permits.

Depth here is around three metres. There is a tidal
range of 3.6 metres at springs, so long mooring
warps laid fore and aft are necessary. Quayside
berths around the north part of the harbour are
reserved for landing fish, so you are likely to be
told to move if you moor here. The centre part of
the west quay and inside the outer end of the
Muelle Sur are the best options.

It may be possible to use the harbour mooring
buoys (moor fore and aft) if not in use by fishing
boats. Some moorings are laid in the bay outside
the harbour, but these are private and usually
occupied. In calm weather, with the swell at a
minimum, there is enough room for one or two
yachts to anchor outside the harbour entrance a
couple of boat lengths south of the lit beacon on
Aislado Rock, or alternatively nearer the moorings.

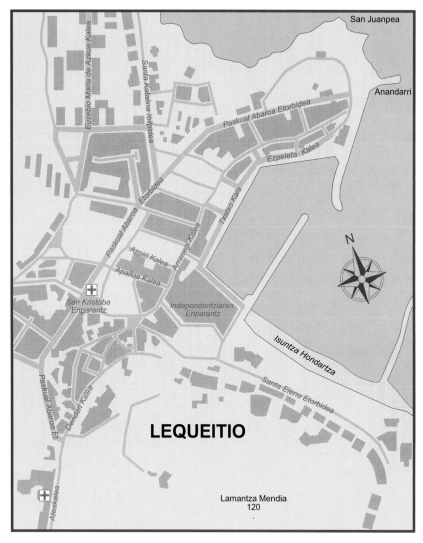

A RUN ASHORE

Wandering about the narrow streets of the old quarter is both pleasant and interesting. A major attraction is the church, which, south of the harbour, is more like a miniature cathedral. Santa Maria de la Asunción will even impress atheists, being late Gothic and elaborate in appearance. The current church dates from the 15th century and was built on the site of one consecrated in 1287. The stunning altarpiece, behind the main altar, is in 16th century Gothic-Flemish style. More worldly pleasures can be found in the bars and cafés along the harbour-front, in the old quarter, and on the beach. The island can be reached on foot at low tide and provides some interesting walks or even climbs.

The local Fiesta (de San Pedro) takes place at the end of June and beginning of July. One remarkable feature of the celebrations is the curious *kaxarranka* dance, which is performed on a wooden chest carried by fishermen.

PROVISIONING

The old quarter of the town, west of the harbour, has a variety of delightful small groceries and bakers. On some mornings a grocery and fish market is held in the narrow street behind the harbour. Supermarkets are in the newer part of town, further inland.

Fish! Just one of the commodities at Lequeitio market

EATING OUT

Lequeitio has many restaurants, some close to the harbour, while bars serve tapas throughout the day (and night). The main meeting place is the Bar Marina at the end of the harbour-front, open from early to late, and offering a wide variety of tasty tapas. An Irish-style pub lies at the other end of the promenade. The restaurant, Kaia Erretegia (near the Bar Marina, Tel: 946 84 02 84) is a good bet for fish. Opposite the church is the restaurant Goitiko, which is a little cheaper. For good, solid Basque food, try Zapirain (Igualdegi 3, Tel: 946 84 02 55), situated a little way into the town, turning right (if coming from the harbour) off the church square.

DAYTIME ANCHORAGES NEARBY

In calm weather, you can anchor east of the Isla de San Nicolas, off the Playa del Carraspio. This

Viewed here from the end of the Muelle Sur, the best berth for yachts is directly opposite the entrance

is good for lunch or swimming when the conditions are settled, but is not really recommended as an overnight anchorage.

A few miles further west, the beautiful Rio de Ea offers a daytime, calm weather anchorage in dramatic settings. A little way up river is the picturesque village of Ea. But be warned, however, the water is extremely shallow and the river dries well to seaward even of the small boat basin outside the village. It is only possible for you to drop anchor off the beach in the river mouth, taking care of the depth, in quiet and settled weather. An overnight stay is not advisable.

Lequeitio's old quarter

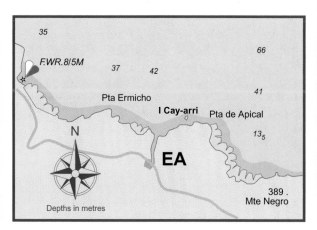

ELANCHOVE (ELANTXOBE)

Elanchove harbour entrance – 43°24'.30N / 02°38'.16W

Elanchove (Elantxobe) is tucked into a corner of the cliffs, a few miles east of Cabo Ogoño, with its harbour and village seeming to tumble down rocks to the sea. It is situated in the Urdaibai biosphere reserve, centred on the Rio de Mundaca.
This is the ultimate sleepy, tranquil fishing village and, being on the road to nowhere – the coastal route passing by further inland, – it has changed little. There is seldom space for visiting yachts, so you mustn't rely on finding a berth in the tiny harbour.

LOCATION/POSITION

Elanchove is east of the wide but unnavigable Rio de Mundaca and its off-lying island of Isla Izaro. Coming from the east, it is not far from the narrow and conspicuous Rio de Ea.

APPROACH AND ENTRANCE

Approach waypoint: 43°24'.47N/02°37'.50W; 070°; 0.5M to harbour entrance.

The harbour approach is south-westerly towards the village, which can be seen from far off, although the entrance itself will only become clearly visible when close in. Both pier-heads are lit, but first-time entry by night would be difficult. Turn to port immediately inside the harbour entrance. The inner harbour is shallow and dries, as is the area behind the northern mole.

Elanchove is one of the smallest harbours on this coast

BERTHING

Moor inside the pier of the outer harbour, the Digue Sur, where depths are around two metres, although care must be taken because of possible underwater obstructions. Creative mooring skills – such as laying a holding off anchor – are definitely necessary. Use fore-and-aft mooring buoys if these are not occupied by fishing boats, or try taking a line to the pier with the other end of the boat moored to a buoy (only of course if this will not block the passage for other craft). There are no harbour facilities.

TRANSPORT

There are buses from the top of the hill to other regional towns. An excursion to Gernika (see below) might be worthwhile, but don't leave your boat unattended. It will be easier to visit Gernika from Zumaya or Bilbao, as there is no secure harbour between these two places.

PROVISIONING

Small shops are scattered along the steep uphill climb towards the top of the cliff.

A RUN ASHORE

The real interest here is a complete absence of touristic features. Although the harbour is at the bottom of a steep cliff, with the village on top, there is really nothing to make you climb the hill, unless you want to enjoy the view or catch a bus. The nearby Gernika is

Elanchove village hangs on the slope above the harbour

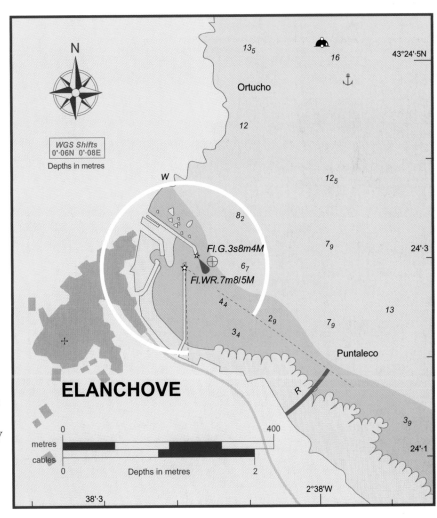

The mouth of the Rio de Mundaca offers a good daytime anchorage

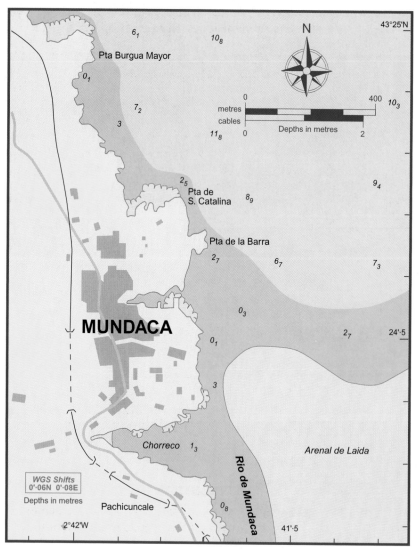

the sacred city of the Basques, who since the 10th century have met below an ancient oak tree for their assemblies. The tree became a symbol of their culture and its remains are now surrounded by an open pavilion, while its successor, grown from an acorn of the original tree, flourishes nearby as a new symbol of Basque freedom. Gernika also has various museums, one of which (Gernika museoa) deals with the younger history of the town and the brutal bombardment by Hitler's Condor legion in 1937 during the Spanish civil war in support of General Franco. Some 80% of the buildings were destroyed and, as market day was chosen for the attack, more than 1,600 of the population were killed with many more seriously wounded.

Picasso took this massacre as the theme of his famous monumental work *Gernika* (*Guernica*), which was returned to Spain after Franco's death, as specified in Picasso's will. It can now be seen in the Centro de Arte Reina Sofia in Madrid.

EATING OUT

The town's gastronomic scope begins and ends with a few basic bars around the harbour.

DAYTIME ANCHORAGES NEARBY

With care in settled weather, you will find a daytime anchorage in the mouth of the Rio de Mundaca, off the village of the same name. There is a tiny port here, but it is too small for comfort and dries out completely.

Bermeo is Euskadi's largest fishing port

BERMEO

Bermeo harbour entrance – 43°25'.4N / 02°42'.4W

Bermeo is a large, commercial fishing harbour with a busy and bustling town. It is not dependent on tourism, for few visitors come here and those who do, don't stay too long. If you want to experience a genuinely normal Spanish provincial town, this would be it.

As the region's largest fishing port, it is, needless-to-say, not ideal for yachts. Although there are two areas allocated to moorings, these are normally occupied by local boats.

LOCATION/POSITION

Bermeo lies east of Cabo Machichaco, which in turn is situated a little over 20 miles east of the Abra de Bilbao.

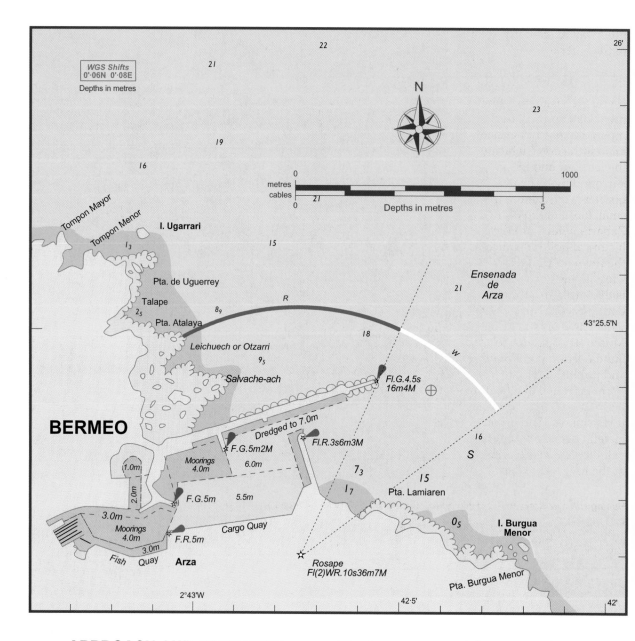

APPROACH AND ENTRANCE

Approach waypoint: 43°25'.75N/02°41'.95W; 225°; 0.5M to harbour entrance.

Coming from the west, the conspicuous Cabo Machichaco, along with its lighthouse, cannot be mistaken. Coming from the east, the Rio de Mundaca and Isla de Izaro are good landmarks. The final approach into Bermeo presents no problems or dangers.

BERTHING

There are no dedicated yacht berths, so go alongside the pier as and where space permits (taking into account the tidal range of about three metres). The south pier of the outer harbour is for large commercial ships, so try the inner basin, again on the south pier, where depths are around three metres. Another small basin branches off to the north, but this is shallow and dries in most places, which maybe explains why it is called Portu Zaharra.

TRANSPORT

There are buses and trains along the coast to other towns, including Bilbao and Gernika (see under Elanchove).

PROVISIONING

Bermeo has a wide selection of shops in the town. A supermarket can be found in Kalea Dolariaga, a little way to the north-west of the harbour.

A RUN ASHORE

If you are visiting in your own boat, you will be moored in one of Bermeo's main attractions, which is the harbour and its surroundings. The old quarter is adjacent to the small basin of the Portu Zaharra, with a number of historical buildings such as the town hall, built in 1732. Close to the Portu Zaharra is the tower Torre Ercilla, dating back to around 1500, which now houses the Museo del Pescador (closed Sunday afternoon, Monday and public holidays). Various fishing and boating items are on display on three storeys. And if you haven't had enough of fish yet, then the biggest fiesta of the town is the fish

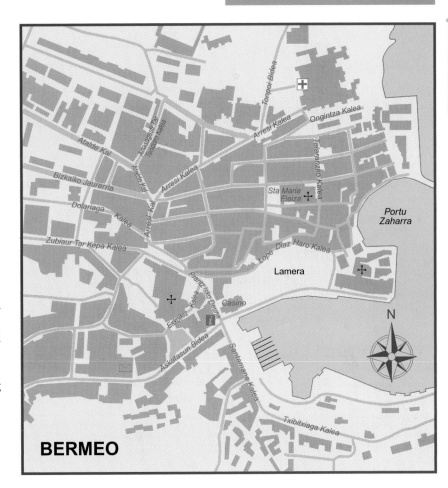

BERMEO

Fishing rules at Bermeo – it is a working town that makes few concessions to tourism, including yachts

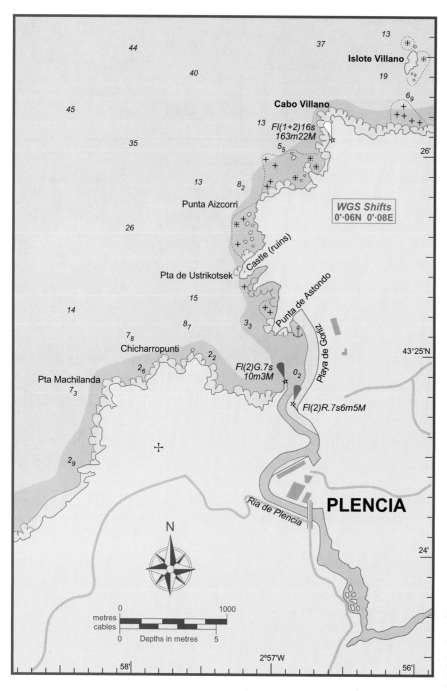

A good one to try is Restaurant Jokin, situated just south of the basin (Eupeme Deuna Kalea 13, Tel: 946 88 40 89, credit cards accepted). Beside the cloister is the restaurant Beitxi (Eskoikiz 6, Tel: 946 88 00 06, credit cards accepted), which is slightly cheaper than Jokin.

DAYTIME ANCHORAGES NEARBY

Around the corner (18 miles further west, past Cabo Machichaco and Cabo Villano) is the Ria de Plencia, which has a long, sandy beach and, as it is the northern terminus of the new Bilbao Metro, is directly connected to Bilbao. Hence the beach is well frequented, especially during sunny summer weekends. The harbour inside the ria is tiny, crowded with local boats and dries out. However, in fine weather the anchorage in the bay just off the north end of the beach, preferably tucked in behind the small jetty at Punta de Astondo, makes for a pleasant bathing or lunchtime stopover if you are *en route* to or from Getxo or Las Arenas in the Abra de Bilbao.

Immediately east of Bermeo you will find the Rio de Mundaca, where there is a possible daytime anchorage (for more information see under Elanchove).

festival held in September. Bang in the town centre, just opposite the small park (Lamera) north of the harbour, is the church and cloister of San Francisco, founded in 1357 and one of the few remaining cloisters. During the course of its long and varied history, it was also once a market.

EATING OUT

Fish restaurants are the main gastronomic attraction here, most of which are scattered around the old quarter near Portu Zaharra.

USEFUL INFORMATION
Harbour master Tel: 946 18 64 45; VHF 09
Tourist office Tel: 946 17 91 54

The Abra de Bilbao. In the foreground is the modern marina at Getxo. Las Arenas is across the bay, beside the river entrance

BILBAO (BILBO)

Bilbao outer harbour entrance – 43°22'.91N / 03°04'.79W

Bilbao, a large natural harbour with two good yacht havens, is the biggest city of the Basque country and is situated a few miles upstream on the river. Although, sadly, it is not navigable as far up as here, yacht harbours are located in the elegant suburbs of Getxo and Las Arenas,

from where the city can be reached by metro or bus. Bilbao, or Bilbo in Basque, is the most interesting and fascinating town in northern Spain, a cultural and commercial centre with a busy ferry harbour, an international airport, universities, a colourful historical centre, theatres, concert halls and the famous Guggenheim museum. Several foreign consulates are conveniently situated in Las Arenas, and Bilbao, with 360,000 inhabitants, has all the major city

facilities as well as many festivals/concerts during the summer .

Getxo hosts its own highly acclaimed music festivals, amongst these the famous jazz festival (July), the blues festival (June), and the folk festival (September).

LOCATION/POSITION

The Abra de Bilbao marks the western end of the Basque country. The entrance to the outer

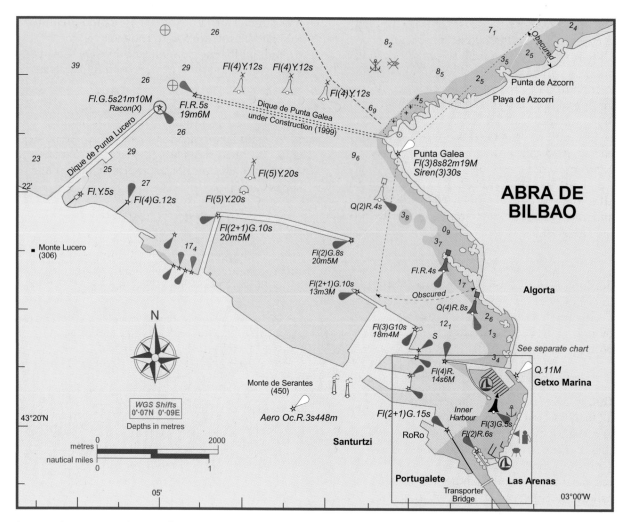

Labels on chart:
- 26
- 39
- 29
- 26
- Fl(4)Y.12s
- Fl(4)Y.12s
- Fl(4)Y.12s
- 8₂
- 7₁
- 2₄
- Obscured
- 2₅
- Fl.G.5s21m10M Racon(X)
- Fl.R.5s 19m6M
- Dique de Punta Galea under Construction (1999)
- 8₅
- 2₅
- 3₅
- Punta de Azcorn
- Playa de Azcorri
- Dique de Punta Lucero
- 26
- 6₉
- 4₅
- Punta Galea Fl(3)8s82m19M Siren(3)30s
- 23
- 29
- 25
- 9₆
- ABRA DE BILBAO
- 22'
- Fl.Y.5s
- 27
- Fl(4)G.12s
- Fl(5)Y.20s
- Fl(5)Y.20s
- Q(2)R.4s
- 3₈
- Monte Lucero (306)
- 17₄
- Fl(2+1)G.10s 20m5M
- Fl(2)G.8s 20m5M
- 0₉
- 3₇
- Fl.R.4s
- 1₇
- Algorta
- Fl(2+1)G.10s 13m3M
- Obscured
- Q(4)R.8s
- 2₆
- 1₃
- N
- Fl(3)G10s 18m4M
- 12₁
- S
- See separate chart
- 3₄
- Q.11M Getxo Marina
- Monte de Serantes (450)
- Fl(4)R. 14s6M
- WGS Shifts 0'·07N 0'·09E
- Depths in metres
- Aero Oc.R.3s448m
- Inner Harbour
- Fl(3)G.5s
- Fl(2+1)G.15s
- Fl(2)R.6s
- metres / nautical miles
- 0 / 2000 / 0 / 1
- Santurtzi
- RoRo
- 43°20'N
- Portugalete
- Las Arenas
- Transporter Bridge
- 05'
- 03°00'W

bay is about six miles south-west of Cabo Villano and from here it is less than 40 miles to Santander. The outer bay has a western breakwater (Dique de Punta Lucero) and a half-built, mostly submerged eastern one (Dique de

The marina at Getxo

Punta Galea). The entrance is between the two pier-heads, which are both lit. The eastern one is effectively an island structure.

APPROACH AND ENTRANCE

Approach waypoint: 43°23'.40N / 03°04'.79W; 180°; 0.5M to outer harbour entrance.

Entry is possible at any state of the tide and weather. Coming from east or north, the Abra is easily identified by the headland of Cabo Villano, with its powerful lighthouse. Care is needed, especially at night or in bad visibility, to identify the entrance to the outer bay between the two pier-heads (see above).

The long, eastern breakwater, as mentioned, is actually incomplete and, while it may be possible to pass through, as some fishermen in small boats with up-to-date, local knowledge sometimes do, it would be downright foolish to attempt to do the same by yacht. Depths and obstructions along this part-submerged breakwater are neither marked nor charted, so enter by the shipping channel, between the two lit pier-heads.

There can be strong tidal streams and, in heavy onshore winds, large seas in the outer entrance. Yacht harbours are located on the port side of the inner harbour, opposite the commercial harbour at Santurtzi. In the north corner is the new and comfortable marina of Getxo, while at the south end of the bay, near the mouth of the river Nervion leading to Bilbao, is the club harbour of the smart and welcoming Las Arenas Yacht Club, although space inside this harbour is restricted and yachts larger than 15 metres are advised to use the marina instead.

BERTHING

Berthing is on pontoons with finger berths in both Getxo marina and Las Arenas Yacht Club. Berths will be allocated by marina or yacht club staff in both harbours.

MARINA FACILITIES

Getxo: this brand new marina offers all facilities and over 800 berths. Water and electricity are on the pontoons, diesel - Gasoleo A is available, along with showers, toilets, shops, restaurants, bars and chandleries ashore. Hoisting out facilities include a travelift and slipway, with mechanics and repair services as well as hard-standing in the marina area.

Las Arenas: this offers fewer facilities, but does have a luxurious clubhouse, incorporating a lounge area, bar, restaurant and a swimming pool, all of which may be used by guests. Other amenities include a travelift, mast crane and a small chandlery. The club employs several full-time boatmen, who are usually helpful should you have technical or other problems. The one drawback, however, is that most of them only speak Spanish.

TRANSPORT

Bilbao, about 10 miles away from Getxo and a little less from Las Arenas, can be reached by the metro from either place. Alternatively, there are buses into town. Bilbao has an international airport, a ferry to Portsmouth and train and bus stations with connections throughout Iberia and mainland Europe. Cars can be hired in the yacht harbours or in Bilbao itself.

PROVISIONING

There are small shops for basic needs in the marina and larger supermarkets in Las Arenas – just a short taxi ride away. Las Arenas also has local shops, elegant boutiques, cafés, tapas bars and restaurants.

A RUN ASHORE

The main attraction is Bilbao, although Getxo is a pleasantly pretty suburb with impressive old villas along the waterfront. Bilbao, granted city rights by Don Diego Lopez de Haro back in 1300,

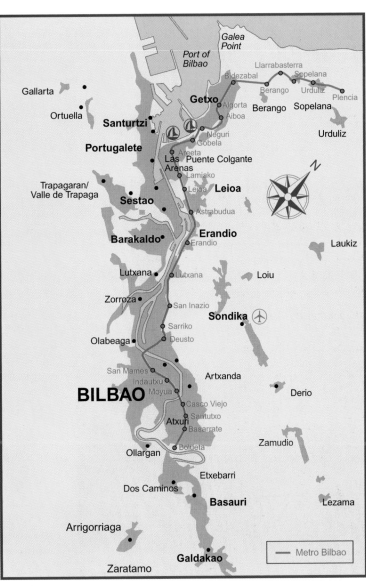

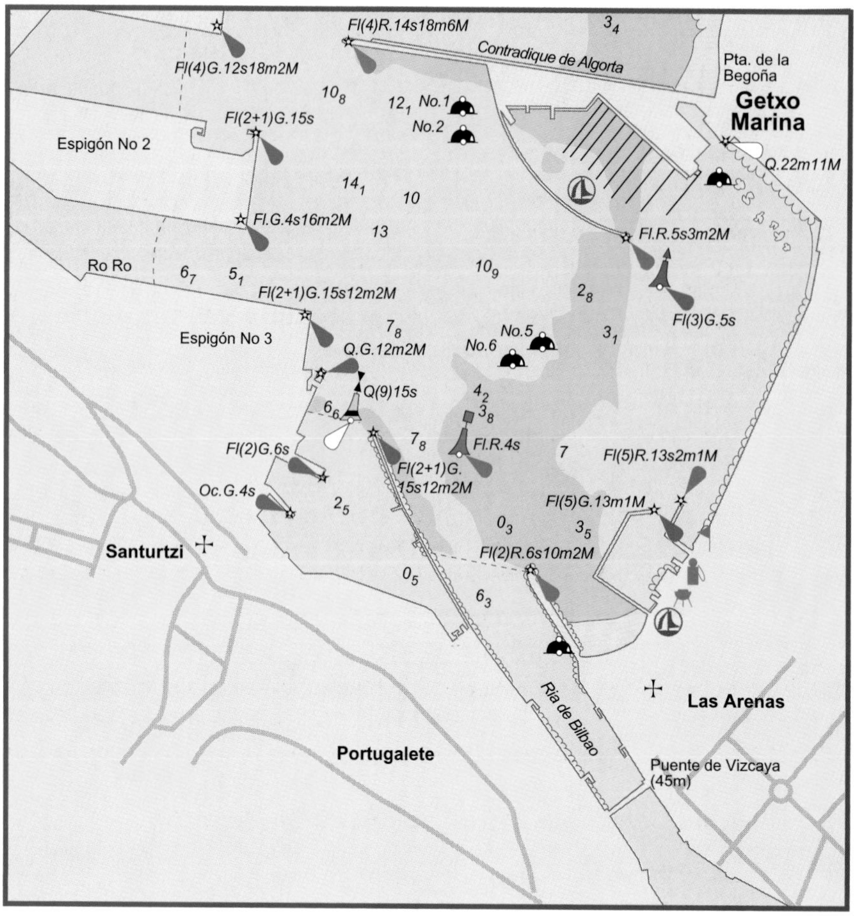
Fl(4)R.14s18m6M
Contradique de Algorta
Pta. de la Begoña
Getxo Marina
Fl(4)G.12s18m2M
Fl(2+1)G.15s
Espigón No 2
No.1
No.2
Q.22m11M
Fl.G.4s16m2M
Fl.R.5s3m2M
Ro Ro
Fl(2+1)G.15s12m2M
Fl(3)G.5s
Espigón No 3
Q.G.12m2M
No.5
No.6
Q(9)15s
Fl.R.4s
Fl(2)G.6s
Fl(2+1)G.15s12m2M
Fl(5)R.13s2m1M
Oc.G.4s
Fl(5)G.13m1M
Santurtzi
Fl(2)R.6s10m2M
Ria de Bilbao
Las Arenas
Portugalete
Puente de Vizcaya (45m)

is squeezed into both sides of the Rio Nervion valley and surrounded by motorways. Well over a million people live in and around the city, which is about half of the population of the entire Basque country. Bilbao used to be industrial, with iron from the surrounding mines the main export, but has changed into the banking and financial centre of northern Spain.

When visiting the centre, use the following metro stations: Moyua is nearest (but not close) to the Guggenheim, where there is also a tourist information office. Abando is near the mainline station in the modern city centre. Casco Viejo, the next stop, is across the river, close to the Plaza Nueva. The main tourist office is located on the river bank at the north end of the small park, not far from this metro station.

Museo Guggenheim. Bilbao's spectacular landmark

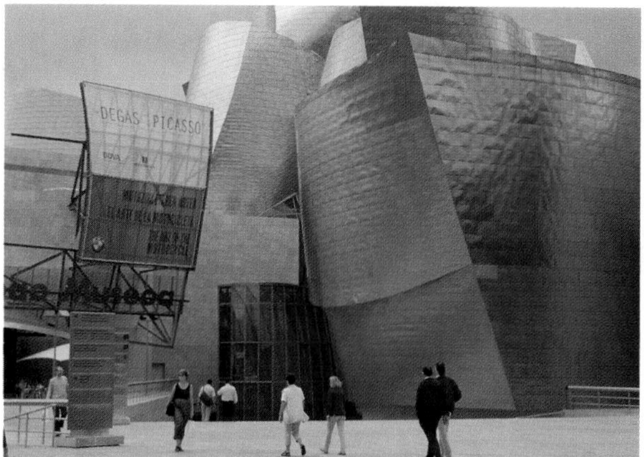
DEGAS PICASSO

One of the predominant attractions is the old city (Casco Viejo). Along the cool, narrow streets are many cosy bars and unusual shops. Plaza Nueva, the main centre here, is a large square surrounded by arcades that house a number of cafés. It is always a good place for a break and a coffee, although things do liven up in the evenings when everyone comes out to meet and have a drink.

On the next square, the Plaza de Arriga, is one of Bilbao's most charming art deco cafés, the Café Boulevard. Other highlights of the old quarter are the cathedral, in the heart of the district, dating back to the 15th century. From here, the Siete Calles (Seven Streets), which have the highest density of bars and clubs, lead to an impressive market, the Mercado de la Ribera, a multi-storey building right at the river's edge.

Also on the Plaza de Arriaga is a monumental opera house and theatre, built along the lines of the Paris opera. Opposite the cathedral is the Basque museum (Museo Arqueologico, Etnografico e Historio Vasco, open Tuesday to Saturday 1000 – 1330/1600 – 1900 and Sunday 1030 – 1330), which is housed in a former cloister. The exhibits give insights into the area's rich history, although in places it can be a bit confusing.

The town's main attraction must surely be the Guggenheim museum (opened 1997) in its spectacular building on the south bank of the river at the northern end of the new city. The building was designed by the American architect, Frank Owen Gehry, and is in itself a piece of art.

Chapter 1

Inside are exhibits from the Guggenheim collection of modern and contemporary art, the world's largest private art collection, which was turned into a trust in 1937 by the American entrepreneur Solomon Guggenheim. (Opening times: Tuesday to Sunday 1100 – 2000 during July, and to 2100 during August).

Art enthusiasts should also not miss the Museo de Bellas Artes in Bilbao, now somewhat overshadowed by the Guggenheim but, with old and modern masters in two separate buildings, is still well worth a visit. It is not far from the Guggenheim on the Plaza del Museo, bordering on the Parque de Doña Casilda de Iturriza. (Open Tuesday to Saturday 1000 – 1330 and 1600 – 1930, Sunday

The view from the transporter bridge takes in both marinas and the harbour entrance

1000 – 1400. Combination tickets to both are available, called Bono Artea).

The Basilica de Begoña is a 16th century church on a hill overlooking Bilbao, surrounded by a pleasant park with good views over the city. It can

Bilbao lies in a deep and winding valley, the sides of which are an effective backdrop to the city buildings

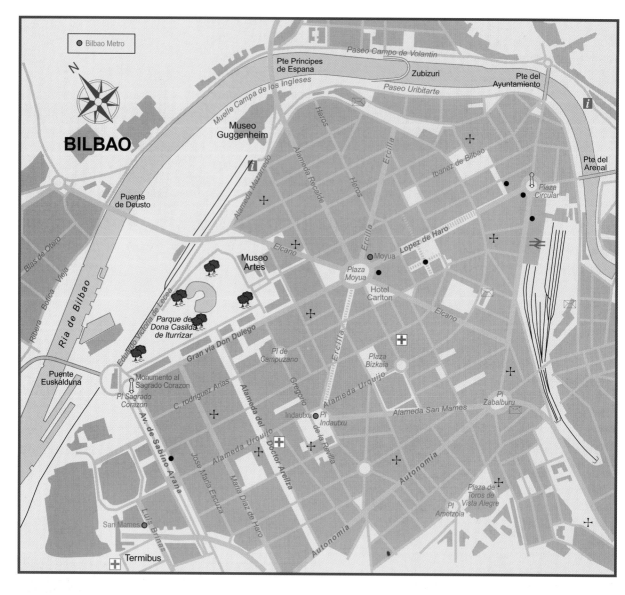

The Guggenheim has echoes of Bilbao's shipbuilding past

be reached from the old town (Plaza del Miguel Unamuno) by a long flight of stairs or by lift (*ascensor*) alongside the San Nicolas church north of the Plaza Nueva.

In Las Arenas, the Puente Bizkaia bridge is an impressive structure. Dating back to 1893, it has a hanging capsule to carry cars and passengers to and from the river banks. This, the oldest transporter bridge in the world, has recently been renovated, with viewing facilities for visitors now added. For a small fee, you can ascend by a lift to the top of either tower, cross the upper support bridge by a walkway equipped with viewing/information points, then descend the other tower. The excursion finishes by re-crossing in the gondola: certainly an experience not to be missed, especially when berthed in Las Arenas, just a few minutes walk away.

The magnificent transporter bridge links Las Arenas and Portugalete

The marina at Getxo and the yacht club in Las Arenas are safe and secure places to leave the boat for awhile, which makes this an ideal base for an excursion by car to the beautiful wine region of La Rioja, situated on a wide plain behind the first range of mountains inland of Bilbao and about three hour's drive away. It is worth, *en route*, visiting the capital of the Basque region, Vitoria-Gasteiz, a city surrounded by a belt of ugly suburban housing estates and industrial developments, but with a small historical centre around the Plaza Virgen de la Blanca and Plaza de España. Narrow streets and Gothic buildings show the age of this place, which was founded by Navarre's King Sancho in 1181.

EATING OUT

There are several restaurants in the Getxo marina area, but for more traditional Basque cuisine, you need to go to the ones in Neguri (just north of the marina) and Las Arenas. From the marina, try the (rather expensive) restaurant Artaza (Avenida de los Chopos 12, Tel: 944 91 28 52) or Jolastoki (Leioako Etorbidea 24, Tel: 944 91 20 31). In Las Arenas, Igeretxe is the up-market option (Calle

In the Casco Viejo, Bilbao

Gexto's elegant waterfront villas

The marina environs are modern and equally elegant

Mayor 28, Tel: 944 64 55 93), while La Estrada (Muelle Tomas Olabarri 4, Tel: 944 64 80 01) is more moderately priced. Las Arenas also has an abundance of attractive tapas bars, where you can enjoy the local custom of drifting from bar to bar, drinking small glasses of wine or beer and indulging in the delicious tapas from the huge platters on the counters.

Much the same applies to downtown Bilbao, especially the Siete Calles area of the old town. However, as there are well over a hundred restaurants of all varieties in the centre, there is every chance of getting a meal of a type and price to suit. For luxurious dining, try the restaurant Zortizo, which boasts a Michelin star and is in the newer part of town, north of the main station and about half way between it and the Guggenheim museum (Alameda de Mazzaredo 17, Tel: 944 23 97 43). The up-market Victor Montes, in the old town on Plaza Nueva (Tel: 944 15 16 78), has an elegant interior and offers freshly cooked Basque cuisine. More moderately priced and very interesting is the restaurant Bikandi, also in the old town, with a crowded bar downstairs and a dining room on the first floor (Calle Somera 21, one of the Siete Calles). Practically opposite the main station is the trendy restaurant Nicolas (Calle Ledesma 10, Tel: 944 24 07 37, closed Sunday nights), which is run by an ambitious local chef in a traditional setting.

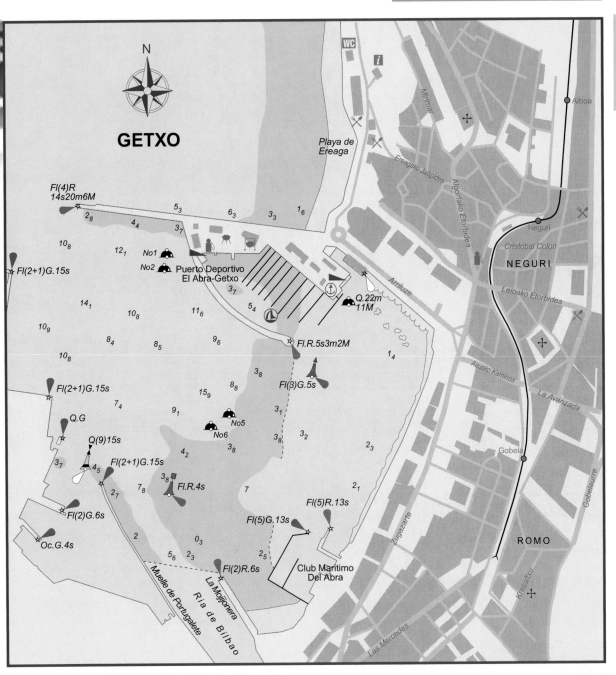

DAYTIME ANCHORAGES NEARBY

Yachts can anchor off the beaches north of Getxo in the outer harbour, but take care not to come too close inshore, as the water is shallow and full of rocks. For daytime anchoring only: off Playa de Ereaga (easily reached on foot from the marina) and one bay further north, off the Playa de Arrigunaga, taking care of the rocks and underwater obstacles that extend north-west from the Punta de San Ignacio. There are numerous local moorings between the marina at Getxo and the yacht club harbour at Las Arenas, where it might be possible to find an overnight anchorage.

THE CANTABRIAN COAST

The striking coastline of Santander

Cantabria is the next province along the coast, west of the Basque country. It begins just after the Abra de Bilbao at the charming seaside town of Castro Urdiales, extending 57 miles as far as the equally delightful fishing village of San Vicente de la Barquera.

Sunset at Rio de Solia, Santander

This too is a fairly straightforward coast, with the headland of Cabo Mayor and the Ria of Santander being virtually the only conspicuous features.

A backdrop of high mountains can be seen far out at sea although, as most of these mountains are in fact quite some way inland, they are predominantly too far from the shore to produce local squalls or such effects. Coastal currents, most likely caused by periods of steady wind from one direction or another, are variable.

This stretch of coastline has a safe, well-equipped marina at Santander, as well as some

The inner harbour at Castro Urdiales

rather more rustic river mouths and fishing harbours, which therefore require a bit more improvisation and seamanship when mooring up or dropping anchor. Santander is a suitable place to leave the yacht for a few days in order to go off and explore the high mountain range of the Picos de Europa, shared between Cantabria and Asturias further west.

Unimproved harbours and rolling hills are typical of Cantabria

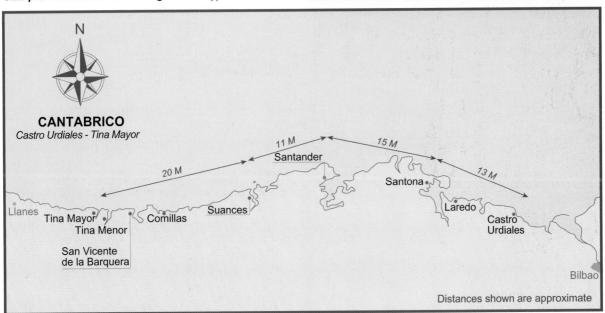

CANTABRICO
Castro Urdiales - Tina Mayor

20 M
11 M
Santander
15 M
Santona
13 M

Llanes
Tina Mayor
Tina Menor
San Vicente de la Barquera
Comillas
Suances
Laredo
Castro Urdiales
Bilbao

Distances shown are approximate

CASTRO URDIALES

Castro Urdiales harbour entrance – 43°22'.89N / 03°12'.38W

Castro Urdiales is a lively, interesting coastal town, boasting a Knights Templar mediaeval castle and a church from the 14th century. Its small historic centre, dating back, as the name suggests, to Roman times, is positioned around a drying inner harbour. Tourism is not as intrusive here as in other places along the coast, such as Laredo, although there are two popular beaches close to the harbour.

The Romans, after exploiting the local iron mines, came to view this area as one of their most important settlements in the northern peninsula. In 1296 the Hermanadad de las Marismas (League of the salt marshes) was founded here. It was an important trading league and a major Atlantic maritime power through the middle ages. Today, Castro Urdiales is chiefly a suburb of Bilbao.

Although this fishing harbour may be in decline, space is still pretty limited, with the whole western half of the outer harbour full of moorings that are either dedicated to fishing boats or occupied by leisure craft. Despite an active sailing club, which is very welcoming to visitors, all the moorings are private and not usually available for visiting yachts.

LOCATION/POSITION

Castro Urdiales is nine miles west of the Abra de Bilbao and about the same distance east of Laredo.

Castro Urdiales harbour. There is ample room for anchoring just inside the entrance

APPROACH AND ENTRANCE

Approach waypoint: 43°23'.21N/03°11'.86W; 230°; 0.5M to harbour entrance.

The entrance is easy and safe at any state of the tide. Coming from the east, the town and castle are easily identified, but from the west they are hidden by the Punta da Rabanal cemetery. A lighthouse on the castle, along with both mole heads lit, make a night approach possible.

Castro Urdiales breakwater.
The nearest yachts are at anchor

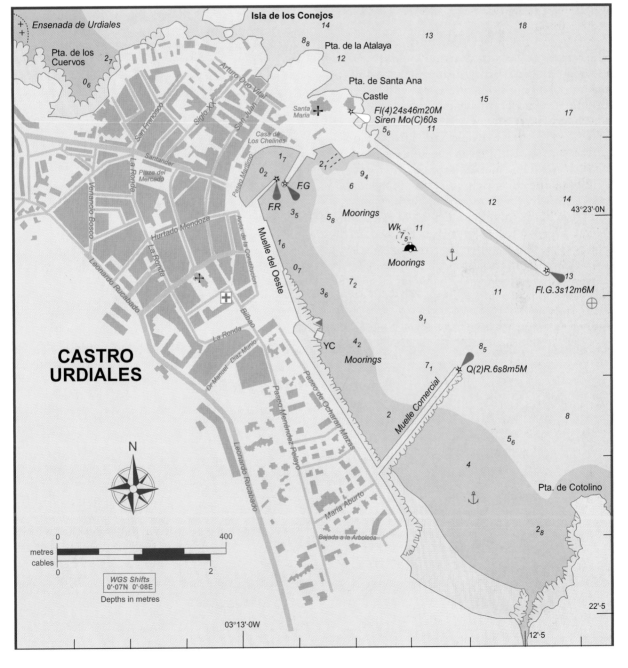

CASTRO URDIALES

Fl(4)24s46m20M
Siren Mo(C)60s

F.G

F.R

Moorings

Wk

Moorings

Fl.G.3s12m6M

YC

Moorings

Q(2)R.6s8m5M

Muelle Comercial

Pta. de Cotolino

Isla de los Conejos
Pta. de la Atalaya
Pta. de Santa Ana
Castle
Santa Maria
Casa de Los Chelines
Ensenada de Urdiales
Pta. de los Cuervos

N

0   400
metres
cables
0   2

WGS Shifts
0'·07N 0'·08E
Depths in metres

43°23'·0N

03°13'·0W

22'·5
12'·5

The old town at Castro Urdiales, full of bars and cafés

BERTHING

The tiny inner harbour dries out and is completely taken over by fishing boats, while the outer harbour is also crowded with larger fishing vessels and private moorings. There is the chance of picking up a mooring, but visiting yachts will be chased away from those that are privately owned and the yacht club has no visitors' moorings marked as such.

The best area to anchor is just inside the harbour, between the northern group of moorings and the entrance, where there is room for a dozen or more yachts. The depth is around 10 metres and, as the bottom is sand or mud on rock, the holding is variable, so dig the hook in well. Unfortunately it's quite a long way in the dinghy to the inner harbour and the yacht club doesn't permit landing

The cathedral of Santa Maria de la Ascunión

on its steps, as these are reserved for a launch service (see below). In quiet weather, an alternative anchorage is outside the entrance, immediately south of the southern jetty, just off the beach. Here, you can drop anchor in a depth of about three metres, although at times it can be very rolly.

HARBOUR FACILITIES

Water is available by can from the yacht club, while fuel is obtainable by can from a filling station on the pier near the inner harbour entrance. The yacht club runs a launch service, which will pick you up and deliver you to your boat if you have found a mooring or anchorage inside the harbour. The club's facilities include showers, toilets, bar and an excellent restaurant.

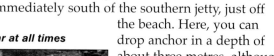

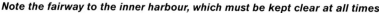
Note the fairway to the inner harbour, which must be kept clear at all times

Beware of fishing lines if approaching the harbour by dinghy

The adjacent mediaeval castle, built by the Knights Templar, has a pentagonal plan with defensive towers at each corner, upon one of which the lighthouse is built.

EATING OUT

Castro Urdiales has many restaurants, with some of the better ones found around the inner harbour. Close to the harbour, by the Plaza de Ayuntamiente and the impressive old town hall, are two noted for traditional cooking: El Segoviano (La Correia 19, Tel: 942 86 18 59) and, a few doors further on, Meson Marinero (La Correia 23, Tel: 942 86 00 05). Both are fairly expensive, although the latter doesn't accept credit cards, and each serves wonderful tapas, a good meal in itself. There are less expensive places, not to mention the many tapas bars scattered around the old part of town, the waterfront and of course the yacht club. One thing is certain: you won't starve in Castro Urdiales.

TRANSPORT

Buses and trains to Bilbao and elsewhere in the region; hire cars available in town.

PROVISIONING

There are numerous shops and small supermarkets in the second and third streets, which run parallel to and inland from the harbour. A major hypermarket outside the town can best be reached by taxi. Ask at the yacht club.

A RUN ASHORE

Castro Urdiales is a vibrant town, with numerous bars, restaurants and shops. Its historic centre is grouped around the tiny inner harbour. The castle-like church (Nuestra Señora de la Asunción) on top of the hill is worth visiting. It dates from the 14th century and, with its flying buttresses, cloisters and large interior, is considered Cantabria's most outstanding Gothic building.

Just one of the many refreshment options

USEFUL INFORMATION

Tourist office Tel: 942 87 13 37
Club Nautico de Castro Urdiales Tel: 942 86 12 34

Santona & Laredo

0.6M north of Canto de Laredo – 43°25'.90N / 03°24'.60W

Laredo, with its yacht club at Punta del Pasaje, Santona and the village of Colindres are all situated close together and share a common approach from seaward. You enter the remarkably scenic bay of Laredo, with high mountains either side and a long, curved beach, behind which the Rio de Ason leads to Santona and, a little bit further along a buoyed channel, to Colindres.

Laredo is a busy, popular holiday resort, developed around an old fishing village with a mediaeval centre. The long, sandy beach, stretching to the west and north-west of the old town, is a magnet for summer visitors, although a row of rather ugly buildings has sprung up along the peninsula behind the beach. There is a fairly crowded and partly drying fishing harbour near the town centre which, although picturesque, has precious little space for visiting yachts. Laredo's yacht club is situated four miles north-west of the old harbour, around the point (Punta del Pasaje) at the end of the beach, and does have an anchorage and mooring buoys. Its clubhouse provides some facilities, although it's a very long way from the town, so you will need to take a bus.

Laredo harbour. Not much room for visiting yachts

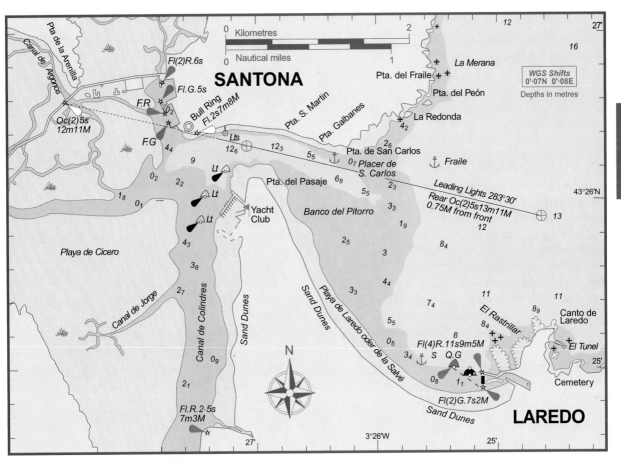

Chapter 2

SANTONA

Pta. de la Arenilla
Canal de Argoños
Fl(2)R.6s
Fl.G.5s
F.R
Oc(2)5s 12m11M
Bull Ring
Fl.2s7m8M
F.G
Pta. S. Martin
Pta. Galbanes
Lts
Pta. del Fraile
La Merana
Pta. del Peón
La Redonda
Fraile
Pta. de San Carlos
Placer de S. Carlos
Pta. del Pasaje
Banco del Pitorro
Leading Lights 283°30'
Rear Oc(2)5s13m11M
0.75M from front
Yacht Club
Playa de Cicero
Canal de Jorge
Canal de Colindres
Sand Dunes
Sand Dunes
Playa de Laredo oder de la Salvé
N
El Rastrillar
Canto de Laredo
El Tunel
Fl(4)R.11s9m5M
S Q.G
Cemetery
Fl.R.2·5s 7m3M
Fl(2)G.7s2M
Sand Dunes
LAREDO

WGS Shifts
0'·07N 0'·08E
Depths in metres

43°26'N

Santona is a rather sleepy, derelict fishing village and a small military post. This lies opposite Punta del Pasaje and has two small harbour basins, both of which usually have enough space for visitors.

Colindres, at the end of a buoyed channel that begins past Punta del Pasaje and Santona, is dull, charmless and off the beaten track for yachts. However it is close to the main coastal road and has a large hypermarket close by.

LOCATION/POSITION

The bay of Laredo and entrance to the Rio de Ason (leading to Santona) are about eight miles west of Castro Urdiales and 17 miles east of Santander.

The Club Nautico overlooks the sheltered waters behind Punta del Pasaje

APPROACH AND ENTRANCE

Approach waypoint: 43°25'.89N/ 03°24'.66W; 283°; 1.8M to the north of Punta del Pasaje: 43°26'.32N/03°27'.01W. The bay is immediately east of the steep and unmistakable Montaña Santona, on the extremity of which is Punta Pescador. Laredo's town and harbour are at the east end of the bay. There are no dangers on entering this bay, but when approaching the harbour at Laredo, take care to stay west of the pier-head as there are rocks and shoals north of the breakwater. To reach the yacht club or the harbours of Santona or Colindres, continue past Punta del Pasaje, the north-west tip of the beach, turning to starboard for Santona, or following the buoyed channel – Canal de Colindres – to Colindres.

The partly-drying, picturesque fishing harbour at Laredo

A shallow area south of the approaches to Santona, between Punta Pescador and Punta de San Carlos, should be given a good offing. The outer approaches to the channel are shallow across to Punta del Pasaje, making entry in strong north to north-easterly winds against the ebb tide difficult. If possible arrive on a flood tide. There is a leading line – 283° – from the point just before Santona harbour, with leading marks that are difficult to see. Inside, the stream can run up to three knots at springs.

BERTHING

Laredo: with a bit of luck you should be able to moor alongside a fishing boat or the outer pier, but only for a short stay. In settled weather, consider anchoring off the beach west of the harbour and using your dinghy. Beware that the area north of the pier is shallow, rocky and foul.

Yacht club: alternatively, pick up a mooring or anchor off the club (inside Punta del Pasaje). If anchoring near the point, keep away from the track used by fishing boats leaving and entering the channel to Colindres, as they are reputed to be intolerant of other craft. Visitors moorings are reported to be two or three cables south of the clubhouse, west of the channel. A bus service runs to and from Laredo.

Santona: primarily a fishing harbour that doesn't welcome yachts, although you might find space alongside a fishing boat in the new (north) basin – the second basin from seaward. When heading for Santona, stay close to the harbour piers, as the estuary shallows dramatically 100 metres or so further west.

Colindres: again a fishing harbour neither geared up for nor welcoming to yachts. The harbour basin to the east is shallow and dries so, if space permits, the pier on the western side is probably a better bet.

FACILITIES

Laredo yacht club: Club Nautico de Laredo has a clubhouse with showers, toilets, restaurant and bar. Water is available by can from ashore. A diesel pump is at the head of the pontoon, but was out of order during our visit and had long been so. The yacht club has a mechanic.

TRANSPORT

A bus goes from Punta del Pasaje (yacht club) to Laredo town centre and from there to the rest of northern Spain. The nearest train station, on the Santander and Bilbao line, is three miles away.

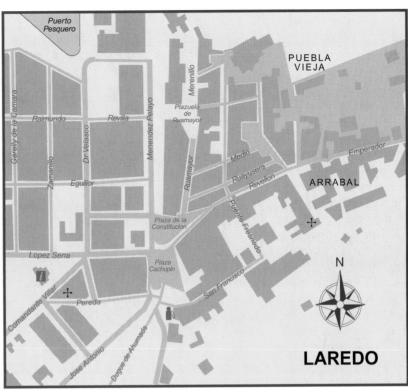

PROVISIONING

Laredo: there are shops in the town centre, with one small supermarket close to the fishing harbour (Calle Zamanillo), along with numerous smaller shops for day-to-day provisioning.
Santona and Colindres: some small shops exist here, but these are unsuitable for provisioning so it is best to use the hypermarket outside Colindres, near the motorway to Santander (a short taxi ride away).

A RUN ASHORE

The mediaeval town centre of Laredo (Puebla Vieja), nestling below the 13th century church of La Asuncion, is well worth seeing, as is the rocky bay on the east side of the hill La Atalaya which, accessed through a pedestrian tunnel, was Laredo's port until 1871. The long beach, Playa de Salve, is pleasant enough, but has lost some of its appeal due to the ugly buildings across the road. In this respect, the beaches on the west side of the peninsular are more attractive. For those of you who like horses, you can book up some horse-riding at the Centro Hipico Laredo (Tel: 942 61 23 09), which is situated inland from the beach about a third of the way to Punta del Pasaje.

EATING OUT

At Punta del Pasaje there are two average restaurants, although there is a wider choice in Laredo itself as well as along the beach. El Pescador (Avenida de la Victoria/Playa Salve, Tel: 942 60 66 38) serves above average seafood and has great views across the bay. Near the harbour in Laredo, El Marinero is particularly noteworthy (Calle Zamanillo 6, Tel: 942 60 60 08). You can also try out one of the many tapas bars in the Puebla Vieja (the old town).

DAYTIME ANCHORAGES NEARBY

Weather and swell permitting, it is possible to anchor on sand off the beach. Once inside the river, you can anchor almost anywhere outside the fairways, but beware it is very shallow and dries out in many places. The best anchorage is probably off the yacht club (or pick up a visitor's mooring if available).

USEFUL INFORMATION

Yacht club (Club Nautico de Laredo)
Tel: 942 60 58 12
Tourist office, Laredo Tel: 942 61 10 96
Local police Tel: 942 60 57 84

SANTANDER

The magnificent entrance to Santander

Santander entrance, south of Punta del Puerto – 43°27'.80N / 03°45'.87W

Santander, the capital of Cantabria, has 190,000 inhabitants, a large commercial harbour and a most attractive town centre. However, the yacht club and its adjacent marina in the Darsena de Molnedo do not welcome visiting yachts, who have to use the newer Marina del Cantabrico.

This is situated close to the airport, another two miles south-west up the estuary, but there is a bus connection to the city, which is well worth a visit.

LOCATION/POSITION

Santander is located 17 miles west of Laredo and immediately east of Cabo Mayor. If using it as a first port of call when crossing Biscay it is 276 miles south of the Chaussée de Sein.

APPROACH AND ENTRANCE

Approach waypoint 0.25M south of Isla de Mouro: 43°28'.08N/03°45'.30W; 236°; 0.5M to harbour entrance. Cabo Mayor, with its distinctive light, is a perfect landmark and there are no special difficulties or dangers in the approach and entrance. In normal conditions the small island of Isla de Mouro can be passed on either side, but should be left to starboard when entering in heavy weather due to rough seas between the island and mainland. The shipping channel into Santander is well marked and lit as well as problem-free.

The Marina del Cantabrico is at the south-west end of the harbour, near the airport. A buoyed channel branches off the main fairway to the marina, almost half a mile past the conspicuous oil terminal jetty. Do not be tempted to cut the corner after passing starboard hand mark No 15, as the water is shallow to the line of the navigation buoys. Stay in the main south-east going channel until half way between starboard-hand marks Nos 15 and 31, and then turn on to the marina leading line – 235° – from the beacons beside the fuelling point. There may be a small north cardinal buoy marking the corner of the shoal.

BERTHING

There are floating pontoons with finger berths for 1,400 boats in the Marina del Cantabrico.

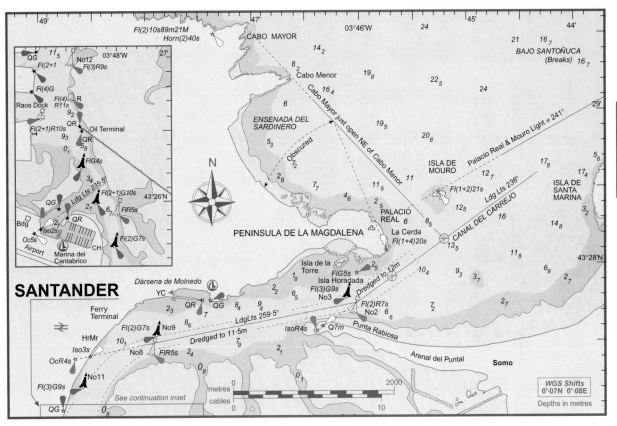

MARINA FACILITIES

Water and electricity are available on the pontoons, with showers, toilets and laundry facilities ashore. There are also a bar and restaurant in the marina building, on the port-hand side as you enter. In 2001 there was another restaurant on the landward side of the marina.

The marina staff are very helpful and usually try to allocate berths conveniently close to the marina office and facilities building. They will also provide some tourist information, including getting to and from the city by bus or taxi, as well as supply you with the latest weather reports. Hauling out is possible, with a travelift and a hard-standing area, alongside which are the chandlers and repair shops.

The city waterfront and the entrance to the Darsena de Molnedo

Isla Horadada, with the city and the Picos de Europa in the background

TRANSPORT

Bus is the cheapest but not always the quickest way into the town centre. A local bus runs up to eight times a day to the Corte Ingles superstore, where you change to the regular city bus. You can also pick up the city bus from a stop about 20 minutes walk from the marina. Taxis may be slow to arrive as they have to be phoned for, and the weekday city traffic is very congested.

The airport is close by, but as the terminal building and the roads leading to it are on the opposite side of the main runway from the marina, this is not as helpful as it sounds. Currently there are no direct flights to Santander from the UK, but you can connect with Barcelona and Madrid.

Both the RENFE (mainline to inland cities) and adjacent FEVE (coastal narrow gauge) train stations are close to the city centre. The FEVE, which runs east to Bilbao and west to Galicia, might seem useful for connecting with harbours along the coast, but it runs inland much of the way, missing many coastal towns as a result. If you enjoy train journeys and are not in a hurry, this is one to consider.

The quickest means of coastwise transport is the inter-city service, which links Galicia with Bilbao and further east. Hire-car information is available from the marina office, where staff can arrange to have a car delivered to the marina. There is also a

tourist office in the city. Brittany Ferries runs a twice-weekly summer service to Plymouth.

PROVISIONING

No shops or other facilities exist near the marina, so all shopping has to be done by bus or taxi. You will find plenty of shops in Santander, including a huge hypermarket in the Corte Ingles shopping centre on the way in to the city.

A RUN ASHORE

Santander is an elegant seaside resort with remarkable beaches close by. The town runs a colourful festival programme in summer. Sadly, in 1941, a huge fire destroyed most of the old city, but despite this there are some elegant boulevards with inviting cafés and shops. The Avenida Alfonso XIII, near the cathedral, is more a square than an avenue and is close to the waterfront. From here, the main shopping street, Avenida Calvo Sotelo, branches off towards the west, with the waterfront Paseo de Pereda leading east in the direction of the yacht club. Approaching the north-east end of the peninsula is the residential area of El Sardineiro, with beautiful Belle Epoque villas and a good beach. The Cathedral dates back to the 13th century, but was rebuilt after the fire of 1941, so only a few parts of it are original. However, it is well worth seeing. A stroll around the centre could also include a visit to the Museo de Bellas Artes (Calle Rubio 6, not far from the market) with exhibits of local, contemporary painters on several floors, as well as 17th and 18th century masters including Goya's portrait of Fernando VII (open Monday to Friday 1000 – 1300 and 1730 – 2000, Saturday 1030 – 1300).

The market is on Plaza de la Esperanza and it opens from Monday to Friday in the afternoons.

Towards the other end of town, past the yacht club, stands the Palacio de Festivales, a modern, ugly building which cannot be missed as you enter the port. Here many concerts and events are staged in the summer.

Further along the road is the Museo Maritimo (Calle San Martin Bajamar, free entry, open Tuesday to Saturday 1100 – 1300 and 1600 – 1900, Sunday 1100 – 1400). It has an aquarium and biological exhibits, including a 24-metre whale skeleton. From here, it is not far to the peninsula de la Magdalena, with a beautiful park, and the Palacio de la Magdalena, which now belongs to the university and has a commanding position overlooking the Isla de Mouro and the port approaches. The park has a small excursion train which takes visitors round it. The trip, incorporating views over the surrounding beaches and coastline and providing information (in Spanish) about its history, terminates at the small sea-animal zoo.

The summer festivals include the Ferias de Santiago, a big fiesta in the Sardineiro area. Usually starting around 25 July, it has bull-fights, fireworks and festivities on the beach. The Festival de Jazz begins at the end of July, an overture to the ever more popular August-long Festival Internacional, now one of the largest in Spain. It offers classical music, ballet, opera, theatre and a famous piano contest in the Palacio de Festivales, as well as many outdoor activities.

EATING OUT IN SANTANDER

Not surprisingly in a city of this size and importance, Santander has many elegant and expensive restaurants. However, there are also many cheap and interesting alternatives for seafood lovers in the fishermen's quarter at Barrio Pesquero, south of the Puerto Pesquero. This area can be found about a mile south of the cathedral along the shore road and is easiest to get to by taxi. Here you will come across about a dozen cheap and cheerful fish restaurants with outdoor charcoal grills, on which the fresh fish is prepared. At weekend lunchtimes and evenings, families gather to enjoy local specialities like *Marmita de Bonito*,

The Marina del Cantabrico is relatively new and well appointed

Peninsula de la Magdalena

a one pot stew with tuna and potatoes.

For more upmarket restaurants, look around in the centre and the Sardineiro areas. The Bar del Puerto (Hernan Cortez 63, Tel: 942 21 56 55), opposite the yacht club harbour, is one of the best places in town. Alternatively you could try the Asador Lechazo Aranda (Tetuan 15, Tel: 942 21 48 23) for very good, down-to-earth regional cooking at moderate prices. For the best night-life, check out the bars and discos around the Plaza Canadio or, a few blocks further away, the Calle Rio de la Pila, both in the old town centre. Bars and inexpensive restaurants are plentiful around Calle Burgos, a couple of blocks west of the Museo de Bellas Artes, where the main road goes underground to create pedestrian areas.

INLAND EXCURSIONS

The Marina del Cantabrico is a good place to leave your boat for a few days. Even if it's not the cheapest option, it is better than leaving it unattended in one of the smaller fishing harbours.

It is a fairly short drive from Santander to the Picos de Europa mountains – a great contrast to the coastal towns. Another option would be to visit the mediaeval village of Santillana de Mar by either hire-car, 'La Cantabrica' bus or train from Santander, although the station at Santillana is about two miles from the town. This picturesque town dates back to the fifth century and has it all: narrow cobbled streets, ancient buildings, palaces and churches. Although named Santillana del Mar, the town isn't anywhere near the sea and is in fact a few miles inland on the C6310 road, close to the famous caves of Altamira. What Jean-Paul Sartre once called 'the prettiest town of Spain' is visited by hoards of tourists in the summer, so if you're planning to stay overnight, which is well worth doing, you should book a room ahead of time.

The most exquisite overnight accommodation is in the local Parador Gil Blas (Plaza Ramon Pelayo 10, Tel: 942 81 80 00). The Hotel Altamira (Calle canton 1, Tel: 942 81 80 25) is also a historic building, but is nearer the town centre and slightly cheaper. Alternative accommodation can be found through the tourist office, Tel: 942 81 82 51.

The famous caves of Altamira are a mile and a half south of Santillana. Although the actual cave is closed to the public, a museum incorporating an exact replica of it is planned for visitors. The caves were discovered by a hunter in 1868, but it was not until 1879 that a local landowner was told about the impressive paintings inside the caves by his eight-year old daughter. It is now known that the cave was inhabited up to 18,500 years ago and that the paintings are about 14,000 years old. The caves were soon dubbed the 'Sistine chapel of prehistoric art'. Replicas of parts of the cave can also be seen in Madrid's archeological museum.

ANCHORAGES NEARBY

There are good anchorages south of the peninsula de la Magdalena, taking care to avoid local moorings and shoals, or off the yacht club, although again be careful to stay clear of local moorings and the race start line immediately in front of the clubhouse. You can continue further upstream past the marina and anchor in the river, but this area is pretty remote.

RIA DE SUANCES

Ria de Suances river entrance – 43°26'.34N / 04°02'.08W

The entrance to Ria de Suances is canalised between two training walls, with a small boat basin inside the river. Outflows from the industrial town of Torrelavega, a few miles upstream, have been known to pollute the river, and the beaches on both sides of the mouth have had to be closed on a couple of occasions. Although the authorities may well be working to minimise this, it would be prudent to make enquiries at neighbouring ports about the present situation if you intend to visit.

LOCATION/POSITION

Ria de Suances is 13 miles west of Santander and 16 miles east of San Vicente de la Barquera.

APPROACH AND ENTRANCE

Approach waypoint: 43°27'.03N / 04°02'.64W, 149°; 0.8M to Ria de Suances river entrance.

This river should never be attempted in heavy weather or if any swell is running. Even in moderate onshore winds and especially on the ebb tide, the seas will break on the bar across the entrance to the Ria de Suances. It is reported to have a minimum depth of around 1.5 metres at LW, although there is more water inside the river.

The river mouth is in a small bay with a sandy beach that can easily be identified from sea, either by the Islas de los Conejos immediately to the east, or by the small headland of Punta de Dichoso and the beach that extends from the beacon east towards its lighthouse. When approaching from the east, stay well clear of the rocks and shoals around the Punta de Cuerno and

Suances entrance and bay. When conditions are like this, entry is feasible

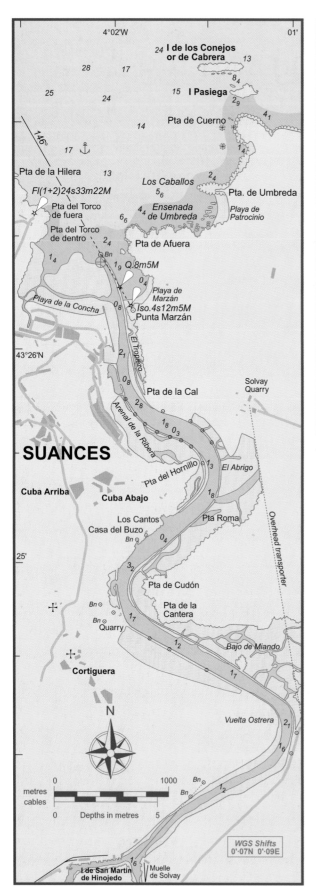

SUANCES

Cuba Arriba

Cuba Abajo

Cortiguera

WGS Shifts
0'·07N 0'·09E

At LW the sand to the west of the entrance is extensive

its off-lying islands. Approach the beacon on the head of the eastern, longer, training wall on a course of 146°, which is the line of the leading marks. These leading marks, one of which is on the training wall about half way between its head and its foot, the other on Punta Marzán, are faded white towers and are both lit, although a night approach is not generally recommended.

Stay close to the training wall when entering, as the deeper channel is very narrow and water shallows rapidly towards the beach to starboard. Entry is preferable on the last third of the flood tide and never on a falling tide due to breakers and danger of grounding.

BERTHING

In Ria de Suances, it is possible to anchor upstream of the small boat harbour in between two and four metres of water at LW. Alternatively, with a small boat, you may be able to find a temporary berth inside the boat harbour, although you should bear in mind that there is less than one metre here at LW.

Deep water is very close to the training wall

FACILITIES

No dedicated facilities, but there are small shops ashore as well as bars, restaurants and hotels.

A RUN ASHORE

Ria de Suances is in a beautiful setting, with fine sandy beaches on both sides of the entrance, but be aware that these have been closed on occasions in the past due to pollution from Torrelavega. This can sometimes spoil an otherwise pleasurable anchorage.

On a calm day, the Ria de Suances is enchanting

EATING OUT

There are several hotels and restaurants around the beach and close to the lighthouse.

DAYTIME ANCHORAGE

If wind, tide height and swell permit, the cove beneath Punta del Torco is a handy stop for lunch. Likewise, if awaiting sufficient water to enter Ria de Suances, it is a good shelter from westerly winds, although the swell will relentlessly find its way around the corner. Depth reduces rapidly towards the beach, which extends a long way out, so be careful if anchoring on a falling tide.

Pretty architecture complements the charming surroundings

A long, sandy beach near the holiday resort of Comillas

COMILLAS

Comillas is an attractive village 10 miles further west of Suances (43°24'N/04°17'W), with a tiny drying harbour. It is therefore recommended solely for a short daytime visit at high tide. The port (about 50 metres by 50 metres) should be attempted only near high water, in calm conditions and good visibility during daylight hours.

The harbour is situated on the east side of the small headland of Punta de la Gerra, which has off-lying shoals and rocks up to about half a mile. Once the bay below the village is identified, approach, sounding carefully, on a south-westerly course, as there are shoal patches with less than two metres of water in places. There are two pairs of leading marks, one to guide you into the bay on 195°, the other to guide you into the harbour on 245°, but they are not easily identified. When entering the harbour, stay close to the pier-head.

The bay is strewn with rocks and shoals, so anchoring here is not possible.

Comillas is an attractive village, which sits on a hill above the small harbour and is popular with people from Santander in summer. Large villas and *palacios* date back to the late 19th century. Comillas has long been fashionable with rich Santander society, so has a good range of restaurants, some of which are well above average. Outstanding is the Capricho de Gaudi (Barrio de Sobrellano outside the village centre towards Cabezon, Tel: 942 72 03 65), a gourmet restaurant in the old palace of the architect Gaudi. Although it isn't cheap, it is considered good value locally and every meal is a real treat. More

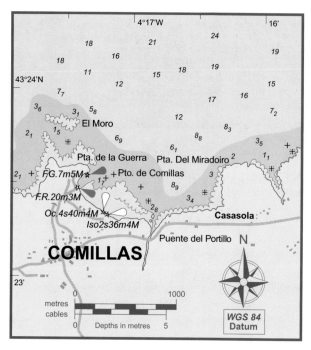

down to earth is the restaurant Gurea in the village centre (Fernandez de Castro 11, Tel: 942 72 24 46), which specialises in Basque cuisine. Another tip is the Bar Filipinas in the centre, an old, unassuming stone house with a rustic interior where good, solid meals at cheap prices are served. It is usually packed, especially at lunchtimes.

USEFUL INFORMATION

Comillas tourist office Tel: 942 72 07 68

SAN VICENTE DE LA BARQUERA

San Vicente de la Barquera entrance – 43°23'.80N / 04°22'.95W

San Vicente de la Barquera is an interesting, sheltered fishing harbour, which lies beneath the impressive backdrop of the Picos de Europa mountain range. It is also a busy provincial town with a picturesque old quarter.

LOCATION/POSITION

San Vicente de la Barquera is situated on the wide estuary of the Ria de San Andres, roughly 30 miles west of Santander and 55 miles east of Gijon.

APPROACH AND ENTRANCE

Approach waypoint: 43°24'.30N / 04°22'.95W; 180°; 0.5M to the harbour entrance.

The entrance itself is not particularly conspicuous, but the spectacularly long beach of Playa de Meron, east of the entrance, cannot be missed, whichever direction you approach from.

There is a bar to cross, and the mouth of the channel sometimes silts up, so entry is not recommended on a falling tide, especially as the ebb can run so strongly that it creates breakers in the entrance. The rocky islets of Pena Mayor and Pena Menor are joined by a breakwater, which forms the west side of the entrance. A shorter rubble training wall, covering at HW, forms the east side. Both are lit at their

Despite the potential difficulty of berthing, San Vicente de la Barquera is a rewarding and interesting port of call

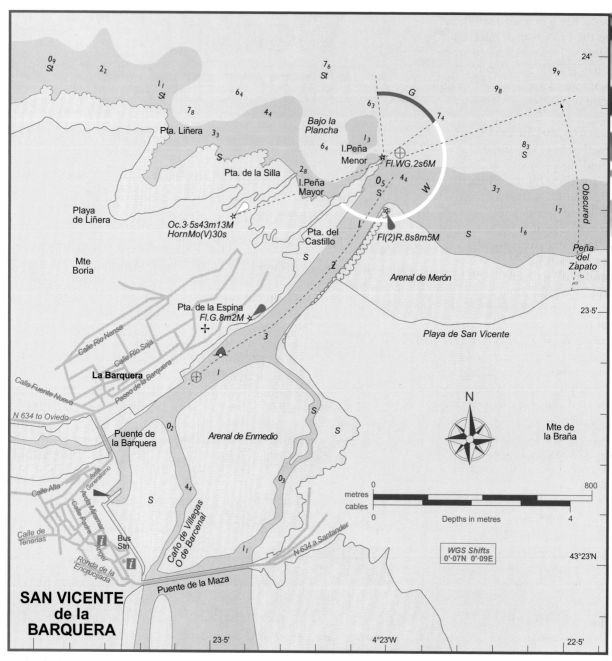

SAN VICENTE
de la
BARQUERA

seaward end and the main light on the western breakwater has a safe approach green sector (Fl WG 2s 6 miles). Make your final approach and entrance on a course of 225° to 220°, sticking slightly to the west of the middle of the channel and also keeping a close watch on your depth. Once past the inshore end of the east side training wall, head for the starboard-hand mark, close to the west shore, and then for the end of the quay. The channel was shallowest (less than two metres at LW) abreast of the starboard-hand mark (2001). A first time night entry is not recommended.

BERTHING

The fishing quay to starboard is usually busy with large fishing trawlers and therefore not available for yachts, although sometimes space might be found at its extreme northern end, where there is less demand for berths by fishing boats.

The small quay underneath the old town, just south of the road bridge, is also taken up by local craft. Vessels not in regular use are often moored to large buoys below the bridge, with lines to the bridge itself. Going alongside one of these, or picking up a mooring buoy and securing a bow or stern line to the bridge, is a practical alternative when the fishing quay is full. Tie up carefully with good springs, as the ebb tide runs strongly through the bridge. Small craft moorings in the middle of the harbour dry out at LW. Finding a place to anchor is difficult, with the edges of the channels already filled with moorings and the remainder of what looks like a large expanse of water drying at LW. However, a multihull or bilge-keeler could anchor almost anywhere in the south part of the harbour, which dries on hard sand. Another anchorage in a narrow channel of varying depth (check by sounding) is behind Punta Espiñha, which is immediately to port when entering. This is convenient for the beach, Playa de Meron, but quite a long way from town.

FACILITIES

There are no dedicated facilities for yachts and the fuel on the fishing pier is for fishing boats only.

TRANSPORT

San Vicente is on the main east-to-west coast road, with buses to most larger towns in northern Spain, including Santander, Oviedo and Gijon. The railway station is under two miles south of the town centre.

PROVISIONING

Many local shops and supermarkets in the town.

A RUN ASHORE

Behind the pretty palm-tree lined waterfront promenade, ugly modern buildings spoil the outskirts of San Vicente, but the old part of town, huddling on a hill south-east of the old road

You can moor downstream of the main road bridge, if there is room

bridge, is worth seeing. It is dominated by the fine Gothic basilica of Santa Maria de los Angeles, dating from the 13th and 16th centuries, the Castillo del Rey and old town walls.

The castle houses an excellent visitors centre, where the town's history can be absorbed. It stresses the town's past importance as a trading port, where the first code of maritime law was drawn up and given royal endorsement. Geographically, San Vicente might seem an obvious choice from which to embark on a land excursion into the mountains, but unfortunately it is not a suitable place to leave a yacht unattended for any period of time.

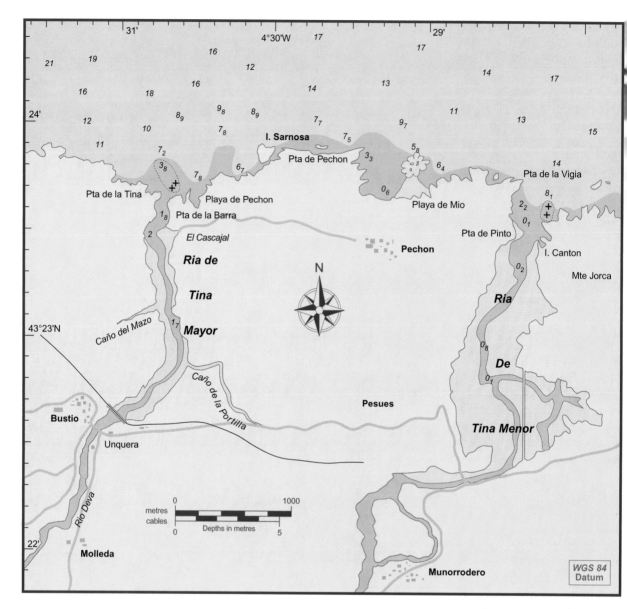

EATING OUT

San Vicente de la Barquera is noted for its fish restaurants and their price ranges. One of the best (at around €20) is the restaurant Maruja (Avenida Generalissimo, Tel: 942 71 00 77), close to the tourist information centre, but there are others nearby and off the main road towards Comillas. Traditional bars with tapas can be found in the pier area below the old town.

ANCHORAGES NEARBY

Rias de Tina Menor and Tina Mayor, both possible anchorages, are only four miles and six miles west of San Vicente de la Barquera respectively. Both are noted for beautiful scenery, but are accessible only at HW in very calm and settled weather when no swell is running. They are recommended as daytime anchorages in the summer, but not in any other season. Shoals shift in the entrances, so a very cautious approach – on a rising tide, and preferably following a dinghy reconnaissance – would be advised. Both Tinas have shallow bars in the entrance, but once inside the water deepens again and it is possible to anchor in depths of between 1.8 and 4 metres (check by sounding, as the situation can change rapidly due to silting).

The narrow entrance of Tina Menor can be spotted only from fairly close inshore, so running the distance from San Vicente or setting up a waypoint ensures you don't miss this entrance. Much the same can be said for Tina Mayor, an approach even more daunting as it is only a

Castillo del Rey once controlled the port and river

narrow gap in the cliffs, another two miles further west from Tina Menor. When entering Tina Menor stay close to the west point, Punta de la Vigia, and carefully sound your way in, always tending more towards the west side, which is steep-to and normally deeper than the other side. Tina Menor is the shallower river of the two once inside, so if planning to stay, work out your depths and tidal ranges very carefully.

Tina Mayor should be entered roughly in the middle of the river, and the sides here are both steep-to in the entrance. Once inside, there is an extensive sand-bank on the east side. Again, you must calculate the depths and tidal ranges if you're planning on staying, as these may not be charted.

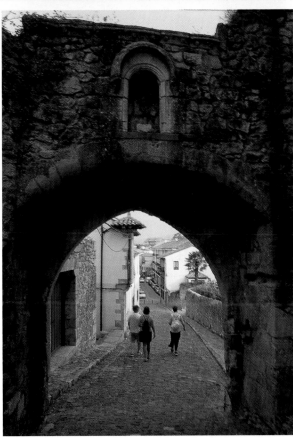

Gates in the old walls lead to the modern town below

ASTURIAN COAST

The coast between Luarca and Cudillero is typical of the region

The coastline of the fairly large province of Asturias, which makes up part of the Costa Verde, the Green Coast, is similar to that of Cantabria further east. However, it changes dramatically at its western end, where the Rio de Ribadeo not only marks the border with Galicia but is also the first of the

Playa de Rodiles near Villaviciosa

the large Galician fjords. The Asturian coast extends from Llanes in the east to Ribadeo in the west, a distance of just under 130 miles. It has picturesque and dramatic harbours, but only one modern marina, Gijon, which is roughly a third of the way along from the east. The foremost navigational feature of this stretch of coastline is the Cabo de Peñas, west of Gijon, which should be given a good offing in rough weather as the seas can break a considerable distance offshore.

The main surface current is west going. The ebb is east going, but is often overridden by the surface current, subject to the strength and duration of recent winds. A powerful

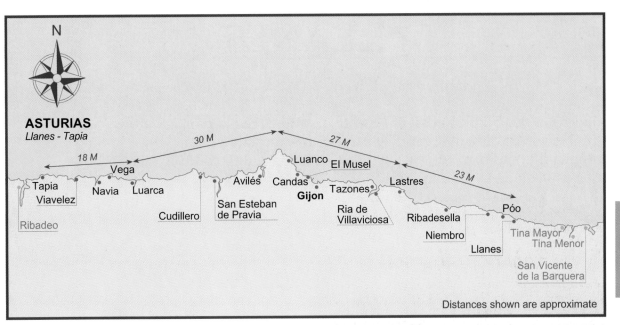

ASTURIAS
Llanes - Tapia

N

Ribadeo

Tapia
Viavelez

Navia

Vega

Luarca

Cudillero

San Esteban
de Pravia

Avilés

Candas

Gijon

Luanco

El Musel

Tazones

Ria de
Villaviciosa

Lastres

Ribadesella

Niembro

Llanes

Póo

Tina Mayor
Tina Menor

San Vicente
de la Barquera

18 M   30 M   27 M   23 M

Distances shown are approximate

Chapter 3

swell, which comes in to the coast from the deep water to the north-west, breaks furiously on submerged rocks as well as over the bars across harbour entrances and river mouths. This swell can also at times create a strong surge inside some of the harbours, often making them untenable or at least uncomfortable in these conditions.

Right: Gijon Marina – one of the few on this coast
Below: the village and old harbour at Cudillero

LLANES

Llanes harbour entrance – 43°25'.38N / 04°44'.89W (approx)

Llanes is a busy little coastal town with an attractive old part that draws a growing number of visitors each year. The harbour has recently been enlarged and now has an outer basin, making it possible to lie alongside a concrete pier, unless occupied by fishing vessels.

The inner harbour, sometimes locked off, is located in the old town centre but caters only for very small open boats.

LOCATION/POSITION

Llanes is almost exactly half way between San Vicente de la Barquera and Ribadesella, about 15 miles from each.

APPROACH AND ENTRANCE

Approach waypoint: 43°25'.70N/04°44'.40W; 225°; 0.5M to harbour entrance.

The approach is straightforward, with no off-lying dangers and a town easily identified from seaward. Aim straight for the head of the breakwater on a south-westerly course. The entrance is lit, so a night entry should be possible with due care. The depth in the approach between Punta de San Antón (on which stands the lighthouse) and the new pier is approximately 2.5 metres, getting shallower towards the pier. Proceed with caution if near to LW.

BERTHING

It is only possible to berth in the small outer harbour, which was built a few years ago. Here, moor up either alongside the concrete pier (taking care to leave enough scope in mooring lines), or outside another vessel. Fishermen will generally indicate where or where not to go. Depth alongside at LW varies between two and three metres (check with echo-sounder or lead line). A surge in the harbour can make

The new harbour at Llanes

lying alongside
rather uncomfortable
at times.

FACILITIES

There are no dedicated
facilities for yachts,
although water and
electricity can be
arranged on the quay.
It is best to ask the
fishermen for help.

TRANSPORT

There are trains to
Santander, Oviedo and
Ribadesella; buses to the
Picos de Europa and
along the coast to San
Sebastian, Bilbao,
Oviedo and Santander.

PROVISIONING

There is a good
assortment of shops in
the town centre. Market
day is Tuesday.

Map of LLANES showing Playa del Sabón, Dique de la Osa (Fl.G.5s5M), Puerto, Ria de Llanes, Fl(2)G.7s, Oc(4)15s16m15M, Playa de Puerto Chico, Lock, depth marks (Dries), 2m, 3₈. Coordinates 25'·4, 25'·2, 43°25'N, 45.2', 4°45'W, 44'·9. Scale in metres/cables 0–200, Depths in metres 0–1. Horizontal datum approximate.

A RUN ASHORE

Llanes is a town of two parts – an area of new
buildings of no great beauty and an old part,
which has some remarkable architecture,
including the Romanesque/Gothic basilica of
Santa Maria, begun around 1240 and completed
in 1480, with a 16th century altarpiece. More
interesting for seafarers is the fishermen's tiny
Capilla Santa Ana, located between the basilica
and the harbour. This church contains numerous
nautical items including model boats.

In the old town, some of the original city wall,
dating back to the 13th century, is still intact, and
the tourist office is housed in a mediaeval tower,
with fine views of the town and harbour from its
upper floors. The Fiesta de San Roque takes place
in mid-August when groups from the region
perform traditional dancing and music.

EATING OUT

Try the Calle Manuel Cue, a tiny street by the
inner harbour, which is almost entirely occupied
by restaurants. The best bet here is probably Casa
Canene, a family-run restaurant which has been
going for three generations, or El Pescador,

**The lighthouse on Punta de San Antón, the southern
point of the harbour entrance**

specialising in seafood. If you would rather
overlook the harbour, there is a good
bar/restaurant beside the quay.

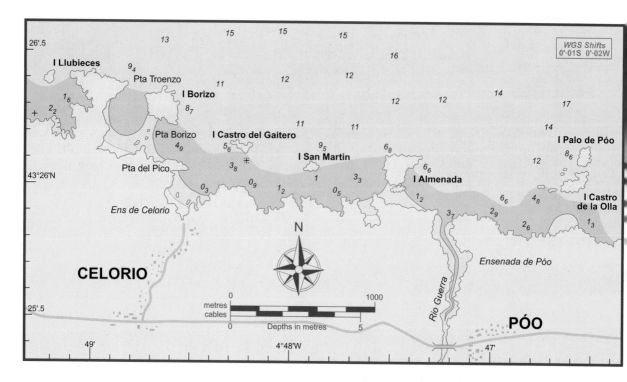

DAYTIME ANCHORAGES NEARBY

Ensenada de Póo is just under two miles west of Llanes, a shallow, almost land-locked lagoon, the approaches to which are somewhat protected by an off-lying island and the Isoletes Palo de Póo. Although the inlet mostly dries, anchorage in the outer bay is possible in quiet weather when the largely unspoilt bay can be explored by dinghy. The approximate position of the approach is 43°26'.1N/04°47'W.

Ria de Niembro is four miles west of Llanes. It is a shallow, winding river that runs between two cliffs, making it rather exciting to enter, especially as there are numerous rocks close to both sides of the entrance where the depth is around 1.5 metres. Beware of silting and shallowing upriver. The river dries at LW, but is a good place for small multihulls or bilge-keelers. Watch out for more isolated rocks on the river bed.

Enter the small bay from the north-east, approaching from the approximate position of 43°27'N/ 04°49'.4W, which is clear to the north of the unmarked La Vaca rocks lying about 500 metres east-north-east of Cabo Prieto and due north of Isla Peyes. At the entrance to the river is a bar that virtually dries. After crossing it, follow the curving river bed, keeping more towards the outside of the bends. Once fully inside, past a 90° turn to port, pick a spot which will probably dry out. There are no facilities apart from a quay, a small village and a large church.

The new harbour is relatively small, but the fishermen of Llanes are friendly and tolerant of yachts

The inner harbour dries, as does the wet basin if the lock (left centre) is not closed

USEFUL INFORMATION

Llanes tourist office Tel: 985 40 01 64

RIBADESELLA

Ribadesella bay – 43°28'.25N / 05°04'.17W

Ribadesella is a bustling, attractive fishing town which, thanks to an enticing beach by the harbour entrance, becomes a busy resort in the summer. The approach and entry must be carefully negotiated, as the safe channel is narrow. It is dangerous to enter in strong onshore winds or when there is a heavy swell running, as this breaks right across the entrance, even at high tide.

LOCATION/POSITION

Ribadesella is situated about 15 miles west of Llanes, at the mouth of the Rio Sella.

APPROACH AND ENTRANCE

Approach waypoint: 43°28'.72N/05°03'.84W; 200°; 0.5M to Ribadesella bay.

Identify the sheer cliffs of Punta del Caballo, which are unmistakable thanks to a small church on top and a light (Fl (2)R 6s) on a small tower. The main light is west of Punta de Somos but it doesn't help with the final approach. The beach and the buildings backing the entrance appear to be west of the cliffs, but in fact form the southern side of the channel. Depths in the entrance are reported to be more than two metres at LW, but it is strongly advised that you enter on the last half of the flood tide. Large breakers form off the beach when swell is running. Entering for the first time at night may be difficult in anything other than ideal conditions.

If making a coastwise passage and approaching from east or west, keep at least two cables off the coast until the Punta del Caballo bears 170° before turning on to this heading. This will avoid the off-lying rocks to the east and shoal water in the bay.

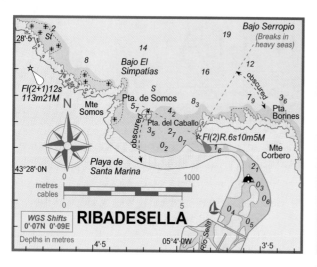

Ribadesella is an attractive town, and is the closest port to the spectacular Picos de Europa

During the final part of the approach on this course, keep close to the headland to avoid the visible rocks at its foot – about 30 metres off – and maintain this distance off as the point is rounded to avoid the shoal water that extends almost all the way from the beach opposite. Once inside the river, keep to the north side – about 25 metres off the promenade – and continue to the town pier, which has about four metres of water at LW.

BERTHING

Look for a berth alongside the town pier or tie up next to the vessels already moored there. The

official Zona Deportivo is below the bridge, although this is not the deepest part of the quay. Alternatively anchor off the pier, clear of the fairway and the shallow central shoal, which extends from the middle of the harbour right up to the bridge.

The ebb flows at two knots at springs, but can increase to as much as five or six knots when the river is in flood during springtime.

HARBOUR FACILITIES

There are none for yachts, although the friendly harbour master will organise almost anything necessary, including fuel (Gasoleo A is not available alongside), water and lubricating oils.

There is a small boatyard on the west side of the river and a three-ton crane at the harbour.

TRANSPORT

FEVE trains run to Santander, Llanes, Oviedo and further west. Buses go to Gijon, Oviedo and Llanes, with connections to Bilbao, Santander and San Sebastian.

PROVISIONING

There are local shops and small supermarkets close to the quay as well as a market every Wednesday.

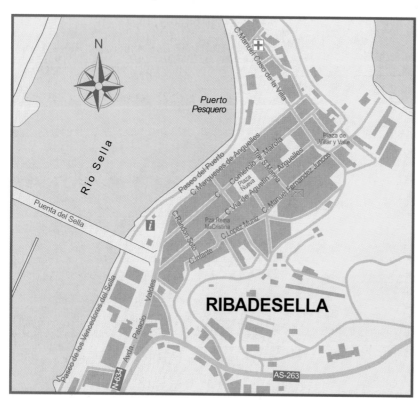

Looking south from Punta del Caballo reveals the narrowness of the channel

A RUN ASHORE

Ribadesella is one of the larger resorts on this stretch of coast, as its fine beach is an attraction for visitors.

The caves of Tito Bustillo and their stone age drawings are about half a mile or so from the town, on the western side of the river, upstream of the bridge. They were only discovered in 1968, and the paintings, 15,000 to 20,000 years old, are well worth seeing. Visit early in the morning during the height of the season, as viewing is restricted to less than 400 people per day. Open summer only from 1000 – 1300 and 1530 – 1715, closed Mondays and also Sundays in July/August.

Walks upriver are enjoyable, particularly along the west bank. Go as far as the village of Cueves where, at the end of the road through an unusual natural tunnel, is a café/bar serving great-tasting, rustic lunches.

The best yacht berth is along the Paseo del Puerto

Once into the river, keep close to the promenade

EATING OUT

There are a number of bars and restaurants in the old part of town. Outstanding for quality and value is La Bohemia (Gran Via 53, Tel: 985 86 11 50). Another good one is the restaurant Nautico (Marques de Arguelles 9, Tel: 985 86 00 42).

USEFUL INFORMATION

Tourist office (summer only) Tel: 985 86 00 38
Cave Tito Bustillo Tel: 985 86 11 18

An attractive overview of the old fishing village of Lastres, situated on a hill just above the harbour

Lastres harbour entrance – 43°30'.93N / 05°15'.78W

This is a beautiful old fishing village in the heart of the Costa Verde, which clings to a hill above the harbour. The historical centre of this small village is remarkably picturesque and is undoubtedly among the most attractive along this stretch of coast.

LOCATION/POSITION

Lastres is positioned about nine miles west of Ribadesella and 16 miles east of Gijon on the Punta Misiera headland.

APPROACH AND ENTRANCE

Approach waypoint: 43°31'.28N/05°15'.30W; 225°; 0.5M to harbour entrance.

Punta Misiera is about two miles east of Cabo Lastres, which is rather inconspicuous but has a major light on it (Cabo Lastres – Fl W 12s 116m 23 miles). A television mast above the village and harbour is easily identified. There are no off-lying dangers apart from Banco de la Plancha, a shoal with about six metres of water where seas break.

The harbour is best approached on a course of 220°, which is on the leading marks or, if these can't be identified, on a more westerly course of

250° – 270°. The leading marks, comprising a piled concrete platform in the water and an isolated white house on the hill behind, are indeed difficult to see. Don't get too close to the pier-head when entering, as you may encounter on-coming traffic leaving at speed. Head north into the new port, as the small boat harbour to the west dries completely at LW and will be crowded anyway.

BERTHING

Moor up next to the pier, if space can be found between or alongside the fishing boats – the depth here is up to seven metres. If alongside the pier, you will need long warps to cope with a tidal range of up to 3.5 metres. You can also tie up alongside the quay, but watch out for possible mooring lines to the numerous small craft that are scattered throughout the harbour basin and be careful not to get entangled in them.

HARBOUR FACILITIES

There are no dedicated yacht facilities, although there is a small slipway and crane. Water and gas are supplied on the pier, however there is no diesel - Gasoleo A available alongside or in the village.

PROVISIONING

There are several small shops in the village, which are adequate for basic provisioning.

A RUN ASHORE

The climb up to the village will take you to what is quite rightly regarded as one of the prettiest places along this stretch of coast. Its historical centre has the status of a protected monument.

EATING OUT

Bars, cafés and restaurants abound, but none are outstanding. The Casa Eutimo has a good reputation for local seafood at moderate prices.

ANCHORING

In calm weather it is possible to anchor in about three metres off the sandy bay, directly below the village. This is south of the harbour entrance, so pick a spot far enough away to avoid obstructing or being disturbed by fishing vessels entering and leaving.

DAYTIME ANCHORAGES NEARBY

Ria de Villaviciosa is about four miles west of Cabo Lastres and is partly canalised by training breakwaters in the entrance. It is rather shallow and subject to silting, with a bar of 1.5 metres across the entrance. It is recommended only in calm, settled weather.

In the approach take care to avoid the shallow Bajas de la Mesnada north of the Punta de la Mesnada, immediately north-west of the entrance. Enter during the last two hours of the flood, keeping close to the west training wall head. The head of the east training wall has crumbled away and is partly submerged at HW. Once inside the river, you will find a silted up harbour basin with

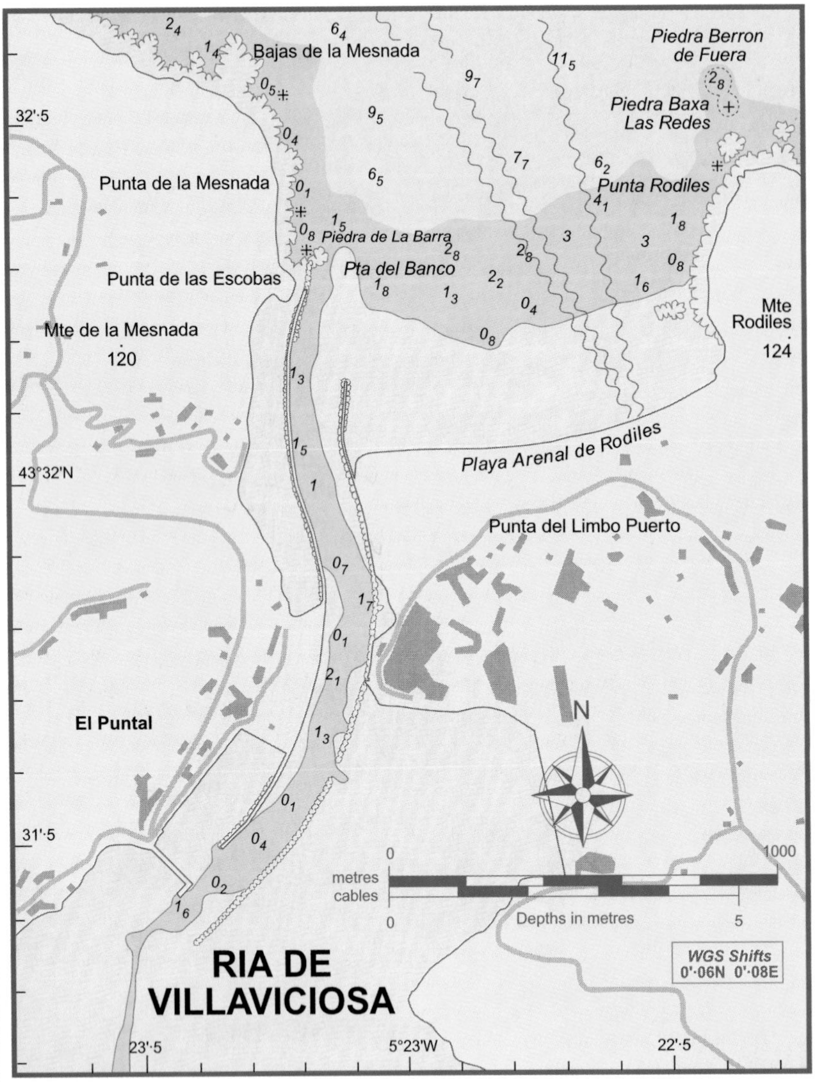

Bajas de la Mesnada
Piedra Berron de Fuera
Piedra Baxa Las Redes
Punta de la Mesnada
Punta Rodiles
Piedra de La Barra
Punta de las Escobas
Pta del Banco
Mte Rodiles
124
Mte de la Mesnada
120
Playa Arenal de Rodiles
43°32'N
32'·5
31'·5
Punta del Limbo Puerto
El Puntal
N
metres
cables
Depths in metres
1000
WGS Shifts
0'·06N 0'·08E
RIA DE VILLAVICIOSA
23'·5
5°23'W
22'·5

concrete piers on the west side at a village called El Puntal, where there is a small craft pontoon largely taken up by local day-boats. As there is no commercial river traffic, it would be better to anchor outside the basin and come in by dinghy. There is a yacht club further upstream, but this has no facilities for visiting yachts.

The river upstream of El Puntal is a nature reserve, to which access in winter is strictly forbidden when numerous birds are nesting there. Villaviciosa, further upstream, is the apple capital of Spain, where *Sidra* (cider) is produced in vast quantities. Accordingly, there is a large number of small *Siderias* scattered throughout the old town around the Plaza Mayor.

Small fishing boats moored up in the bay at Tazones

Chapter 3

With great seafood restaurants, Tazones is a popular weekend destination

The town can best be visited by taxi or bus from the harbour basin at El Puntal.

Further west, around the Punta and Bajas de la Mesnada, is the bay and fishing village of Tazones, a popular place at weekends, as it has some very good (and often crowded) restaurants specialising in seafood. It's an unsuitable overnight anchorage but makes a very good lunch stop if you want to venture ashore to eat.

When approaching from the east, take care of the shallow Bajas de la Mesnada. It's best to aim for the breakwater head on a south-west course and anchor just south of it on to sand, paying attention to the depth. This anchorage is open to the north and north-east and often rolls with the incoming swell even in north-westerly winds.

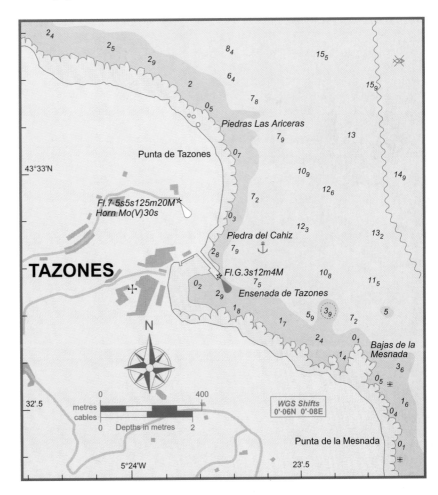

GIJON

Gijon marina entrance – 43°32'.85N / 05°40'.17W

Boasting a population of 260,000, Gijon (pronounced something like Hee-hon) is the largest city in Asturias, with a vast commercial harbour west of the city and a pleasant, busy marina in the old city harbour. It was largely destroyed during the Spanish Civil War, although much of its old part is still standing close to the marina on a headland called Cimadevilla. The new and bustling centre lies to the south.

The marina offers superb shelter and can be entered in almost any weather, although the entrance could be rather hair-raising in certain conditions.

LOCATION/POSITION

Gijon is located roughly half way along the Spanish north coast, a little less than 10 miles east of Cabo Peñas.

APPROACH AND ENTRANCE

Approach waypoint: 43°33'.85N / 05°40'.17W; 180°; 1M to marina entrance.

The marina of Gijon – the Puerto Deportivo – is on the promontory of Cerro de Santa Catalina, which features a striking sculpture, while the commercial harbour is about two miles west. Unless you have a 50 metre-plus superyacht, there is no reason to visit this commercial harbour.

Gijon's skyline and the headland can be clearly seen from the sea as you approach on a southerly course. Take care, however, to avoid Serrapio de

Gijon's excellent yacht harbour is in the former commercial harbour. Care is needed in the approach

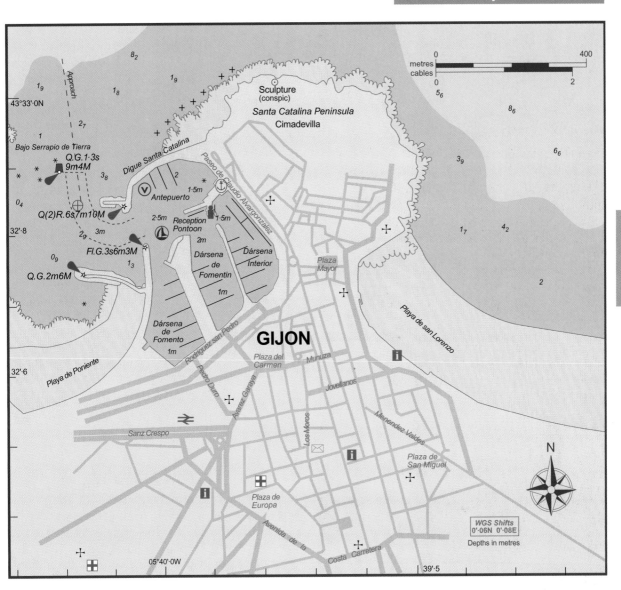

Tierra, a shoal marked by a green light-tower (Piedro Sacramento, QG 1-3s) off the marina entrance, where there is a rubble extension to the main harbour wall. In heavy swell or strong onshore winds, seas break viciously on this bank, which is uncomfortably close (150 metres) to the marina entrance.

Regardless of weather, it is imperative to keep between Piedro Sacramento and the rubble breakwater extension, marked by a red tower (Q(2)R 6s). When approaching, note that this rubble extension to the harbour wall, and the longer rubble breakwater beyond (marked by a green column: QG 1s) are difficult to distinguish from one another until you get quite close. The entrance is wide and easy to negotiate. Once inside the marina, the fuel, reception berths and office are straight ahead on the short pier.

BERTHING

Mooring is to floating pontoons with fingers. Visitors' berths are located to port on the first pontoons behind the outer breakwater, as you enter the basin.

MARINA FACILITIES

Water and electricity are on the pontoons, while showers and toilets are ashore (in the marina office building, which shuts at night), along with a diesel fuelling station (Gasoleo A) and petrol (just past the reception berths). Marina staff are friendly and helpful, although unlikely to speak English, and usually hand out city maps when you book in. You will be asked to deposit your ship registration documents while in port. Repairs can be arranged through the marina staff.

Yachts in the visitors' berths (see chart). The marina office and facilities building is on the central pier, in the background

from the sea. The Picos de Europa are about two hours drive away (for details see under 'Major Attractions' on p13 of the introduction). Bear in mind that Gijon is in the centre of an industrialised area and the city's surroundings are not worth seeing. If you do decide to tour, take the motorway or a coastal route and go for miles before stopping! Car hire firms (a full list is available from the tourist office) include: Atesa 985 15 41 00; Avis 985 34 08 09; Hertz 985 35 50 50; Budget 985 13 11 13.

PROVISIONING

There is a superb selection of shops, supermarkets and every kind of facility in the new part of town, south of the marina.

A RUN ASHORE

A small tourist information booth is on the promenade south of the marina office, but the main tourist office, which is more enterprising than usual, is in the square immediately behind the inner harbour basin. Here you will get all the information you need to make the most of a visit to Gijon and the Principado de Asturias.

The old part of town, Cimadevilla, on the promontory between the marina and the Playa de San Lorenzo, is the most scenic area. You can wander up to the top of the hill to the park-like area of the Cerro de Santa Catalina, which offers panoramic views along the coast and across town. The huge sculpture here, a useful landmark, is called *Elogio del Horizonte* (praise of the horizon) and was created by the Basque sculptor Eduardo Chillida. By evening this area becomes lively and busy, with pubs, bars and restaurants galore to choose from.

For train fanatics, the new Museo de Ferrocantil is an attractive option. Situated in the old station Estacion del Norte, whose main hall, built in 1873, still stands, it houses an exhibition of all things that run on rails. This depressed area is gradually being upgraded.

On the east side of Cerro de Santa Catalina, overlooking Playa de San Lorenzo

The Piedro Sacramento shallows lying to the north-west of the harbour approach can be clearly seen

TRANSPORT

Trains and buses to other major cities as well as a full selection of hire car companies make Gijon an excellent centre for taking a short break away

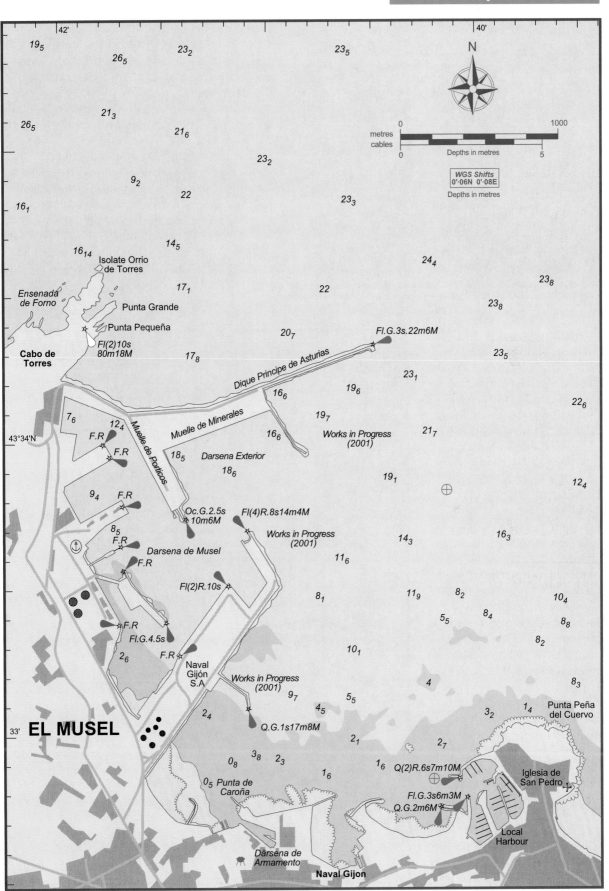

19_5

26_5

23_2

23_5

N

21_3

26_5

21_6

9_2

23_2

22

23_3

metres
cables

0   1000

Depths in metres   5

WGS Shifts
0'·06N 0'·08E
Depths in metres

16_1

14_5

24_4

23_8

16_{14} Isolate Orrio
de Torres

17_1

22

23_8

*Ensenada
de Forno*

Punta Grande

20_7

Fl.G.3s.22m6M

23_5

Punta Pequeña

17_8

Dique Principe de Asturias

23_1

**Cabo de
Torres**

*Fl(2)10s
80m18M*

16_6

19_6

22_6

7_6

12_4

Muelle de Minerales

19_7

21_7

43°34'N

F.R

18_5

Darsena Exterior

16_6

Works in Progress
(2001)

12_4

Muelle de Porticos

F.R

18_6

19_1

9_4 F.R

Oc.G.2.5s
10m6M

Fl(4)R.8s14m4M

14_3

16_3

8_5 F.R

Works in Progress
(2001)

11_6

Darsena de Musel

F.R

11_9 8_2

10_4

Fl(2)R.10s

8_1

5_5 8_4

8_8

F.R

8_2

Fl.G.4.5s

10_1

2_6 F.R

EL MUSEL

Naval
Gijón
S.A

Works in Progress
(2001)

4

8_3

9_7 5_5

3_2 1_4 Punta Peña
del Cuervo

2_4

4_5

Q.G.1s17m8M

2_1

2_7

3_8 2_3

1_6

1_6 Q(2)R.6s7m10M

Iglesia de
San Pedro

0_8

0_5 Punta de
Caroña

Fl.G.3s6m3M

Q.G.2m6M

Local
Harbour

*Darsena de
Armamento*

Naval Gijon

33'

Foundation Museum (Plaza de Villamanin), set in beautiful gardens full of sculptures. Inside is an exhibition of paintings, drawings and manuscripts documenting the artist's literary works.

Finally, the painter Juan Barjola is represented in the Barjola Museum (Trinidad, 17), housed in the 17th century chapel and palace of the Jove Huergo family. The exposition depicts the development of the artist from the fifties through to today and his main subjects, which include bullfights, suburbs and erotic themes, evolve from abstract art to expressionism.

EATING OUT

Close to the marina is the cheap and cheerful bar and restaurant El Planeta. This is a good

The church of San Pedro and the Real Club Astur de Regatas on Cerro de Santa Catalina. The Roman baths are beside the church

Other museums include the Roman Baths, the Termas on Campu Valdes, which were the city's public baths in the Roman period between the first and fourth centuries. Archaeological remains tell of the building techniques, including the heating system, as well as the daily lives of that era.

The Casa Natal de Jovellanos is the birthplace of Jovellanos (1744 – 1811, writer, politician and minister of justice during the reign of Carlos IV). Located in the Cimadevilla on Plaza Jovellanos, it is also a museum exhibiting Asturian art from the 19th and 20th centuries and holds exhibits of earlier European art. Another museum is entirely dedicated to the Asturian painter Nicanor Piñole (1878 – 1978). This exhibition is housed at 28 Plaza de Europa, where oil paintings, sketches, drawings and notes illustrate this artist's long career. His colleague, the Gijon painter Evaristo Valle, (1873 – 1953) also has his own museum, the Evaristo Valle

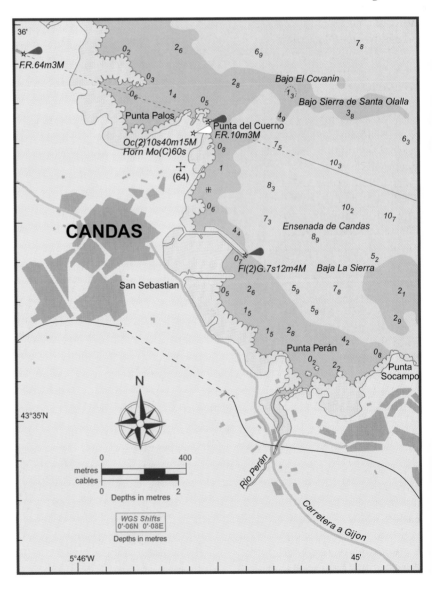

option if meeting crews from other yachts in the marina. There are plenty of alternative eating places within a few hundred yards. After the meal, you can wander off to the bars in the Cimadevilla – if you're still up to it, bearing in mind Spanish eating times.

In the marina office building is the rather smart El Puerto (Tel: 534 90 96), which is expensive, quiet and serves high quality food. A little further away, in the new part of town, are a number of good restaurants, of which La Marmita (Begona 20), El Retiro (Begona 28) and Casa Victor (Carmen 11) stand out.

ALTERNATIVE HARBOURS CLOSE BY

The main commercial harbour of Gijon, the Puerto de Musel, is unsuitable for and unwelcoming to yachts, especially as there is a first-class marina virtually next door. It can, however, be used as a port of refuge in an emergency, in which case call VHF Ch 11, 12, 14, or 16 – Gijon Practicos (Gijon Pilots).

Candas is a rather pretty provincial town a few miles further north-west, but has no special facilities or berths for yachts. Its harbour was being completely rebuilt in February 2002, so it might be possible to go alongside the quays. Phone the tourist office to find out about events taking place in Candas. Luanco is also an attractive little town. Only nine miles from Gijon, it is home to the Maritime Museum of Asturias (not far from the south-west end of the inner harbour). It has an active Club Maritimo, located in the tiny south basin. This bay is full of small craft moorings, so it is not easy to find a space to anchor here. It is more feasible to do so behind the outer mole, but only in settled weather and not if the wind is anywhere east of north. There is an eight-ton crane on the pier by the yacht club, as well as a diesel pump for yachts.

You will come across several inviting restaurants ashore, among which are the rather elegant Guernica and the Restaurant La Riba, with its romantic courtyard. The lively bar El Puerto, opposite Guernica, serves tapas as well as drinks and seems to be the unofficial clubhouse of the yacht club. From here, as well as from the terrace, you can enjoy views across the inner bay.

A large Consum supermarket is only five minutes away by taxi.

Chapter 3

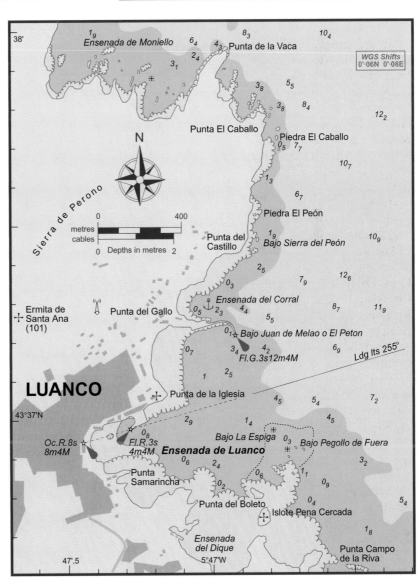

AVILÉS

Avilés river mouth – 43°35'.70N / 05°56'.47W

Avilés is predominantly an industrial town, but does have a small historic centre around the Plaza de España. Still giving a faint hint of the city's mediaeval past, it may be of interest to some visitors. The river leading to Avilés is deep and easily accessible, but at the time of going to press was still fairly polluted and doesn't offer particularly comfortable berths for yachts.

A shipyard on the river may be able to carry out yacht repairs, and the river itself could be useful as a refuge in heavy weather.

LOCATION/POSITION

Avilés lies just west of Cabo de Peñas.

APPROACH AND ENTRANCE

Approach waypoint: 43°35'.37N/05°57'.13W; 110°; 0.5M to river mouth.

The Playa de Salinas, a beach with factories and flats at its west end, is easily identified, as is the promontory of Punta del Castillo, with its lighthouse and signal station. Keeping a safe distance from the headland, the final approach into the river is on an easterly course, sticking to the middle of the river. A red light from the signal mast on the headland indicates that a large vessel is leaving the river, so make sure you stand off until she has passed.

BERTHING

It may be possible to lie alongside another vessel at the town quay, which is upriver past the new

Avilés is a fine natural harbour, but its predominantly industrial environs are less attractive

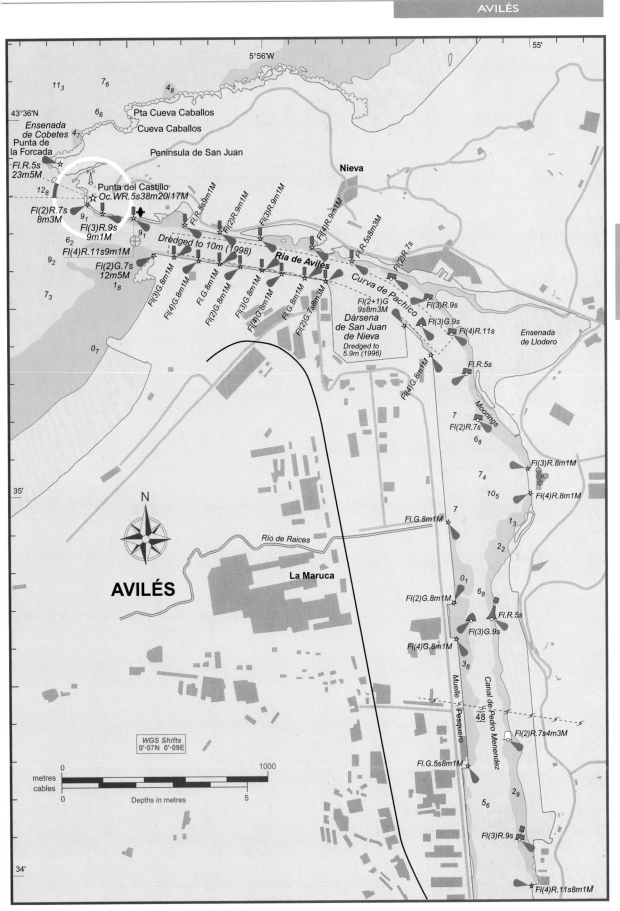

PONTOONS 2.1 KM UP RIVER ON W BANK

Chapter 3

5°56'W

43°36'N

Ensenada de Cobetes
Punta de la Forcada
Fl.R.5s 23m5M

Pta Cueva Caballos
Cueva Caballos
Peninsula de San Juan
Nieva

Punta del Castillo
Oc.WR.5s38m20/17M

Fl(2)R.7s 8m3M
Fl(3)R.9s 9m1M
Fl(4)R.11s9m1M
Fl(2)G.7s 12m5M

Fl.R.5s9m1M
Fl(2)9m1M
Fl(3)R.9m1M
Fl(4)R.9m1M
Fl.R.5s8m3M
Fl(2)R.7s

Dredged to 10m (1998)
Ria de Avilés
Curva de Pachico

Fl(3)G.8m1M
Fl(4)G.8m1M
Fl.G.8m1M
Fl(3)G.8m1M
Fl(2)G.8m1M
Fl.G.8m1M
Fl(4)G.8m1M
Fl(2)G.7s8m3M

Fl(2+1)G 9s8m3M
Dársena de San Juan de Nieva
Dredged to 5.9m (1996)

Fl(3)R.9s
Fl(3)G.9s
Fl(4)R.11s

Ensenada de Llodero

Fl(4)G.8m1M

Fl.R.5s

Moorings
Fl(2)R.7s

Fl(3)R.8m1M
Fl(4)R.8m1M

N

AVILÉS

Río de Raices

La Maruca

Fl.G.8m1M

Fl(2)G.8m1M

Fl(4)G.8m1M

Fl.R.5s
Fl(3)G.9s

Muelle Pesquero
Canal de Pedro Menéndez

48

Fl(2)R.7s4m3M

Fl.G.5s8m1M

Fl(3)R.9s

Fl(4)R.11s8m1M

WGS Shifts
0'·07N 0'·09E

metres
cables

0   1000

0   5

Depths in metres

Punta del Castillo, with its lighthouse, and Avilés' signal station, viewed from the east

EATING OUT

Of the restaurants in the town centre, the rustic Casa Tataguyo is well worth a visit. (Plaza del Carbayedo 6, Tel: 985 56 48 15)

ALTERNATIVE ANCHORAGES

Ria de Pravia, or Rio Nalon, is about six miles to the west. There is a disused commercial harbour here (Puerto de San Esteban de Pravia), but both the river and the basin are now subject to heavy silting. Enter with extreme care in quiet weather on the last third of a rising tide, as there is a bar across the mouth of the river on which the seas tend to break, even in calm conditions. The entrance is reputed to be rough and downright dangerous at times.

On your approach and also once inside the training walls, keep more towards the west side of the channel. Depths vary, but should be around two metres until you get near to the small harbour of the village of San Esteban de Pravia, again on the west side.

There is a pontoon in the southern part of the old harbour, but enter with care as the channel leading to this is not marked. Keep more towards the starboard, shore side, as the south part, inside of the mole, is very shallow and dries completely at LW. The depths along the pontoon and about a hundred metres off are reported to be around two metres at LW, but this is subject to rapid change. If there is no space on the pontoon, or if your boat is too big (anything longer than 30 feet will be too big for the finger pontoons), you can anchor off but stay as close as possible, as the depth dwindles very swiftly. The pontoon has water and electricity, but there are no facilities ashore. In the village are a few intimate bars and restaurants as well as two or three small shops. There are bus and rail connections to the larger towns in the area.

fish quay, or moor directly alongside the pier, although this is high, rough and dirty. Alternatively, you might find an anchorage in the river, around the first bend on your port side, past a very shallow bay and off a small sandy spit. However, beware of fishing vessels, which frequently pass at full speed.

FACILITIES

There are none ashore, although diesel - Gasoleo A and petrol are available at the Lonja, near the southern end of the harbour.

TRANSPORT

Trains and buses connect Avilés to other cities along the coast.

PROVISIONING

There is a wide variety of shops in the attractive town centre, a few minutes walk away from the river, as well as a large market.

A RUN ASHORE

Other than the historic town centre already mentioned, Avilés has nothing to offer tourists. The outskirts of the town and the areas along the river are industrial or derelict and are therefore not particularly attractive.

USEFUL INFORMATION
Avilés tourist information Tel: 985 54 43 25

Chapter 3

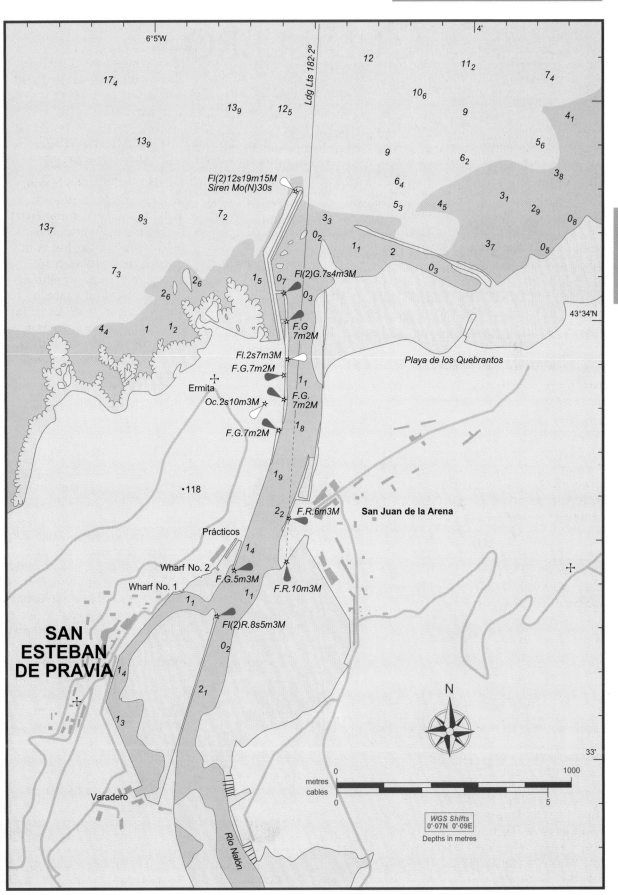

6°5'W

4'

17_4

12

11_2

7_4

13_9 12_5

10_6

9

5_6

4_1

13_9

9

6_2

3_8

8_3 7_2

13_7

Fl(2)12s19m15M
Siren Mo(N)30s

3_3

0_2

5_3

4_5

3_1

2_9

0_8

6_4

3_7

0_5

7_3

2_6

1_5 0_7 Fl(2)G.7s4m3M

0_3

1_1

2

0_3

2_6

2_6

4_4 1 1_2

F.G
7m2M

43°34'N

Playa de los Quebrantos

Ermita

Fl.2s7m3M
F.G.7m2M

Oc.2s10m3M

F.G.7m2M

1_1

F.G.
7m2M

1_8

1_9

•118

2_2 F.R.6m3M   **San Juan de la Arena**

Prácticos

1_4

Wharf No. 2   F.G.5m3M

Wharf No. 1

1_1 1_1 F.R.10m3M

**SAN
ESTEBAN
DE PRAVIA** 1_4

Fl(2)R.8s5m3M

0_2

2_1

1_3

N

33'

Varadero

metres
cables

0

0

1000

5

WGS Shifts
0'·07N 0'·09E

Depths in metres

Río Nalón

CUDILLERO

Cudillero harbour entrance – 43°34'.10N / 06°08'.65W

Cudillero – known locally as Cuideiro – is a very picturesque fishing village. It sits in a gorge between two mountains, where the houses spill down the slopes to the recently extended harbour. A popular place with tourists and day trippers, this small village often becomes crowded and its restaurants, especially those down by the old harbour, are at times extremely busy.

Mooring in the harbour can be tricky, thanks to a heavy surge which finds its way in if the north-west swell is running outside.

LOCATION/POSITION

Cudillero is just under 15 miles west of Cabo Peñas and almost exactly 5 miles east of Cabo Vidio.

APPROACH AND ENTRANCE

Approach waypoint: 43°34'.60N/06°08'.65W; 180°; 0.5M to harbour entrance.

A first time approach can appear difficult, with several rocks on both sides of the harbour entrance. However there are no off-lying dangers and, as you get closer to the entrance, the safe channel becomes obvious. A night entry is definitely not recommended.

Approach the narrow entrance on a course of approximately 200° and, for the new harbour, turn sharply to starboard as soon as you're inside the entrance. Depths here and in the harbour are between four and five metres.

BERTHING

Berthing is on to pontoons with fingers, but it can be difficult to moor up if there is a swell.

Cudillero's new harbour offers good shelter, but is subject to surge. The village climbs the hill behind the old harbour

Alternatively, anchor in the area south-west of the pontoons, using a tripping line to ensure that your anchor can be recovered. There isn't a great deal of room here, but there's no real alternative, except possibly a place on the fish quay. The swell inside this harbour is typical of this part of the coast, although it is not usually a problem during settled weather in summer.

FACILITIES IN THE HARBOUR

A Volvo Penta mechanic is based here, along with a small yard that builds fishing boats. Ice can be obtained from the ice factory in the fishing harbour. You can find a chandlery a little way up the hill towards the village, which is in turn about twenty minutes walk from the yacht pontoons. To get to the village, take the pedestrian tunnel near the new harbour entrance, which runs uphill through the rock. Alternatively you could always go by dinghy to the small, drying boat harbour.

CUDILLERO

On map:
6°9'W · 8'·5 · N · 36 · 39 · 35 · 34 · 23₅ · 36 · 33 · 34'·5 · metres · cables · 0 · 400 · 0 · 2 · WGS Shifts 0'·06N 0'·08E · Depths in metres · 19₅ · 20₆ · 15₁ · 3₂ · 16₅ · 13₅ · 4₇ · 8₃ · Piedra la Corbera · 15₄ · 17₂ · 7₆ · Piedras las Colinas · 2₁ · 3₂ · 12₄ · 12₅ · 8 · 5₆ · 7₃ · 0₂ · 6₂ · 7 · 3₅ · 2₁ · 10₄ · 1₈ · Punta Rebollera · Fl(3)G.9s5m2M · 3₂ · 43°34'N · 3₄ · 2₆ · Fl(3)R.9s10m2M · Oc(4)16s44m16M SirenMo(D)30s

CUDILLERO

TRANSPORT

The bus station is about 500 metres up the hill from the harbour, from where buses go to Avilés, Oviedo and Gijon. There is also a train station, although this is a considerable way south of the town.

PROVISIONING

A good selection of small local shops is scattered around this pleasant village.

A RUN ASHORE

There are no special sights other than the village itself, and time is well spent sitting in a taverna by the old harbour with a coffee, brandy or wine, watching the world crawl by.

EATING OUT

The menus get progressively cheaper when ascending the road up into the village, away from the harbour. Having said this, it is very pleasant to sit by the small boat harbour, perhaps in the Taberna del Puerto, which has outside tables, or in the restaurant El Remo.

DAYTIME ANCHORAGES NEARBY

Rio Nalon (see under Avilés).

LUARCA

Luarca entrance – 43°33'.09N / 06°32'.08W

Regarded by many as the most pleasant town along the northern Spanish coast, Luarca is indeed a remarkable place although, sadly, the berthing for visiting yachts is not ideal. Cut in half by the Rio Negro (the black river), the historical centre, with its narrow, winding alleyways, is squeezed in between the harbour and a loop in the river.

LOCATION/POSITION

Luarca is tucked in between Cabo Busto and Punta de Cuerno, about four miles west of Cabo Busto and just under 20 miles from Cudillero.

APPROACH AND ENTRANCE

Approach waypoint: 43°33'.58N/06°32'.20W; 170°; 0.5M to harbour entrance.

The headlands Cabo Busto, with its lighthouse (coming from the east,) or Punta de Cuerno (coming from the west) can be readily identified from sea. Both have off-lying shoals and covered rocks, so keep a safe distance off of at least a mile.

Be careful when nearing the bay and harbour off Luarca, as there are islets, rocks and shoals close to the approach. It is important to identify the leading marks – two tall red and white lattice beacons – bearing 170°, and to keep an eye on the depth. Don't approach the harbour in strong northerly winds.

Once inside, turn to port to get to the innermost harbour, which reportedly has a depth of around

Puerto de Luarca is a busy fishing harbour set in an attractive town

The inner harbour is unlikely to have space for a visiting yacht. Wave refraction is clearly visible in the outer harbour

Do not attempt to lie alongside this breakwater as the bottom is obstructed by boulders

two metres in places but, due to silting, is often less. This basin is overcrowded and partly dries, but if you're happy to take the ground or dry out alongside the pier, a space might be found (see below). The entrance is lit, although a first-time night entry is not recommended.

BERTHING

The inner harbour is congested with fishing boats, which occupy the only quay with adequate depth for a cruising yacht. The other quays dry, or almost dry. Any remaining space is taken up with moorings and floating pontoons. The curved quay leading to the inner harbour has drying rocks extending two to three metres from its base, as does the mole opposite, ruling them out except for a brief stop at HW. The outer breakwater, where visitors are expected to moor up, has drying rocks extending up to three metres from its base and strange steel structures projecting at quay level.

The visitors' buoys here are (or were in 2001) made of sheet and strip steel and are therefore lethal to the topsides of yachts. The six buoys are placed so close together that the only practical way of using them is to moor bow or stern to one, taking a line ashore to reduce the amount of room needed. It also helps to keep the boats away from the buoys at the

same time. You will, of course, need your dinghy for this operation, as well as for getting ashore later on. Unfortunately, the swell tends to curl around the breakwater, affecting the yachts

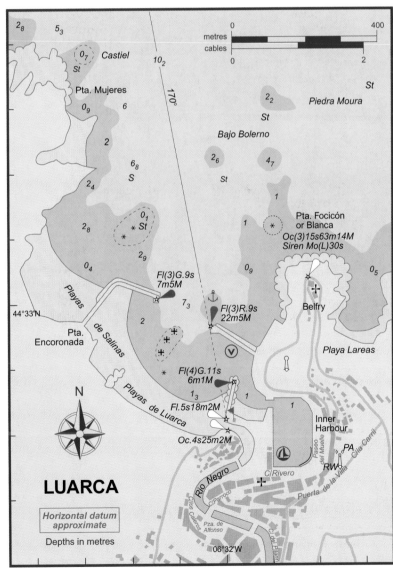

LUARCA

Horizontal datum approximate

Depths in metres

The Rio Negro cuts through the middle of Luarca

The inner basin is generally too shallow for a cruising yacht

moored in this way beam on and, at times, can even make the berths too uncomfortable, especially around HW.

FACILITIES IN THE HARBOUR

You can get water ashore (tap at the fish auction shed). There is also an eight-ton crane and a small craft slipway.

TRANSPORT

Buses go to to Oviedo, Gijon, Ribadeo, La Coruña and Santiago. The train station is on the line from Oviedo to El Ferrol and is about one and a half miles south of the town.

PROVISIONING

There is a wide variety of small shops and supermarkets as well as a colourful local market.

A RUN ASHORE

Luarca is an inviting place to just wander around. The town had its heyday around the turn of the last century and many of the old buildings have, strangely, a Swiss flair about them. The town's main square is Plaza Alfonso X. El Sabio, located opposite the old quarter on the other side of the river, is named after the town's founder, a Castilian nobleman, who was also a German king from 1257 to 1282. The grandiose architecture along the river gives an indication of Luarca's prosperity in former times, when it was a significant whaling and trading port.

The climb up through the old quarter to the lighthouse is a pleasant walk, rewarded by impressive views along the coast and over the

Atmospheric streets and old buildings overlook the inner harbour

roof-tops of the old village.

Luarca also has good beaches close to the harbour, on the west side of the river (Playas de la Salinas and Playas de Luarca).

The town's main fiesta takes place between El Rosario on 15 August and San Timoteo on 22 August, starting with a colourful parade of the fishing fleet.

EATING OUT

Luarca has a good number of bars and restaurants, some of which are along the harbour front. The restaurant Sport (Calle del Rivero 8, Tel: 985 64 10 78) is in the more expensive category of restaurants in Luarca, as is Villa Blanca (Avenida de Galicia 25, Tel: 985 64 10 79). For a cheaper meal, try La Darsena on Paseo del Muelle 11.

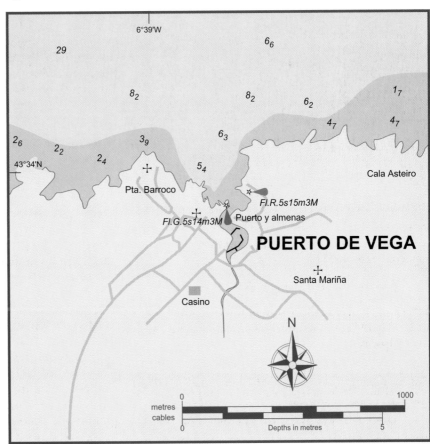

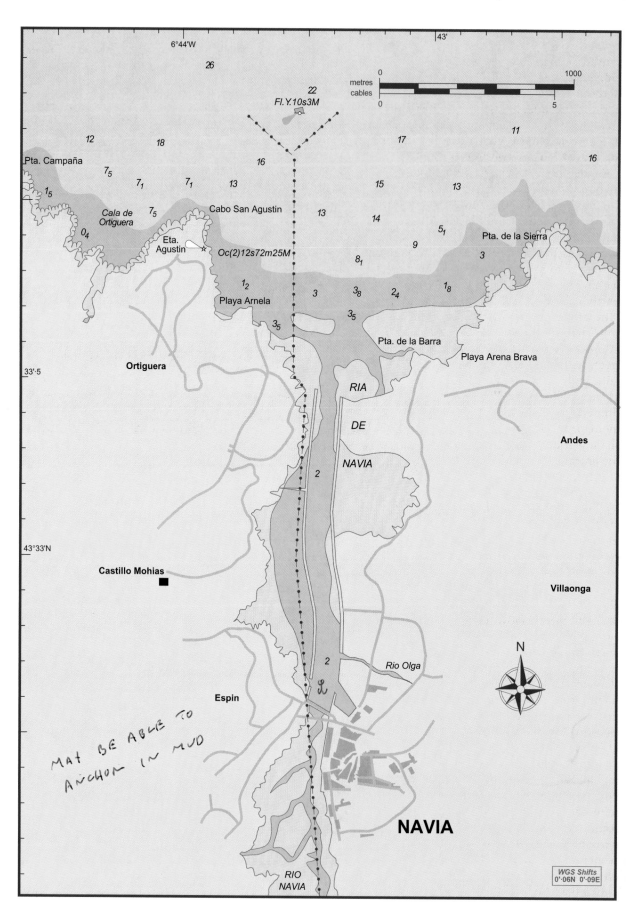

DAYTIME ANCHORAGES NEARBY

Puerto de Vega, a good five miles west along the coast, is a tiny drying fishing harbour, sheltered by a breakwater. Ancient and picturesque, it is merely suitable for small craft that can dry out. The approach and entry are narrow and should only be attempted in calm conditions.

Ria de Navia, which is situated about eight miles to the west, is a shallow bay where you can anchor off the river mouth, but it is only advisable to do so during the daytime and in settled weather. There are some pleasant beaches nearby, although an industrial area a few miles upriver makes bathing here a bit dubious. The river itself is partly canalised and navigable as far as the little provincial town of Navia, which has a small harbour but nothing else of real interest. There is not much depth in the river, with less than one metre at LW (although the harbour basin at Navia is supposedly dredged to about two metres), and it is even shallower at the bar across the entrance, on which the seas frequently break.

Puerto de Viavelez, about 13 miles west of Luarca, is another small fishing harbour that dries completely, although the bay itself is sheltered by two breakwaters and has about one to three metres of depth at LW. However, as with the previous anchorages, you should only approach Puerto De Viavelez on a calm day, paying careful attention to the many shoals and rocks close by. In any strength of wind, the sea will break all around the entrance, making it untenable unless you are a Spanish fisherman with nerves of steel and a sound knowledge of the harbour. Once inside, the scenery is romantic and pleasant, but again this is only a place for small boats.

Gasoleo A is available in this harbour (close to the white motorboat) on the east quay

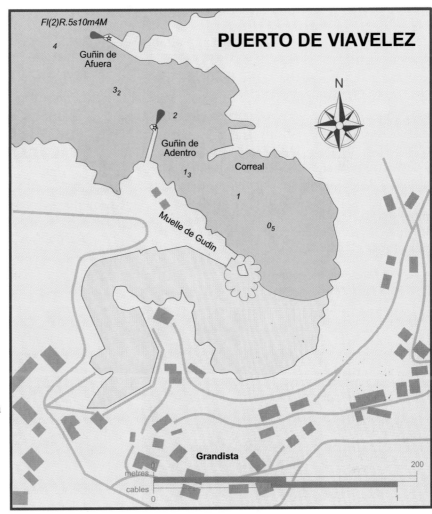

The rugged coastline of Tapia

TAPIA

Tapia harbour entrance – 43°34'.40N / 06°56'.95W

Tapia is another pretty little fishing village, but is difficult when it comes to berthing. It's been discovered by the surfers, who invade this small town during the summer months. They of course are attracted by the one feature we cruisingfolk dislike along the Spanish north coast, namely the big swell, which can make entering and mooring inside tricky or outright impossible at times. When conditions are best for the surfers (i.e. strong onshore winds and big seas), it is more than advisable to continue the few miles to Ribadeo, although you would then unfortunately miss Tapia's lively bars.

A view of Tapia from the north-east

LOCATION/POSITION

Tapia is tucked around the corner immediately west of Cabo San Sebastian, just under five miles east of the Rio de Ribadeo.

APPROACH AND ENTRANCE

Approach waypoint: 43°34'.40N / 06°57'.65W; 090°; 0.5M to harbour entrance.

Tapia is easily and unmistakably identified from the sea. Prominent landmarks include the headland Cabo San Sebastian, along with its lighthouse, and the island of Tapia, which has a rather conspicuous church as well as another islet lying just off it. When coming from the north or east, take care to keep well clear of this islet, as the area north of it is full of rocks and shoals. Final approach is from the west on a course of roughly 100°, keeping the breakwater heads in line.

BERTHING

The harbour is small and crowded and berths are rare. The piers are obstructed by underwater ledges and fixed mooring lines, so the best bet might be to go alongside a fishing vessel, checking first when it plans to leave. In calm weather only, with no swell running into the harbour, it might be possible to lie alongside the fuel pier – but ask the locals about possible underwater obstructions at LW.

FACILITIES

There are no dedicated yacht facilities.

TRANSPORT

Buses run to Ribadeo and Oviedo.

PROVISIONING

Small shops spread out around the town.

A RUN ASHORE

Tapia is a very picturesque town and well worth a visit. The centre comprises a church as well as several shops and restaurants. There are also some pleasant bars at the inner end of the harbour.

Paths along this rugged coastline, mainly to the west of the town, lead to some spectacular beaches, although these probably get quite crowded in the summer.

EATING OUT

Apart from the lively bars, Tapia has a good number of fish and seafood restaurants, among which are the Palermo (Bonifacio Amago 13, Tel: 985 62 83 70) or the Galeria El Bote (Calle Marques de Casariego 30, Tel: 985 62 82 82).

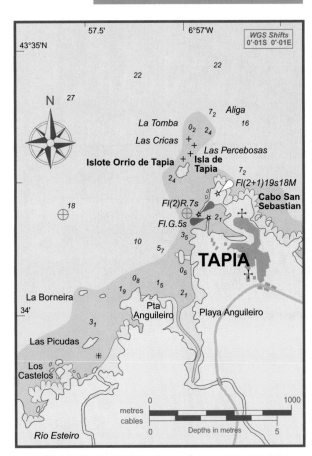

DAYTIME ANCHORAGES NEARBY

See under Luarca.

USEFUL INFORMATION

Tourist office Tel: 985 47 29 68,
but only open at the height of summer.

The swell attracts many surfers to Tapia during the summer

NORTH GALICIA
THE RIAS ALTAS & THE RIAS DA COSTA DA MORTE

The spectacular coastline of the Isla Sisargas

The geographical term 'ria' describes a drowned rivercourse, a name taken directly from the rias of north-west Spain, which are completely typical of landscapes that have suffered a rise in sea level. Fortunately for us they make ideal cruising areas to be thoroughly enjoyed.

The rias are most dramatic along the north coast of Galicia, beginning in the east with the Ria de Ribadeo. The next major one (after a minor estuary at Foz) is the Ria de Vivero and, just a hop around the corner, is the Ria del Barquero. Past the daunting cape of Punta de la Estaca de Bares lies the Ria de Santa Marta de Ortigueira, which is followed, after the next majestic promontory, Cabo Ortegal, by the small but scenic Ria de Cedeira. Heading south-west past Cabo Prior, you then enter the Golfo Artabro, which is home to three large estuaries – the Ria de Ferrol, Ria de Betanzos and Ria da Coruña itself. Finally, heading due west past the Islas Sisargas and Cabo de San Adrian, there are two smaller but again very beautiful bays, which make up the Rias Gallegas: the Ria de Corme y Lage and the Ria de Camariñas.

Generally speaking, this is a wild country, with dramatic scenery. Large capes mark mainland Spain's northernmost points – namely Cabo Ortegal and Punta de la Estaca de Bares. This north-west tip of Spain takes the full force of the Atlantic's winter gales, and the coast further west, around Cabo de San Adrian and Cabo Vilan,

Ribadeo, located in the Ria de Ribadeo, the easternmost of the Rias Altas

The beautiful Ria de Cedeira

is aptly named the Costa da Morte, the Coast of Death. This refers not only to the many shipwrecks of the past, but also to more recent deaths of local fishermen, who worked along this coast even during the rough winter months. However, if you are port-hopping during the friendly summer season, you needn't be alarmed by this sinister name. Besides, in heavy weather, you can always run for shelter into one of the rias.

A traffic separation scheme (TSS) exists about 20 miles off Finisterre, but yachts engaged in coastal cruising will almost automatically be in the inshore traffic zone. The TSS is marked on the relevant charts and should be avoided if at all possible. Finisterre Trafico monitors the area and all vessels over 50 metres are obliged to report on

entering the TSS (VHF Ch 11 and 16 as well as 2182 and 2187.5 kHz – yachts are advised to keep a listening watch when in the area). You should also note that shipping into and out of the bay of La Coruña is heavy at times, so you need to keep a good watch.

The main surface current inshore along the North Galician coast is west-going, with an average rate in summer of less than 0.5 knots. In mid-winter it can reverse for a time during long periods of strong westerly winds. The flood stream runs to the east along this stretch of coast, and the ebb to the west. However, these weak streams are at times overridden by the surface current, particularly after prolonged, strong winds.

Chapter 4

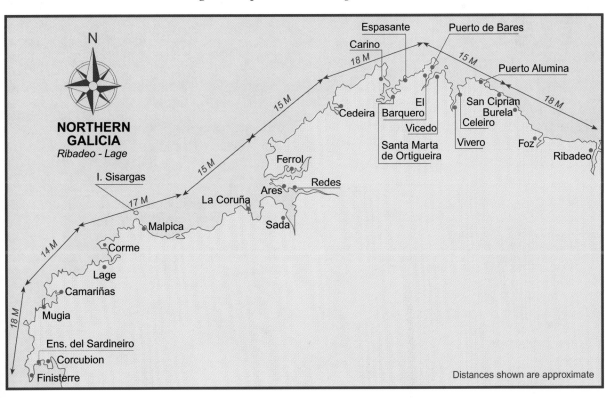

RIBADEO

Ribadeo ria entrance due east of Isla Pancha – 43°33'.45N / 07°02'.09W

Ribadeo is an interesting town and, although somewhat past its best, its fading elegance hints of its former affluence. The Ria de Ribadeo is the easternmost of the Rias Altas, the northern Galician fjords. Easy to enter, except in northerly storms, it is scenically very attractive.

The harbour offers excellent shelter, although visiting yachts are obliged to moor against the rough pier and are not allowed on the floating pontoons of the local yacht club.

LOCATION/POSITION

The Ria de Ribadeo lies about 33 miles east of Punta de la Estaca de Bares, Spain's northernmost headland, and just four miles west of Tapia.

APPROACH AND ENTRANCE

Approach waypoint: 43°33'.95N/07°02'.20W; 171°; 0.5M to ria entrance.

With no off-lying dangers, the entrance is easily identified by lighthouses on each headland at the mouth of the ria, the larger structure being on Isla Pancha (Fl(3+1)W 20s 26m 21 miles), which from some aspects looks like a promontory. The high (30-metre) road bridge across the ria, just north of the town and about a mile from the open sea, dominates the approach.

Shallows and rocks lie on both sides of the entrance, most hazardous of which is the reef of Las Carrayas, approximately halfway between Isla Pancha and the bridge. It can be a danger as it projects into the fairway and covers at HW. You therefore need to identify and follow the leading marks on the east shore (red diamonds on white towers 18/24m: QR/OcR), although these are difficult to see at times. If in doubt, stay well in the middle of the ria, preferably entering on 140°

Visiting yachts berth inside the mole of the Darsena de Porcillan, almost under the bridge

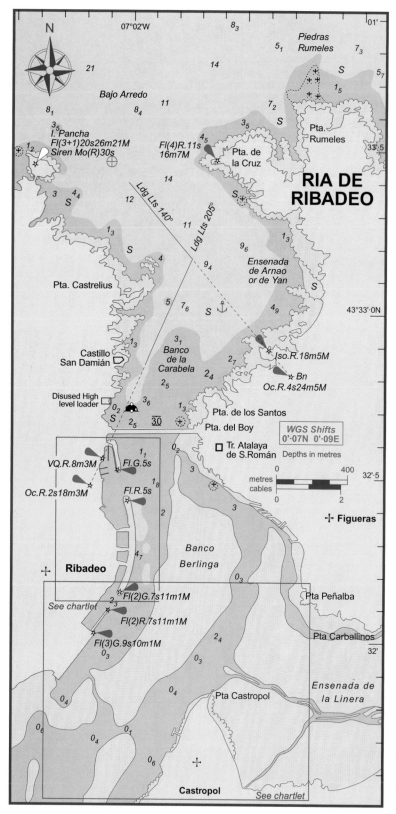

The town of Ribadeo stands on high ground to the south of the harbour

the harbour of Ribadeo just beyond.

The inner leading marks are also red diamonds on white columns (VQR/OcR2s), the lower, nearer one of which is close to the small yacht club crane, visible over the root of the north breakwater. The upper mark is in front of and below a distinctive hexagonal white building. Both were in need of painting (Feb 2002) and hard to identify, although the approach is not difficult and you don't have to be precisely on the line. If you can't manage to pick them up immediately, proceed on a bearing of 205° from the root of the breakwater – the Muelle de Garcia.

BERTHING

Although the local yacht club has floating pontoons in the northern half of the Darsena de

(which is the leading line) to avoid the west side.

Once the lighthouse on Punta de la Cruz – the eastern headland – bears about north from astern, turn towards the western end of the bridge and

Chapter 4

Porcillan, visiting yachts for some reason are not allowed to berth there. Instead you have to moor along the inner side of the Muelle de Garcia, which forms the basin, using a fender-board and long warps to cope with a tidal range of up to 3.5 metres. There are very few ladders on this quay, which was not really designed as a berth, so getting ashore near LW may mean using a ship's ladder (which you probably don't have), climbing the rigging or using the dinghy. The south part of the harbour is shallow and dries in parts, although small craft or those without a big draught may find a mooring or a space to anchor.

FACILITIES

Water is available on the pier (enquire with the fishermen) or from the yacht club on the other side of the basin, but there is no Gasoleo A – diesel here is for fishing and commercial craft only. Showers and toilets are available at the yacht club.

Berthing in the Darsena de Porcillan

A fleet of local boats race enthusiastically

TRANSPORT

The bus station, on the northern fringe of town towards the main road, has connections to La Coruña, Santiago, Lugo, Vivero, Oviedo and Gijon. The railway station is about two miles south-west of the town centre, with trains to El Ferrol and Oviedo.

PROVISIONING

There are plenty of shops and stores in the town centre, which is, however, a steep climb of about

Interesting buildings line the Praza de España

15 minutes from the harbour. There is also a large supermarket just to the north of the town centre.

A RUN ASHORE

Despite the climb, a visit to the town centre is well worthwhile. Ribadeo was once an important commercial harbour and its trade with the Baltic countries was the reason for its early development, although the harbour is in fact built on the remains of an ancient port dating back to Roman times. A small fleet of local traditional

Market day

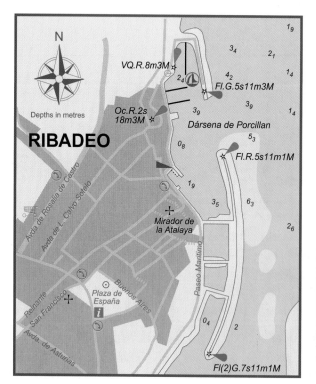

Steep, narrow streets lead from the harbour up to the town

lugsailed boats go back and forth in the wide estuary.

The lively old town lies around the main square of Plaza España, on top of the hill above the harbour. Its formal public gardens, filled with palm trees, is overlooked by some fine Spanish Colonial-style buildings. The tourist office can be found on the opposite side of the square to the town hall and provides the usual selection of leaflets about the town and its surroundings.

If you have time to spare, a visit to the Mirado de Santa Cruz (a round trip of about four miles) or along the cliff top road to Isla Pancha (approximately three miles) will be rewarding.

Ribadeo's fiestas include Nuestra Señora do Carme,

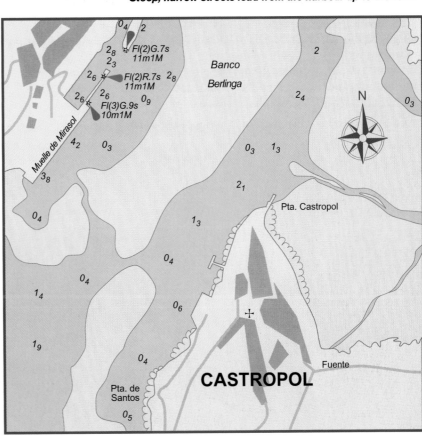

One of the two small basins at Foz, a small fishing harbour not far from Ribadeo

on 16 July, to honour the patron saint of the seafarers and fishermen, and the Xira de Santa Cruz, which takes place every first weekend in August when a large number of folk musicians gather to play Galician bagpipes, clearly demonstrating their Celtic connections.

A visit to Castropol, just across the ria, is to be highly recommended. Indeed, a stroll through the old alleyways, lined with the houses of the

The diesel - Gasoleo A pump at Foz is only for use by fishing boats

formerly rich and aristocratic families, is an interesting experience, as is sampling local delicacies in the waterfront tapas bars down by the little quay.

Castropol can be reached by ferry, tender or, if your boat is small or of shallow draught, under your own steam (see page 147).

EATING OUT

Ribadeo has a number of restaurants and bars, including Parador (Amador Fernandez 7, Tel: 982 12 88 25), where you might go for a special treat. Specialising in seafood is the Mediante on the main square (Plaza de España 16, Tel: 982 13 04 53).

ALTERNATIVE ANCHORAGES

Due to the constant swell, anchoring to seaward of the bridge cannot be recommended. Upriver from Ribadeo, the Rio Eo shallows quickly, but if you

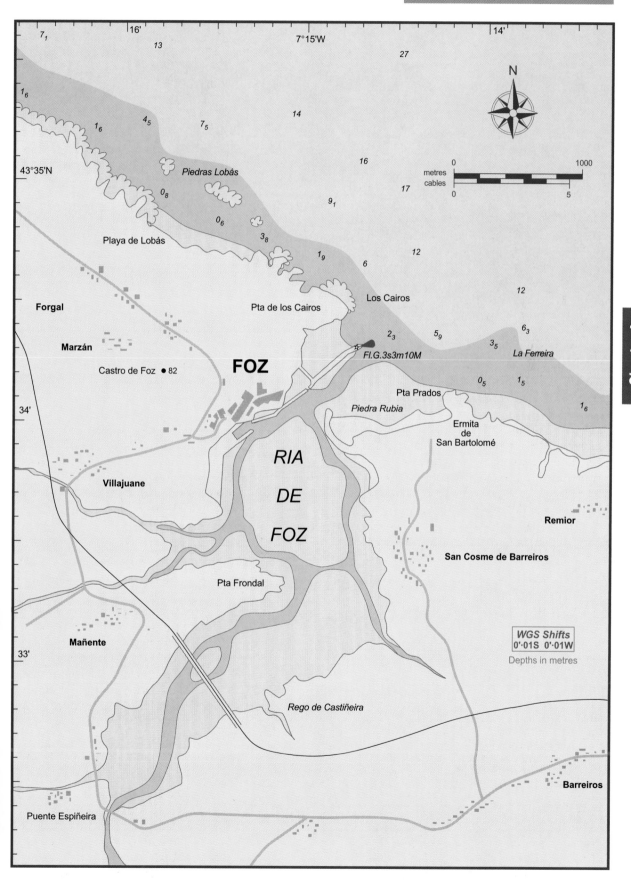

43°35'N

34'

33'

7°15'W

Piedras Lobás

Playa de Lobás

Forgal

Marzán

Castro de Foz ● 82

FOZ

Pta de los Cairos

Los Cairos

Fl.G.3s3m10M

La Ferreira

Pta Prados

Piedra Rubia

Ermita
de
San Bartolomé

RIA

DE

FOZ

Villajuane

Remior

San Cosme de Barreiros

Pta Frondal

Mañente

WGS Shifts
0'·01S 0'·01W

Depths in metres

Rego de Castiñeira

Barreiros

Puente Espiñeira

N

metres
cables

0   1000

0   5

Chapter 4

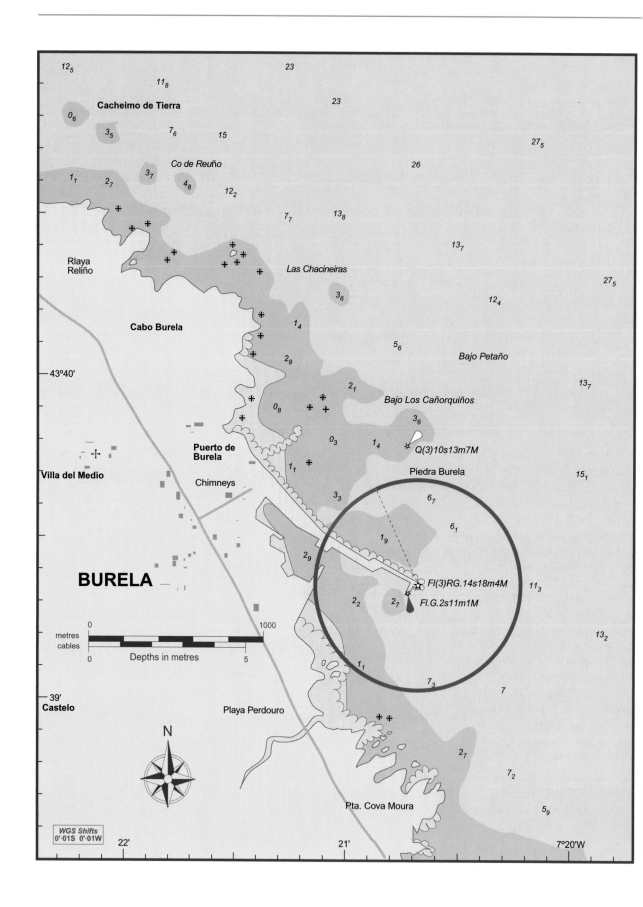

12₅

11₈

23

23

Cacheimo de Tierra

0₆

3₅

7₆

15

27₅

Co de Reuño

26

1₁

2₇

3₇

4₈

12₂

7₇

13₈

13₇

Rlaya
Reliño

Las Chacineiras

27₅

3₆

12₄

Cabo Burela

1₄

5₆

2₉

Bajo Petaño

13₇

43°40'

2₁

Bajo Los Cañorquiños

0₈

3₆

0₃

1₄

Q(3)10s13m7M

Villa del Medio

Puerto de
Burela

1₁

Piedra Burela

15₁

Chimneys

3₃

6₇

6₁

1₉

BURELA

2₉

Fl(3)RG.14s18m4M

11₃

metres
cables

0   1000

2₂

2₇

Fl.G.2s11m1M

Depths in metres   5

1₁

13₂

39'
Castelo

0

7₃

7

Playa Perdouro

N

2₇

7₂

Pta. Cova Moura

5₉

WGS Shifts
0'·01S 0'·01W

22'

21'

7°20'W

The second set of leading lines into Ribadeo. The upper one is just below the hexagonal building

proceed with caution and careful sounding, anchorages can be found. Beware, as the river is not marked at all above Ribadeo, which makes exploring here a real adventure.

You might try to anchor off the south end of the Muelle de Mirasol, or north-west of the point at Castropol (in both places in varying depths on sand), failing which it may be possible to moor alongside the drying quay or pontoon at Castropol – again checking the depth, which varies with the silting and dredging of the river. There are no facilities for yachts. Another option is just north of the shipyard at the village of Figueras (the depth here is about three to four metres).

HARBOURS BETWEEN RIBADEO AND VIVERO

The coast west of Ribadeo is not particularly attractive, especially compared to the beautiful rias further west. There are only a few small,

primarily industrial harbours here, which you may consider worth visiting, although some should only really be used as a port of refuge.

Foz is a small, historic town, situated at the mouth of a shallow river. A drying bar lies across the entrance and the channels vary and are

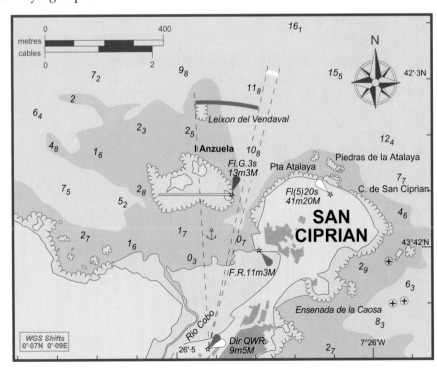

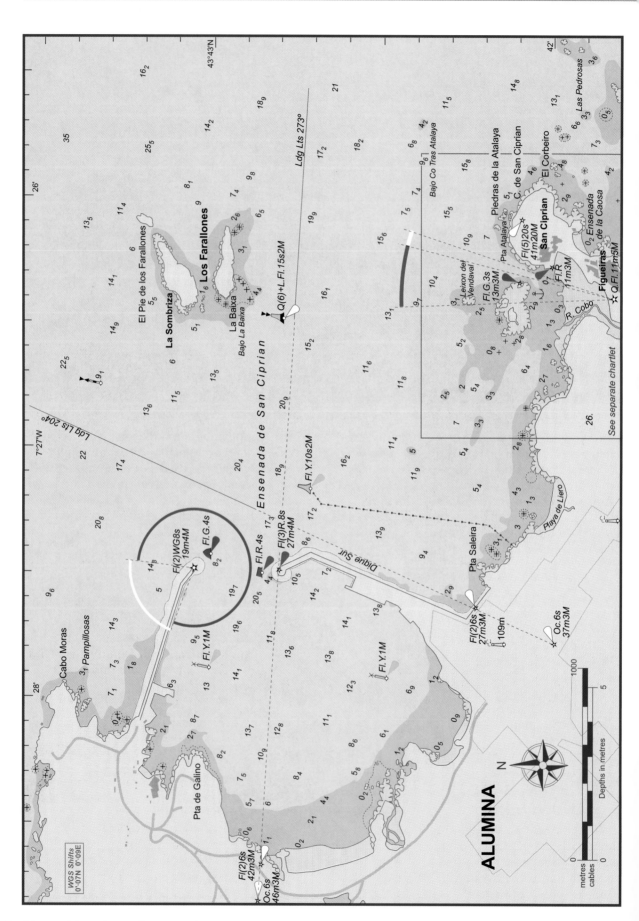

ALUMINA

N

Depths in metres

metres
cables

WGS Shifts
0'·07N 0'·09E

Cabo Moras

Pampillosas

Pta de Galino

Fl.Y.1M

Fl.Y.1M

Fl.Y.1M

Fl(2)6s
42m3M

Oc.6s
46m3M

Fl(2)6s
27m3M

109m

Oc.6s
37m3M

Fl(3)R.8s
27m4M

Fl.R.4s

Fl(2)WG8s
19m4M

Fl.G.4s

Fl.Y.10s2M

Dique Sur

Pta Saleira

Playa de Liero

Ensenada de San Ciprian

Ldg Lts 204°

7'27'W

Ldg Lts 273°

Q(6)+L.Fl.15s2M

El Pie de los Farallones

La Sombriza

Los Farallones

La Baixa

Bajo La Baixa

26'

7'27'W

28'

43°43'N

42'

Bajo Co Tras Atalaya

Piedras de la Atalaya

C. de San Ciprian

El Corbeiro

San Ciprian

Pta Atalaya

Leixon del
Vendaval

Fl(5)20s
41m20M

Fl.R
11m3M

Fl.G.3s
13m3M

Figueiras
Q.Fl.11m5M

Ensenada
de la Caosa

R. Cobo

Las Pedrosas

See separate chartlet

26.

1000

5

Chapter 4

Sunrise over the Ria de Ribadeo

subject to silting. The estuary is actually very scenic and ideal for multihulls or other craft able to dry out at LW. Otherwise, it is possible to berth along the outside of the quay.

There are two tiny harbour basins at Foz. The first one incorporates two small craft pontoons, which are entirely occupied by local boats, although if you're lucky you might find a berth along the inner quay. The second basin is very shallow and dries in places at LW. There is an eight-ton crane, but no Gasoleo A – the diesel pump is only for use by fishing boats.

The town itself is not wildly interesting, but has the usual assortment of small bars and cheap restaurants.

Burela is a fishing harbour that provides very good shelter, thanks to its huge breakwater. However, it is always full with fishing craft and doesn't cater at all for yachts, which are in fact not encouraged to come here. This place should therefore only be considered in an emergency, to which end there is a large hospital near the harbour.

San Ciprian is a rather scenic old village, which sits on a promontory connected to the mainland by a sandy spit and a road. Its harbour is nothing more than a protected anchorage, which is full of moorings. There is an eight-ton crane on the pier and the diesel pump sells Gasoleo B for fishing boats only.

Alternatively, you can anchor in the little bay east of the village, but beware the shallows and rocks all around. The old village on the promontory has a few bars and restaurants, while in the new town, situated on the mainland just across the sand spit, you will find a post office and small supermarket.

About two miles further north-west is a huge commercial harbour called Alumina, which again is unsuitable for yachts, but could possibly provide a refuge in emergency conditions. There are no facilities here whatsoever.

USEFUL INFORMATION

Ribadeo tourist office Tel: 982 12 86 89
www.ribadeo.com
Castropol tourist office Tel: 985 63 50 01
Club Nautico Tel: 982 13 11 44

RIA DE VIVERO

Ria de Vivero entrance – 43°43'.02N / 07°35'.57W

Ria de Vivero is the easternmost of the large Rias Altas and, although scenic, it is not as remote as the others. Its wide entrance is virtually free of hazards and the new marina should, by now, be offering all services to yachts. It is also conveniently close to the attractive and interesting historic centre of Vivero.

This area is perhaps the start of the most beautiful part of northern Galicia, with its high, rugged coasts, dark cool woods and eucalyptus plantations, not to mention its countless sandy coves and beaches either inside the rias or tucked between the cliffs. The pretty Ria del Barquero, the shallow and winding Ria de Santa Marta de Ortigueira and the more dramatic Ria de Cedeira, with its excellent anchorage, all lie further to the west.

LOCATION/POSITION

Ria de Vivero is only five miles south-east of Punta de la Estaca de Bares.

APPROACH AND ENTRANCE

Approach waypoint: 43°44'.02N / 07°35'.57W; 180°; 1M to ria entrance.

The approach presents no real problems, as there are no off-lying dangers, and the ria is easily identified by several headlands, lighthouses and islands. The outer approach is situated between Isla Coelleira and Punta Roncadoira (both of which have lighthouses), with the inner approach being between Punta Socastra and Punta de Faro (also with lighthouses). The small, unlit Isla Gabeira lies close to the western shore, just south of Punta Socastra.

The approaches to Vivero. The modern fishing port of Celeiro is in the foreground and the new marina at Vivero is in the basin to port, just past the bend in the river. Beyond lies the town.

BERTHING

Yachts should keep out of Celeiro fishing harbour, which is commercial, busy and intolerant of visitors. The new marina is a few hundred metres up the river towards the town. Its basin has a depth of two metres at LW and it should, by now, have six pontoons with finger berths.

FACILITIES

The marina offers all services and facilities, including water and electricity on the pontoons, an eight-ton crane, showers and many more amenities in the nearby yacht club, including internet access, bar, restaurant, fitness room and tennis courts.

The marina staff assured us that by June 2002 there would be diesel - Gasoleo A for yachts on the new reception pontoon and a travelift with a hard-standing area, complete with all repair facilities. Even if all these amenities don't actually appear – seeing is believing – the marina already offers the main essentials. You can find a small chandlery across the road, in the colourful new row of buildings called Edificio Mirador.

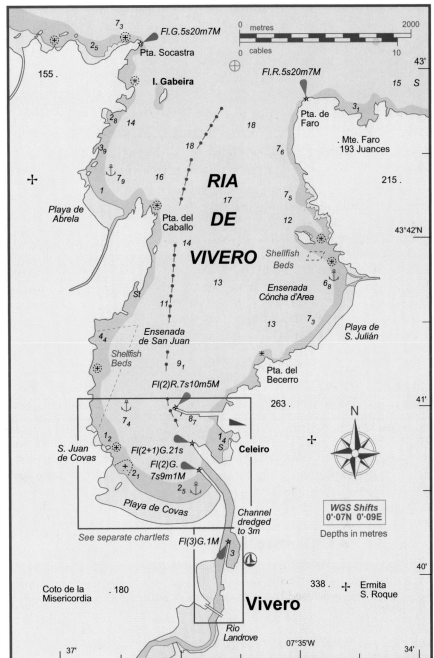

TRANSPORT

The bus station, about 300 metres north of the bridge, provides regular services to La Coruña, Lugo and Ribadeo. The railway station is south of the town, with services to El Ferrol and Oviedo.

PROVISIONING

A large hypermarket, Haley, is just 250 metres away, with a post office and tourist information centre on the opposite side of the road to the

The new marina lies close to the historic town

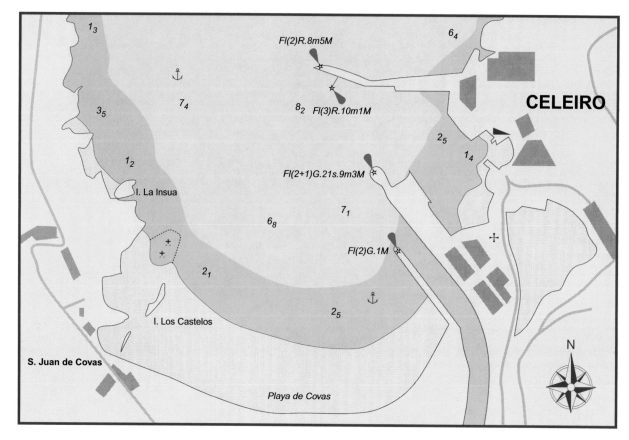

In the map:

1_3

Fl(2)R.8m5M

6_4

3_5 7_4

8_2 Fl(3)R.10m1M

CELEIRO

2_5

1_2

1_4

I. La Insua

Fl(2+1)G.21s.9m3M

7_1

6_8

Fl(2)G.1M

2_1

2_5

I. Los Castelos

S. Juan de Covas

Playa de Covas

N

marina. There are many local shops and a delightful market in nearby Vivero town (Mon, Thurs, Sat). If fresh fish is your thing, go to the daily market at Celeiro, which is just a short walk to the north.

A RUN ASHORE

Although modern housing is spreading outwards from the town, the old centre of Vivero is beautiful. Partly enclosed by the mediaeval town wall, into which some of the ancient houses are integrated, and rising up the hill on the east side of the ria, it is a particularly pleasant place to wander around.

The Santa Maria church dates back to the 12th century, the Puerta de Carlos V was built in 1548, the Puerta del Vallado is from the 13th century and the Porta da Vila was constructed as long ago as 1217. Another asset might be the beach on the other side of the river, off which you can anchor.

To walk around the old town, it is best to enter

The mediaeval gate leads to the beautiful old quarter

The town pool is for small craft only

the old quarter through the Puerta de Carlos V, having come from the waterfront promenade along the river. From here, you will reach the main square, Plaza Major, where you will see the town hall, dating back to the 16th century, and the ruins of a burnt-out church behind. Several old houses are actually derelict, although some are now being restored. A market is held underneath and around the statue of the local politician and poet, Pastor Diaz. Further on, along Calle Teodoro Quidos, you will come across the church of Santa Maria del Campo, while further east, around the Plaza de Fontenova, are the typical, narrow alleys and streets of the old quarter, complete with bars and restaurants.

Vivero also has a few annual fiestas to offer: the Fiesta de San Roque takes place on the hill of Monte San Roque each year for a few days around 16 August, with folklore and religious activities. The Romeria de Naseiro, held around 25 August, is noted for its huge feast of *pulpo* (octopus).

EATING OUT

Good and reasonably priced restaurants in the old town include the particularly cheerful and rustic Laurel (Calle Meliton Cortiñas). Another one not far from the marina is O Muro (Margarita Pardo de Cela 28), which specialises in fish. For a more exclusive treat, try the Hotel Ego, (Restaurant Nito, Hotel Ego, Praia de Area, Tel: 982 56 09 87) overlooking the beach of Praia de Area about two miles north of Vivero. Its prices *à la carte* are not cheap.

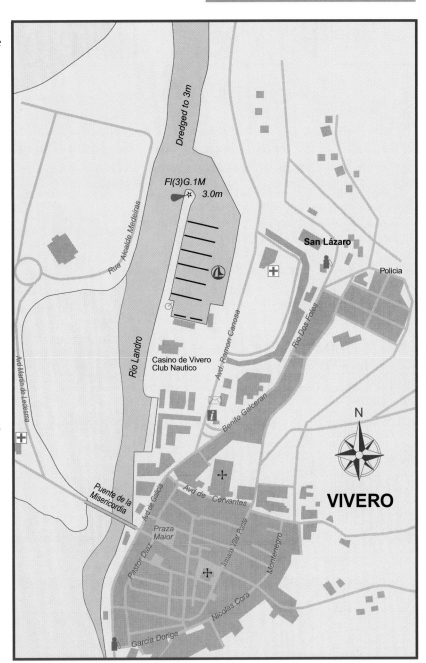

Chapter 4

ALTERNATIVE ANCHORAGES

There are several anchorages in the Ria de Vivero, all open to northerly winds, but some tenable in either north-westerly or north-easterly winds. One of the most attractive is off the beach of Area, just south of the small islet Insua d'Area. Here you can drop anchor onto sand in depths of between two and 10 metres. Other options are off the beaches of Abrela (on the west side, just behind Punta del Cabello), although these are wide open to northerly and north-easterly winds, or at the very end off the beach of Playa de Covas just west of the river and town, but only in fair weather.

RIA DEL BARQUERO

Ria del Barquero 0.5M NE of Punta del Santo – 43°44'.89N / 07°40'.68W

Ria del Barquero is another delightful ria, with the small but attractive village of El Barquero at its head. This ria is, however, exposed to northerly and north-easterly winds and, although the sheltered river anchorage just above the village is wonderfully idyllic, it is only suitable for shoal draught vessels.

Vicedo has a new, purpose-built fishing harbour on the east side of the ria, although this is very busy and should only be used if you need shelter in heavy weather. You would therefore be better off in one of the scenic anchorages nearby, which are secure in all winds blowing from the south-east through to the north-west or even the north.

LOCATION/POSITION

The Ria del Barquero is immediately east of Punta de la Estaca de Bares and just around the corner from Ria de Vivero.

APPROACH AND ENTRANCE

Approach waypoint: 1M east of Cabo de Bares - 43°46'.67N / 07°38'.24W; 225°; 2.5M to waypoint 0.5M NE of Punta del Santo.

Another easy approach without any off-lying dangers and one that is quickly identified by Punta de la Estaca de Bares on one side and the Isla Coelleira, with its lighthouse, to the east. Due to shoals and overfalls, Punta de la Estaca de Bares should be given a wide berth, at least one mile off and significantly more in heavy weather. The same applies for Cabo Ortegal, with its two little headlands Punta de los Aguillones and

There are many pleasant anchorages around the beautiful Ria del Barquero. Vicedo harbour is on the farther shore, and Cabo de Bares and Concha de Bares are at the top left

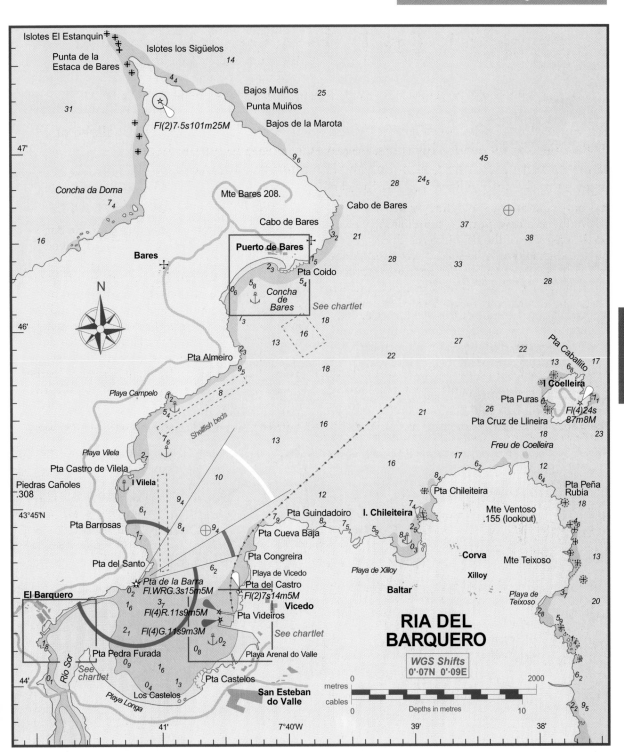

Islotes El Estanquin
Islotes los Sigüelos
Punta de la
Estaca de Bares
14
Bajos Muiños
Punta Muiños
Fl(2)7·5s101m25M
Bajos de la Marota
31
9₆
47'
45
Concha da Doma
28   24₅
7₄
Mte Bares 208.
Cabo de Bares
16
Cabo de Bares
37
Bares
Puerto de Bares
3₂   21
1₅
2₃   Pta Coido
28
33
46'   0₆ 5₈   5₄
Concha
de
Bares   See chartlet
1₃
18
16
18
27
Pta Almeiro
2₃
13
22   22   13   17
9₅
18
Playa Campelo   Pta Caballito
I Coelleira
8   Pta Puras 6₈
5₄   26   Fl(4)24s
7₆   Pta Cruz de Llineira 87m8M
Playa Vilela   18   23
2₇   13
Pta Castro de Vilela   Freu de Coelleira
Piedras Cañoles   17
.308   16   12
I Vilela   10   8₄ 6₂   Pta Peña
6₁   9₄   Pta Chileiteira 6₄   Rubia
43°45'N   12   Mte Ventoso   18
Pta Barrosas   8₄ 9₄   Pta Guindadoiro I. Chileiteira .155 (lookout)
1₇   7₉   8₂ 7₅   7₄
Pta Cueva Baja   5₉   Corva   Mte Teixoso   13
Pta del Santo   6₂   2₅ 8₄   Xilloy
Pta Congreira   Playa de Xilloy   Baltar   Playa de
Pta de la Barra   Playa de Vicedo   Teixoso
Fl.WRG.3s15m5M   Pta del Castro   RIA DEL
El Barquero   0₂   3₇ Fl(2)7s14m5M   BARQUERO
1₆   Vicedo
Fl(4)R.11s9m5M   Pta Videiros   WGS Shifts   2000
2₁   Fl(4)G.11s9m3M   0'·07N 0'·09E
0₈ 0₂
Pta Pedra Furada   0₉   Playa Arenal do Valle   metres
1₆   0
Río Sor   0₄ 1₃   Pta Castelos   cables
See   San Esteban   Depths in metres   10
44'   0₁ chartlet   do Valle
Playa Longa   Los Castelos
41'   7°40'W   39'   38'

Punta del Limo, which is further west. Finally, approach and enter on a south-westerly course, keeping in the middle of the ria.

BERTHING AND ANCHORAGES

The new harbour of Vicedo is purely a commercial fishing port, where yachts are probably unwelcome. The berths inside are taken up by fishing craft, but if space and the locals permit, try mooring alongside the south quay or the outer mole, immediately to starboard as you come in. Be aware that the village of Vicedo is quite a long walk from here.

Alternatively, in settled easterly conditions,

The entrance to Puerto del Barquero

inside the sand bank, which forms the western part of the Playa Longa, and is entered close to the south of the Punta de la Barra.

You may be able to moor alongside a fishing vessel inside El Barquero's tiny fishing harbour, or outside the pier (in calm and settled weather only), with long warps and preferably a fender-board. Alternatively, anchor just below the bridge, but make sure that the anchor is well dug in as the ebb runs very strongly. In settled weather, you can anchor off the Playa Longa without actually entering the Rio Sor. At the north-east end of this bay is a small quay, but here the anchorage is taken over by numerous small craft moorings.

Other daytime anchorages may be found along the west coast of the ria, between Bares in the north and the Punta del Santo, which is where the inner bay begins. These are sheltered from west winds but are otherwise quite open. Depths vary according to the spot chosen.

depending on the state of the swell, you can anchor in the bays north or south of the harbour, but bear in mind that the water off the beach south of the harbour shallows rapidly.

If your yacht's characteristics permit an approach to El Barquero village, enter the Rio Sor at the end of the Ria del Barquero on the last of the flood. The channel runs near to the shore

There are two other possible anchorages along the west shore of the ria, off the beach at Playa Campelo or south of Isla Vilela, but neither is really sheltered. If you manage to land on the beach in Vilela unscathed by the surf pounding onto it, you will at least be rewarded by drinks

Puerto del Barquero is very pretty, but it has only about a metre depth. Anchoring in the river may be better

Looking west over Vicedo reveals the shallow, shore-hugging channel to Puerto del Barquero

and tapas from Meson Vilela, a bar and restaurant conveniently positioned just a few steps uphill from the water. In the outer ria, anchor in the circular bay off the pier and village of Bares, which is Spain's most northerly harbour. It's one of the best beaches for miles around and is sheltered from most wind directions (except south to south-east). There is, unusually, enough space between and around the local small craft to anchor onto sand.

FACILITIES

No facilities other than a crane and a slipway at Vicedo harbour.

PROVISIONING

There are a few small shops in the villages of Vicero and El Barquero. Bares has only one shop, which calls itself a supermarket, and two restaurants on the beach plus another one further up in the village.

A RUN ASHORE

The main attractions here are the spectacular scenery and the often virtually deserted beaches of Bares, Playa Longa (opposite El Barquero on the other side of the river) and several smaller ones tucked between the cliffs.

EATING OUT

El Barquero has a few basic bars and two restaurants, as does Bares. Several bars and cafés can be found in Vicedo.

Puerto del Barquero from upstream

SANTA MARTA DE ORTIGUEIRA

Santa Marta de Ortigueira close W of Isla San Vicente – 43°42'.60N / 07°50'.40W

The Ria de Santa Marta de Ortigueira is one of the most beautiful and unspoilt rias on this part of the coast. This is partly because the access is a little difficult, which has consequently led both to a decline in commercial fishing and a distinct lack of leisure boating. Once inside the entrance, the ria winds through wooded hills and is completely sheltered from the elements. The only significant settlement is the town of Santa Marta itself which, although appearing remote when approaching from the sea, in fact lies on the main coastal road route and has more than adequate facilities.

LOCATION/POSITION

The entrance to the ria is in the inner part of the Ensenada de Santa Marta o de Carino, which lies between Punta de la Estaca de Bares and Cabo Ortegal, the northernmost points on the Spanish coast. Position 43° 42'.8N / 07° 50'.25W is two cables north of the west end of the Isla San Vicente (58 metres), which in 2001 defined the start of the entrance channel. Spanish Chart 931 refers to, but should not be used for, crossing the bar.

APPROACH AND ENTRANCE

Approach waypoint: 43°43'.60N / 07°50'.40W; 180°; 1M to waypoint close W of Isla San Vicente.

The approach in the Ensenada is generally hazard-free, except near the shore. A group of rocks on the north-east approach, just off the harbour at Espasante, is marked by an unlit west cardinal mark, but in the north-west approach, the shoal and rocks off the point approximately half way between Carino and the ria's entrance are not marked and should be given a wide berth. If leaving Carino for the ria, head for Espasante until Isla San Vicente bears approximately south.

The entrance should not be attempted in an onshore wind of any strength, a heavy swell or at any time other than approximately the last two hours of the flood tide (depending on draught).

Santa Marta is well worth the effort of getting there. The yacht club pontoon is private, but you may be invited to use it

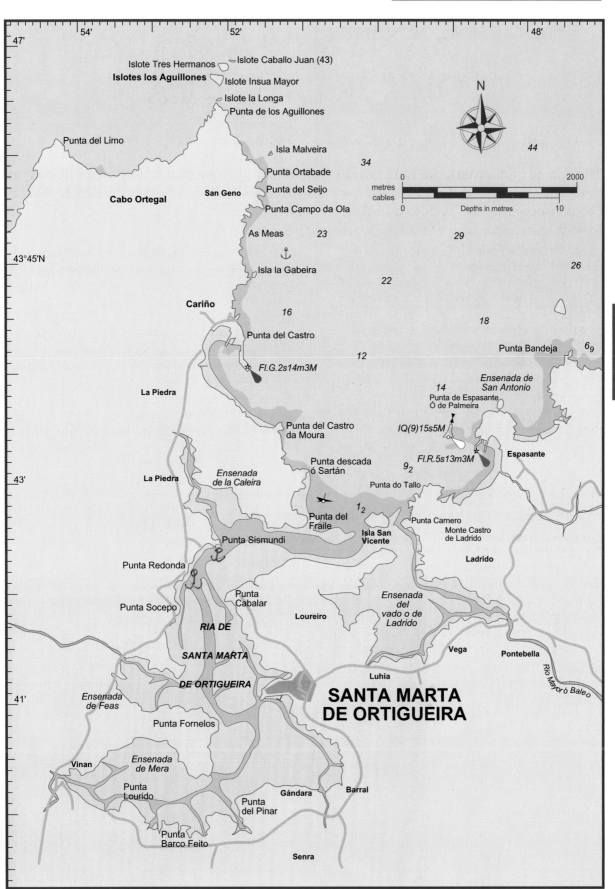

47'

54'

52'

48'

Islote Tres Hermanos ⌒ ⌒ Islote Caballo Juan (43)
Islotes los Aguillones ▽ ⌒ Islote Insua Mayor
⌒ Islote la Longa
Punta de los Aguillones

Punta del Limo

⌒ Isla Malveira
34
44

Cabo Ortegal   San Geno
Punta Ortabade
Punta del Seijo
0   2000
metres
cables
0   10
Punta Campo da Ola
Depths in metres

As Meas   23
29

43°45'N
⚓
Isla la Gabeira
26
22

Cariño
16
18

Punta del Castro
12
Punta Bandeja   6₉

✴ Fl.G.2s14m3M ⬤
**Ensenada de
San Antonio**
14

La Piedra
Punta de Espasante
Ó de Palmeira
IQ(9)15s5M
Espasante

Punta del Castro
da Moura

43'
Punta descada
ó Sartán
Fl.R.5s13m3M ⬤
La Piedra
*Ensenada
de la Caleira*
9₂
Punta do Tallo

1₂
Punta Carnero

🛬 Punta del
Fraile
**Isla San
Vicente**
Monte Castro
de Ladrido

Punta Sismundi
Ladrido

Punta Redonda ⚓
*Ensenada
del
vado o de
Ladrido*

⚓
Punta
Cabalar

Punta Socepo
Loureiro

RIA DE
Vega   **Pontebella**

SANTA MARTA
Luhia

41'
DE ORTIGUEIRA
SANTA MARTA
DE ORTIGUEIRA

*Ensenada
de Feas*

Punta Fornelos

*Ensenada
de Mera*

Vinan
Punta
Lourido
Gándara   **Barral**
Punta
del Pinar

Punta
Barco Feito
Senra

Rio Mayor ó Baleo

STA MARTA DE ORTIGUEIRA

The position of the sand-bar, which stretches between Isla San Vicente and a point six cables to the west, changes regularly, so don't rely on charts and sketch plans.

You can either survey the entrance in advance by dinghy, or in calm conditions slowly feel your way in. In either event, there are often locals out on their boats, who will generally offer information about the best depths. Once inside, the start of the deep water channel is located about a cable to the south of the point of land directly west of Isla San Vicente (Punte del Fraile on some charts). As soon as you're safely in the channel, stay fairly close to the northern shore as far as the mouth of a north-west arm of the ria, then head south-west towards the prominent Punta Sistmund and on to the next point, Punta Redonda. Moorings give a good indication of the line of the channel.

At Punta Redonda, alter course towards Punta Fornelos, which is prominent, wooded and about 1.5 miles away, opposite the now visible town of Santa Marta. After a short distance, the channel is marked by red plastic floats, some of which have been painted green to serve as starboard markers, although in 2001 a good

deal of this paint had fallen off, requiring a certain amount of judgement as to which buoys were meant to be green. The buoys continue almost to Santa Marta quay.

BERTHING

There is virtually no commercial fishing traffic in this ria, so you can anchor where depth permits. You will come across various quiet spots on the way in, although nearer the entrance the tide runs strongly. If visiting the town, keep going until you get to between 300 and 100 yards south-west of Santa Marta quay, where there is an area clear of obstructions and with adequate depths of around four to five metres. Alternatively, berth alongside the quay, where there is between two and three metres of water.

The small pontoon beyond the quay belongs to the local yacht club, but visiting yachts are sometimes offered a berth. Depth here is two metres at LW. Beyond (east of) this point, the depth becomes less, and in fact the marina in the bay below the town is only suitable for shallow draught or small craft.

Time your departure carefully to allow for incoming tide (which may run at two to three knots, or even stronger locally) when *en route* to the entrance. If you arrive at the bar too early, anchor in the pool south of the point before the entrance.

FACILITIES

These include a crane on the quay and a slipway at the small boat harbour.

The channel from the sea is as charted, but the bar mouth may not be

TRANSPORT

There are bus and train connections.

PROVISIONING

There are many shops and supermarkets, which can be found past the small boat marina, up the hill to the right.

A RUN ASHORE

Santa Marta de Ortigueira, a pleasant, bustling country town, is the centre of this region. The church, visible from the water, is in a quiet, more residential part of town, while the shops are along the main road (see above). A market on the square in front of the small craft marina takes place on Thursdays and Saturdays. The waterfront promenade is a pleasant place to amble along on a sunny day, unless you feel the urge to march a mile or two to the beaches on the peninsula Minado.

EATING OUT

It is not a place for lavish wining and dining, although several bars cater at least for the former. There is one restaurant, Meson Soilan, which is uphill from the small craft marina. Otherwise try the bars and cafés, one of which is conveniently placed opposite the yacht club pontoon near the quay.

DAYTIME ANCHORAGES NEARBY

Outside the entrance of the ria, the Ensenada de Espasante is a mile to the north-east and offers reasonable shelter from all but westerly winds. There is a small fishing harbour here, but this is taken up by moorings and fishing craft. Anchor off the eastern, inner breakwater, or you might find a short term berth at the quay. The village is about 500 metres from the harbour, with various bars and shops scattered around it. Either this bay or the bay at Carino are good places to await the tide before entering the Ria de Santa Marta de Ortigueira.

Santa Marta's elegant town centre

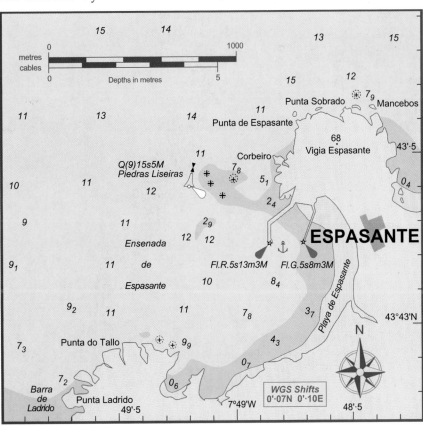

Chapter 4

CARIÑO

Cariño harbour entrance – 43°44'.07N / 07°51'.48W

Cariño is a fairly busy fishing harbour tucked away below Cabo Ortegal which, during the summer, becomes a holiday village as well. The bay at Cariño is sheltered by the substantial outer breakwater and quay, stretching around 500 metres to the south of the main harbour buildings.

The only exposure here is to winds from the north-east to the south-east, although an ever present swell may penetrate from other directions.

LOCATION/POSITION

Cariño is situated underneath the east side of Cabo Ortegal.

APPROACH AND ENTRANCE

Approach waypoint: 43°44'.78N/07°50'.51W; 225°; 1M to harbour entrance.

This bay is easy to enter in all weather except north-easterly gales. Identified by Cabo Ortegal and Punta de la Estaca de Bares, the place cannot be mistaken. In heavy weather or poor visibility, take care not to get too close to Cabo Ortegal or Punta de la Estaca de Bares. Both have off-lying islets and rocks as well as overfalls and rough seas, so keep at least one to three miles off.

There are some rocks and shoals off the eastern part of the bay, both to the north and south of the breakwater. Therefore when heading for the breakwater, stay on a course of anything between 010° and 050° to keep clear of these. The end of the harbour breakwater is lit (Fl G 2s).

The port of Cariño, with the Ria of Santa Marta de Ortigueira in the background

BERTHING

Alongside the floating pontoons in the north part of the harbour, or inside the breakwater if space and the local fishermen permit. Alternatively, an anchorage may be found anywhere behind the breakwater, but take care not to come too close to the moorings or to obstruct the approach to the breakwater. It's a good idea to use a tripping line on the anchor, as the ground is likely to be foul in places.

FACILITIES

Water can be had from the pier but not on the floating pontoons. There is a chandler, principally catering for the fishing fleet, as well as a mechanic.

PROVISIONING

Cariño has plenty of shops as well as a local market near the slipway.

WGS Shifts 0'·07N 0'·09E

Playa Mallorquín

Cariño

44'·5

Pradra Juana

7·5 Pta del Castro

14

3·4

11

Ensenada de Cariño

10

13

6·5

7m

9m

Fl.G.2s12m3M

Moorings 6

0·3

43°44'N

La Piedra

7·8

9·1

11

11

7·6

8·9

3·5

2·4

11

10

7·5

3·5

1·2

2·4

6·2

9·2

Pta Serrón

0·9

Pta del Castro da Moura

2·6

PUERTO DE CARIÑO

219 52' Mte. Mazanteo

7·6 7°51'W

8·6

metres / cables / Depths in metres 18 5 / 0 1000

A RUN ASHORE

Cariño is a busy provincial town which, although not wildly attractive, is very lively during the summer. One of the attractions seems to be the Playa del Forno, about two to three miles from town, but it is not served by public transport. For night-life, there are several bars and discotheques near the waterfront.

EATING OUT

The fish restaurant, Méson O Barrometra, is near the harbour, with several other restaurants and bars thereabouts.

Cariño's moorings, anchoring space and pontoon

The pontoon at Cariño

Fishing, as in most places in NW Spain, is the main activity

Chapter 4

RIA DE CEDEIRA

Cedeira breakwater and fishing quay. Yachts can anchor on approximately the line of the right hand margin

Ria de Cedeira entrance due E of Punta Fulgoso – 43°40'.19N / 08°04'.80W

A beautiful natural harbour where, on first sight, you could be forgiven for thinking you had sailed to Scandinavia rather than Spain: steep, densely-wooded hills surround this deep, clear bay, at the end of which is a fine beach and a friendly, bustling holiday village.

LOCATION/POSITION

Ria de Cedeira, about half way between Cabo Ortegal and Cabo Prior, is approximately 25 miles north-north-east of La Coruña.

APPROACH AND ENTRANCE

Approach waypoint: 43°41'.09N / 08°05'.38W; 155°; 1M to entrance waypoint.

This ria is tucked away in the highland tumbling down to the sea and is not easy to recognise until you are fairly close in. Coming from the north, the lighthouse clinging to the cliffs at Punta Candelaria gives a good indication that you are nearly there, as does the unusual lighthouse-like church on Punta de la Frouseira, when approaching from the south-west.

From the north, keep a good distance from the coast, as squalls come off the high cliffs. Likewise from the south, you should stay well clear, as there are many off-lying rocks, especially off Punta Chirlateira, the western side of the entrance to the outer ria, which should be given a wide berth of at least a mile to ensure you clear the sunken rocks. Approaching from due west, keep north of 43°41'.0N until on the 155° transit of Punta del Sarridal light under Punta Promontorio.

Apart from this, entering is easy in nearly all conditions. Once inside the ria, identify the beacon on the rocks in the middle (Piedras de Media Mar), sticking more closely to the eastern side of the ria to avoid these.

BERTHING

You can anchor almost anywhere in the bay east of the breakwater, taking care not to foul moorings or blocking the direct approach to the quay. Holding is good in around three to four metres of sand, although it can be poor on patches of weed.

FACILITIES

You will find a slipway, workshops and marine mechanics, who service the small fishing fleet.

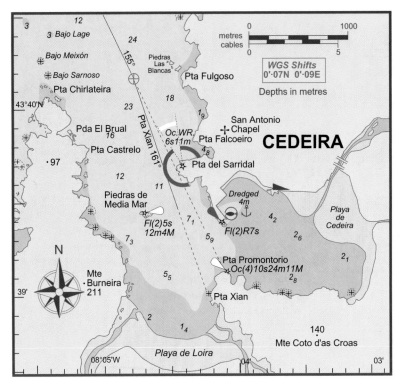

it becomes very busy, although still manages to remain friendly. A stroll through the village and along the banks of the Rio Condomiñas is very pleasurable, but the real treat lies in the extended walks around the bay, through cool, shady woods along the waterfront to the small lighthouse on Punta Promontorio, for example.

The Mirador de Peña Edrosa and Punta Candelaria are also good walks to go on, but if you fancy something shorter, then visit the chapel of San Antonio, which overlooks the harbour approaches and is about a half mile away (albeit uphill).

There are also two attractive beaches: the Playa de Cedeira, just south of the town, and the wild, romantic and often completely deserted Playa de Loira (most easily reached by dinghy from the anchorage) on the other side of Punta Promontorio.

PROVISIONING

There is a good range of shops and small supermarkets in town.

A RUN ASHORE

Cedeira is a lovely, sleepy village, apart from in August at the height of the holiday season, when

EATING OUT

As is to be expected of a holiday village, there is an adequate number bars, cafés and restaurants around the town. The best is probably Avenida (Calle Cuatro Caminos 66, Tel: 981 49 21 12), which is reflected in its prices.

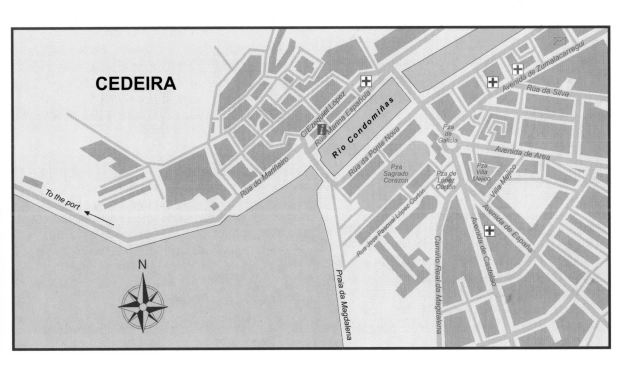

EL FERROL

El Ferrol entrance three cables NW of Punta del Segaño – 43°27'.46N / 08°19'.03W

With its name derived from the Spanish for lighthouse, *faro*, El Ferrol is one of Spain's major naval bases. Now simply known as Ferrol, it is situated in an attractive ria, although, being close to both La Coruña and the new marina at Sada, few yachts have cause to venture into it. The city itself is not

significantly attractive but does have a working feel to it.

LOCATION/POSITION

The ria is roughly half way between Punta de la Estaca de Bares and Cabo Villano, just to the north of La Coruña.

APPROACH AND ENTRANCE

Approach waypoint: 43°27'.00N/08°21'.00W; 072°; 1.5M to entrance waypoint.

There are no off-lying dangers apart from the busy shipping lanes and the shallow Banco de las Laixiñas (19 metres), over which seas break in heavy weather. This bank is about three miles west of Cabo Prioriño Chico. If coming along the coast from the north-east in heavy weather, keep a good distance off, as there are other banks on which seas can break.

The deep and straightforward entrance to the ria is just around Cabo Prioriño Grande and Cabo Prioriño Chico. In settled weather, when coming from the north, these points can be rounded fairly

Darsena de Curuxeiras is central to the city, but the pontoons are not available for visitors, so berth on the NE quay

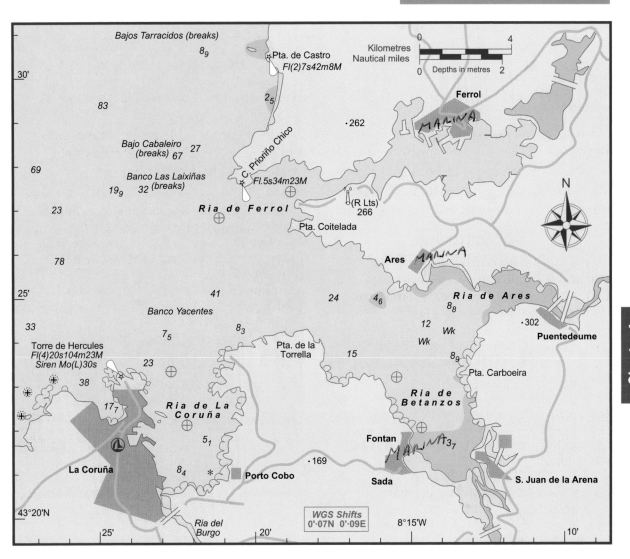

closely (two to three cables off), but in heavy weather stay further off.

The approach from the west is perhaps even simpler. A course of 070° will clear the southern edge of Banco de las Laixiñas, allowing a clear run into the ria.

Like all naval ports, Ferrol is generously endowed with lights and navigation aids. The main leading line is 085° on Punta de San Martin, taking you safely past the twin castles that once defended the port, into the narrows and insight of the city and docks.

BERTHING

Small craft can berth in the Darsena de Curuxeiras, the first small basin as you approach the town. This can be identified by the tower-like building at the end of its eastern pier, as well as the Repsol fuel station and the floating pontoons

for small craft inside. Find a berth alongside the piers as and where the harbour officials and space permit. Yachts are prohibited from entering the other commercial or naval harbour basins further to the east.

Alternatively, there is a small marina at A Graña, which is directly west of the dock. It is publicised as having 60 berths with water, shorepower, fuel (type unspecified) and a ferry link to Ferrol, but the number of actual visitors' berths is unknown. Depending on the local moorings situation, there may be space to anchor off A Graña in three to five metres of water.

FACILITIES IN DARSENA DE CURUXEIRAS

There are no dedicated facilities for yachts. The diesel pump on the small middle pier sells Gasoleo A to yachts, as well as supplying fishing boats and commercial vessels with a larger Gasoleo B hose. If there is nobody around, telephone Ferrol (981) 649 13 04 51 or (981) 696 36 67 63. For any kind of yacht services, chandlery items or repairs, you are far better off at Sada (see section on Sada for details).

TRANSPORT

A train runs along the coast to Gijon, while bus connections, hire cars and taxis are also available. There is a regular ferry service to La Coruña and to the adjacent parts of the ria.

PROVISIONING

All the shops and stores of a large city are available in Ferrol, although the newer, commercial part of town is rather a long walk from the Darsena de Curuxeiras (15 to 20 minutes or so).

A RUN ASHORE

Even the residents say that the best thing about Ferrol is the beautiful surrounding countryside. Having said that, a stroll around the town can be rather pleasant, although there are few significant monuments or historical buildings other than the military architecture. Much of the waterfront is hidden behind a high wall, where the navy has its quarters. Parts of this military arsenal are now open to the public, including the Museo Naval (open 0900 – 1400 except Sundays and public holidays).

Ferrol was the birthplace of Franco who, born in 1892, was the son of a naval purser. During his dictatorship he had the suffix *del Caudillo* added to the city name, which was then dropped after his death and the subsequent return of the

The entrance to the Ria de Ferrol, flanked by the Castles of La Palma and San Felipe

country to democracy. A statue of Franco riding high, covered in a green patina, can still be seen today on the Plaza de España. Many street names have been changed back to their original pre-Civil War names, but not all maps of the town are up to date, so be prepared for some confusion.

From the Darsena de Curuxeiras, you can wander through the old town to the convent San Francisco, which is now partly taken over by the luxurious Parador do Ferrol. Opposite the Parador is the Admiral's palace, from which visitors are obliged to keep their distance, even today. You then come to the new quarter, the Magdalena, built towards the end of the 18th century. It is laid out in a grid pattern and is the main shopping and commercial area.

EATING OUT

For a gourmet treat, why not try the Parador (Tel: 981 35 67 20). Casa Rivera is an

Fishing boats rafted up in Darsena de Curuxeiras

Small craft can berth in Darsena de Curuxeiras

Chapter 4

alternative option, which is less expensive and always worth its money (Galiano 57, Tel: 981 35 07 59). Some regard Pataquina (Dolores 35, Tel: 981 35 23 11) as one of the best value fish restaurants in Ferrol, with the menu being around €15. Bars and night-clubs can be found in Calle Sol.

DAYTIME ANCHORAGES IN THE RIA

Tucked in below Castillo de San Felipe, which is currently not open to the public, lies a very pretty anchorage. It is sheltered from all but easterly winds, which are funnelled down the ria. Holding is variable with some stones, so make sure your anchor is set well before going ashore.

There are other anchorages on the south side of the ria. Try behind Punta Redonda off the sandy beach at Ensenada de Baño, or in the next bay to the east, off the village of Mugardos, from where there is a ferry service to Ferrol. Mugardos is famous for its unique way of cooking octopus.

El Ferrol has 18th century neoclassical buildings as well as a mediaeval quarter

USEFUL INFORMATION
El Ferrol tourist office (Magdalena 12)
Tel: 981 31 11 79

SADA

Marina Sada entrance – 43°21.77'N / 08°14.46'W

A major tourist centre, this busy little town is bustling in summer. It is close enough to La Coruña – only 20 minutes by bus – to be regarded as something of a suburb. The main attraction is the large marina, which is probably the best organised in the entire area.

It is certainly an ideal spot to berth when visiting La Coruña or to leave the boat unattended for longer forays into Galicia. You may even want to consider this marina if you are looking for a place to lay up for the winter.

The Ria de Ares, at the south end of which Sada is located, is very pleasant and boasts two attractive anchorages, Ares and Redes (see below for details).

LOCATION/POSITION

The marina is positioned at the south end of the Ria de Ares, which is sandwiched between Ferrol and La Coruña.

APPROACH AND ENTRANCE

Approach waypoint: 42°23'.18N / 08°15'.17W; 160°; 1.5M to harbour entrance.

The entrance to the ria is wide and presents no problems. Once inside, head south for the Ria de Betanzos and the marina, keeping a safe distance both from the shore and the numerous viveiros (mussel-rafts) anchored there.

BERTHING

The marina has 700 berths for yachts up to 20 metres in length, all on floating pontoons with fingers. Marina staff will allocate a berth (VHF 09). Depths are between two and four metres.

The Ria de Betanzos and the excellent modern marina at Fontan, close to Sada

FACILITIES IN THE MARINA

Facilities include water and electricity on the pontoons, toilets, showers and washing machines ashore. Also on the marina complex are a cafeteria, a supermarket, two chandlers, various mechanics and repair shops. The friendly staff, comprising the harbour master and his assistant, speak English and will help in any way they can. Telephone and fax facilities, along with timetables for buses to La Coruña, are all available in the office, while a weather report is posted up daily.

TRANSPORT

A bus service runs to La Coruña, plus there are taxis and hire-cars. Bicycles can possibly be hired at the marina, but you need to inquire at the office.

PROVISIONING

A supermarket is conveniently situated in the marina area. The town has several shops as well as a market on Saturdays (on Linares Rivas), selling food, clothing and other items.

A RUN ASHORE

Although the town is of limited interest, it does have some traditional fishermen's homes that have been rebuilt on the hillside at Fontan. Also visit La Terraza, allegedly the finest modern building in Galicia. Sada has two beaches, and the five-to-ten minute walk into town along the Paseo Maritimo is very pleasant. The Fiesta del Carmen (held on the Sunday evening after 16 July) has a sea-going, maritime procession that is well worth seeing.

You can, of course, visit

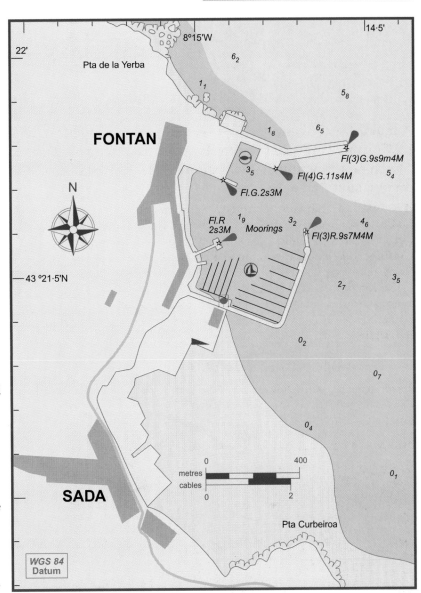

Sada marina has 250 berths and, unlike La Coruña, generally has room for visitors

Chapter 4

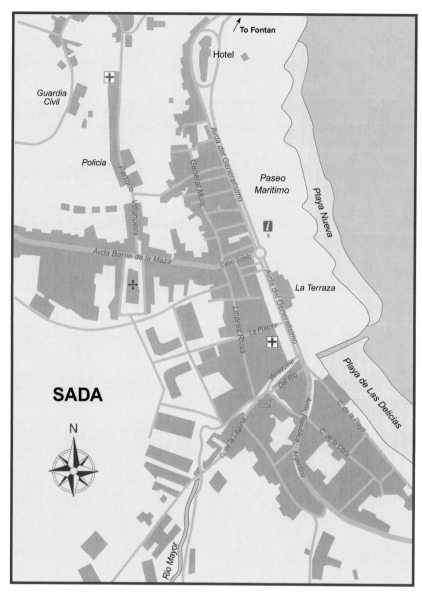

SADA

N

EATING OUT

Sada has a fairly wide choice of bars and restaurants, not all of which are located in the town. There are many good fish restaurants close to the marina, along the road leading from the marina to the fishing pier, including El Pescador, Meson Manel or Restaurante Licar.

If you are anchored at Ares (see below), Bitakora is a wonderful restaurant with very good cuisine, friendly service and a convivial atmosphere.

ALTERNATIVE ANCHORAGES

Ares: this charmingly sleepy village remains comparatively quiet, even in summer. It is located on the north shore of the Ria de Ares, in a half-moon bay behind a sheltering breakwater. The approach is easy and, although the bay is full of moorings, there is space to anchor on a secure holding ground of sand and mud. There is good shelter, except in strong south-westerly to southerly winds. Ares has its own Club Nautico (CN de Ria de Ares), a little

nearby Betanzos, a remarkable, ancient town which was the capital of this northern part of Galicia in the 15th and 16th centuries. Before that it was the Roman port of Brigantium Flavium, which in turn was built on the remains of an ancient Celtic settlement.

The old town, around the Plaza de la Constitucion, certainly deserves a mention. Every year during the last week of July, a mediaeval market takes place, where people dress up in period costume, while arts and crafts are put on display. Also, the world's largest paper balloon, painted with historic scenes, is sent off from here each year on 16 August, and on 18 and 25 August, the Romieria Os Caneiros occurs, which is a special maritime treat when picnics and parties are held on extravagantly-decorated river-boats.

village and, best of all, the aforementioned restaurant, which is at the very eastern end of the waterfront promenade, in a little garden with a shady terrace. Bitakora has wonderful food and service, although it is not cheap by Spanish standards.

Plans have been put forward to build a marina at Ares, but apart from a large notice at the pier announcing the intention, there are no signs of the project actually getting underway. Many of us would no doubt prefer to go on anchoring in this quiet spot rather than moor up in a marina. The next bay east is **Redes**. This is a small, picturesque waterside village, but offers very little else – just two bars at the pier/slipway and a bus-stop.

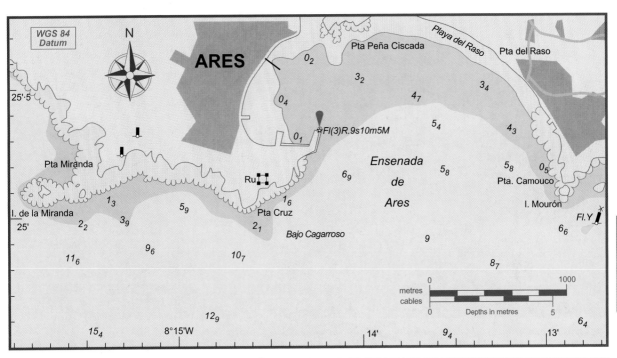

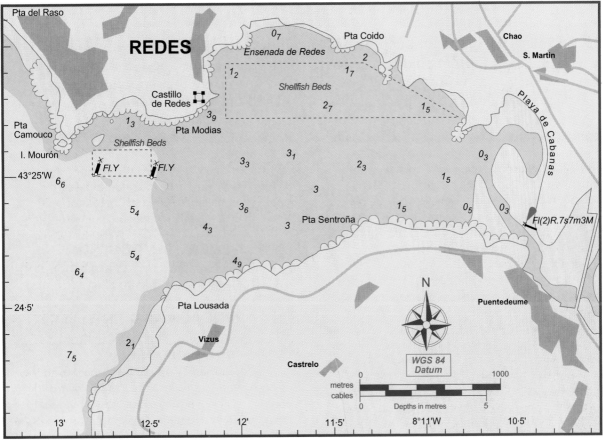

Chapter 4

LA CORUÑA

La Coruña's entrance is open and straightforward in virtually any weather

La Coruña harbour entrance – 43°21'.87N / 08°22'.18W

La Coruña is the capital of the province and very much a favourite with visiting yachts. It has a charming old quarter with colourful bodegas, more festivals and fiestas than you can count, an interesting history, including the world's oldest lighthouse (originally built by the Romans and still in working order),

two hospitable yacht clubs and generally most of the facilities that a crew licking its wounds after a rough crossing of the Bay of Biscay would want to find. In yachting terms, however, it is the

La Coruña's famous lighthouse – the Torre de Hercules

victim of its own popularity, as the limited facilities are often overwhelmed by the number of visiting boats.

This city also has elegant restaurants and a thriving night-life, in contrast to most of the smaller towns along the coast, which are somewhat rustic in comparison.

LOCATION/POSITION

La Coruña is roughly half way between Punta de la Estaca de Bares and Cabo Villano.

APPROACH AND ENTRANCE

Approach waypoint: 43°23'.21N/08°22'.12W; 182°; 1.34M to harbour entrance.

There are no off-lying dangers apart from the busy shipping lanes and the shallow Banco de las Laixiñas (19 metres), over which the seas break in heavy weather. This bank is about three miles west of Cabo Prioriño Chico (for more

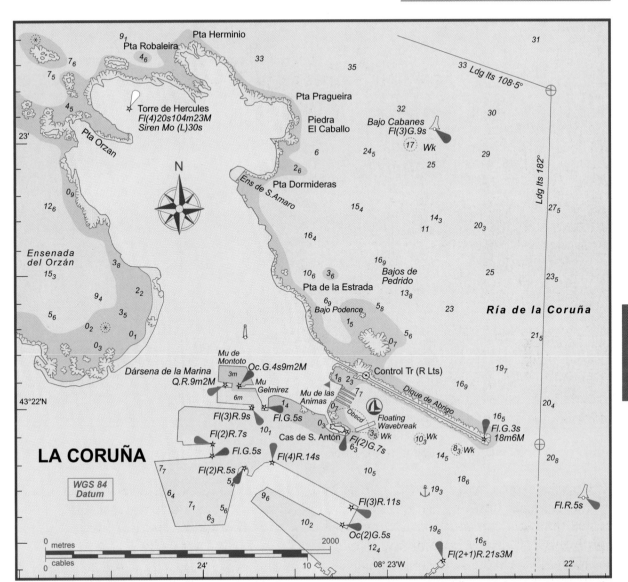

31

33 Ldg lts 108·5°

Pta Herminio

9₁
Pta Robaleira

7₆

4₆

7₅

33

35

Pta Pragueira

32

30

Torre de Hercules
Fl(4)20s104m23M
Siren Mo (L)30s

Piedra
El Caballo

Bajo Cabanes
Fl(3)G.9s

4₅

23'

6

24₅

17   Wk

29

25

Ldg lts 182°

Pta Orzan

2₆

Pta Dormideras

27₅

0₉

Ens de S Amaro

15₄

14₃

20₃

12₆

16₄

11

Ensenada
del Orzán

16₉

Bajos de
Pedrido

25

23₅

15₃

3₈

10₆   3₆

Pta de la Estrada

13₈

9₄

2₂

6₉

5₈

23

Ría de la Coruña

5₆

3₅

Bajo Podence

1₅

21₅

0₂

0₁

5₆

0₃

0₇

43°22'N

Mu de
Montoto

Oc.G.4s9m2M

Control Tr (R Lts)

19₇

Dársena de la Marina
Q.R.9m2M

3m

Mu
Gelmirez

1₈ 2₃

7₁

Dique de Abrigo

16₉

20₄

6m

1₄

Mu de las
Animas

0₇

Fl(3)R.9s

Fl.G.5s

0₃

Obscd

Floating
Wavebreak

16₅

Fl.G.3s
18m6M

Fl(2)R.7s

10₁

Cas de S. Antón

3₅ Wk

10₃ Wk

20₈

LA CORUÑA

Fl.G.5s

Fl(2)G.7s

6₃

8₃ Wk

14₅ Wk

7₇

Fl(4)R.14s

10₅

18₆

WGS 84
Datum

Fl(2)R.5s

5₄

6₄

7₁

5₆

9₆

Fl(3)R.11s

19₃

6₃

Fl.R.5s

10₂

Oc(2)G.5s

19₆

0   metres

2000

12₄

16₅

0   cables

24'

10

08° 23'W

Fl(2+1)R.21s3M

22'

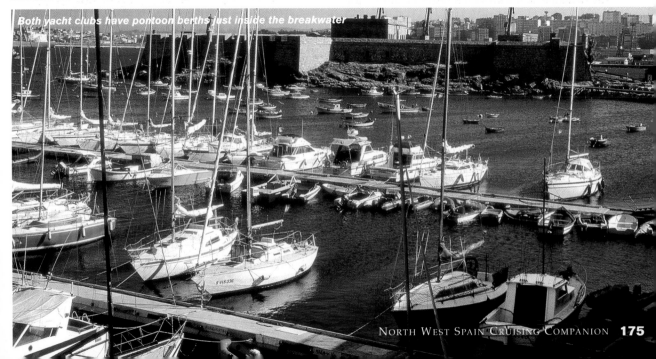

Both yacht clubs have pontoon berths just inside the breakwater

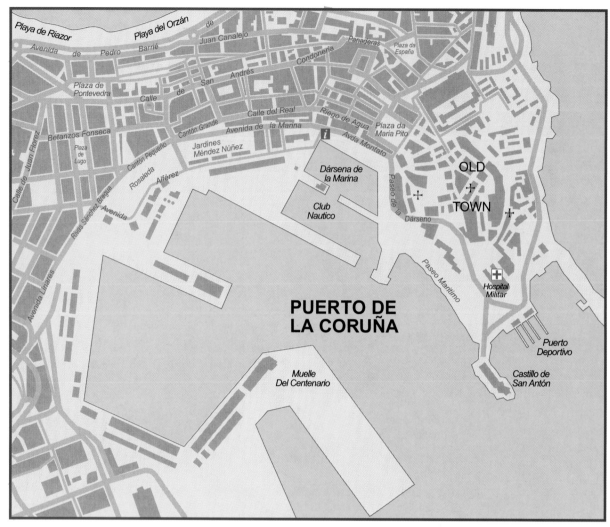

details see section on El Ferrol). Whether you are approaching La Coruña from the west or the north, you won't encounter any off-lying hazards. The long breakwater, with its futuristic-looking harbour control tower, is an unmistakable landmark, with the yacht clubs and moorings/anchorage hidden behind it.

Give the breakwater end an offing of 50 – 100 metres. If entering at night, take care of anchored, unlit yachts as well as unlit mooring buoys behind the breakwater. You can anchor in about 12 – 15 metres of water, pick up a mooring or proceed to the floating pontoons of the two adjacent yachts clubs.

BERTHING

It is possible to anchor behind the breakwater (Digue de Abrigo), taking care not to foul other yachts or mooring buoys. Alternatively, pick up a buoy (there is a modest fee on these) or moor to the floating pontoons of the two yacht clubs, which is actually less expensive than you might think. If moored to a buoy or on the pontoons, you are of course entitled to use all the clubhouse facilities.

The outer basin of Darsena de la Marina is a busy, open, working dock

There are plans to create a new marina in Darsena de la Marina

The Real Club Nautico (RCN) has two club-houses, one at the root of the main harbour breakwater, next door to the other yacht club (Sporting Club), and another in the Darsena de la Marina, close to the Plaza Maria Pits in the city centre. Demand clearly seems to exceed supply during the summer at the Digue de Abrigo facilities, and it can be difficult to find a free mooring buoy or a place on the pontoon. There are plans to install 500 pontoon berths in the Darsena de la Marina which, when it happens, will ensure an adequate supply of visitors' berths.

Until that time, Darsena de la Marina is a sheltered and centrally-located alternative, so long as you can actually manage to get a berth (albeit expensive) on the small number of club pontoons. You can also lie alongside the quays, although unfortunately there is a good deal of wash here from the continuous stream of assorted commercial boats and ferries.

FACILITIES AT DIGUE DE ABRIGO

Water and electricity are on the pontoons and diesel - Gasoleo A is at the southern end of the quay, on which the clubs stand. Both clubs have their own boatmen, mechanics and workshops and there is a good chandlery a little way along the road towards the new town.

The Torre de Hercules. Well worth a visit

FACILITIES AT DARSENA DE LA MARINA

Water and electricity are on the pontoons and there are toilets in the adjacent club. Crews wearing smart clothes can use the bars and dining facilities, but there are no showers or other yachting amenities, as this is really the 'city branch' of the club.

TRANSPORT

La Coruña has a national airport, with international connections via Madrid. There are also bus and train connections to most other major towns, although both the bus and railway stations are a long way from the yacht clubs in the southern part of the new town.

PROVISIONING

The shops are in the town itself, but some are a fair walk away. For major provisioning, take a taxi to one of the huge supermarkets (Hipermercados) a little way out of town – inquire at the yacht club.

A RUN ASHORE

La Coruña's natural harbour has been used by the Phoenicians, Celts and Romans. The town saw its

Castillo de San Antón houses the Archaeological museum

best times in the 14th and 15th centuries, when it was the main port of arrival for pilgrims *en route* to Santiago de Compostelo from the British Isles.

In 1588, the Armada set sail from here to invade England, but their attempt was thwarted by Sir Francis Drake, who bombarded the town with his ship's cannons in 1589, destroying much of it, but failing to actually capture it outright.

Today, with around 250,000 inhabitants, La Coruña is a lively and fascinating city. It is also known as *Ciudad de Cristal* (crystal city), derived from the many glazed balconies (*galerias*)

The Ciudad Vieja (the old city) is a charming contrast to the newer glass-fronted galleries of the 'crystal city'

Chapter 4

The inner basin of Darsena de la Marina is overlooked by the glass façades of the city

that cover entire rows of frontages. The Avenida de la Marina, the spectacular main street running parallel to the inner harbour, is famous for these *galerias*, which have become something of a trademark for the city.

The old town, Ciudad Vieja, is close to the breakwater and the yacht club moorings on the highest part of the peninsula. In contrast to the new city behind, it is fairly peaceful. Narrow, cobbled streets, ancient churches and hidden plazas make this a pleasant area to stroll around, with plenty of bars to serve as pit stops on the way.

Another enjoyable walk is along the newly renovated Paseo Maritimo, a waterfront promenade running right around the peninsula.

The main square, Plaza Maria Pita, is named after the heroine of the Drake invasion, who not only raised the alarm when she saw the English ships sailing into the bay, but somehow also managed to swipe Drake's battle flag. The Plaza is surrounded by arcades and many houses with *galerias*, and is a good place to be in the early evening, when the bars and cafés around the square start to fill up.

The market, held in the attractive market hall on Plaza San Agustin, north of the Calle Franja, is open only in the mornings. Another interesting place nearby is the Museo de Bellas Artes, on Plaza del Pindor Sotomayor / Calle Panaderas, but it is closed on Mondays. The art museum exhibits works by the Spanish masters, including Goya, Velaquez, Ribera and Murillo, as well as those by foreign artists such as Breughel and Rubens.

At the northern extremity of the peninsula is the Torre de Hercules, allegedly the world's oldest lighthouse to still be in working order. In reality, only the foundations still remain of the original 2nd century Roman tower, the rest having been rebuilt in the late 18th century. There are impressive views from the tower, which are further enhanced by modern sculptures. The tower is open daily from 1000 – 1900 and, during the summer only, it also opens on Friday and Saturday nights from 2300 – 2400. More or less on the other side of town, in the park of Santa Margarita, is the Science Museum, which includes a planetarium (closed Mondays).

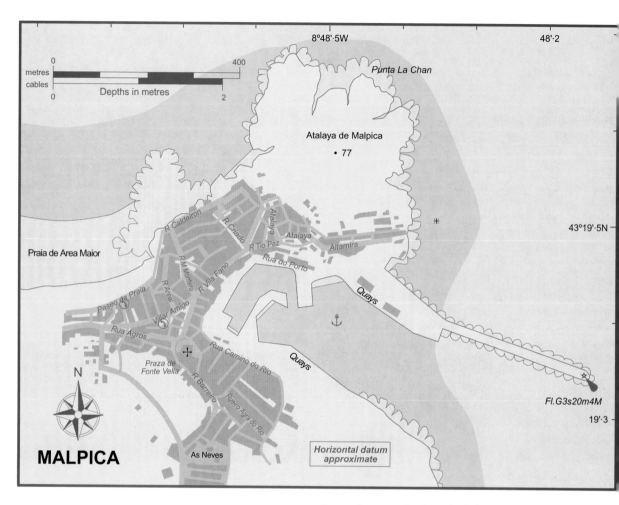

MALPICA

EATING OUT AND NIGHT-LIFE

Restaurants in La Coruña abound, but the main
areas for eating out are Calle Estrella, Calle Real
(both of which are behind Avenida de la Marina)
and more notably Calle Franja, which branches off
Plaza Maria Pita. Casa Pardo (Novoa Santos 15,
Tel: 981 28 00 21, credit cards accepted, closed
Sundays as well as from 15 June to 30 June)
is a long way from anywhere, but is worth the
taxi ride if you want a real treat – it is one of the
very few restaurants in this part of the world
with a Michelin star. Needless-to-say, the prices
are accordingly stiff.

For good quality, but a little less financially

damaging, try La Panela (Plaza Maria Pita,
Tel: 981 20 92 00, closed Sundays). Another
gourmet haunt is the Coral (Calle Estrella 4,
Tel: 981 22 10 82, closed Sundays). For cheap and
cheerful tapas, squeeze with the crowd into the
Meson O'Calexo in Calle Franja 34, or wander off
to Plaza de España in the old town to dip into the
cosy bar, O Trotumundos.

The night-life usually starts with tapas and
drinks in the bars of the Calles Olmos, Estrella
and Franja. From 0200 onwards, the crowd drifts
either to the more modern bars around the Calles
Juan Canalejo and del Orzan, or to the older bars
around the Plaza España in the old town. If
you have managed to get a pontoon berth or a
mooring, La Coruña is a good place to leave the
boat for a day to go by bus to Santiago.

ALTERNATIVE HARBOURS
AND ANCHORAGE

To the west of La Coruña, 20 miles from Torre de
Hercules, are the Islas Sisargas, just off the tiny
fishing harbour of Malpica. Malpica is an
overcrowded harbour, but the islands, a seabird's

Malpica is a former whaling port

Malpica is not a recommended haven for yachts

paradise, offer a lovely daytime anchorage, albeit in calm weather only. You should take care to avoid the rocks of Gran Campana which, unmarked, are 12.5 miles west of Torre de Hercules and about four miles off the coast.

The approach to the Sisargas should only be attempted with large scale charts, taking care to watch out for the rocks off the south tip of Sisarga Chica. In heavy weather, you should avoid using the channel between the islands and the mainland altogether, as the tide runs strongly and the seas often break in these conditions. In calm weather, however, it is possible to anchor south-east of Sisarga Grande, although the holding is not always good – make sure that the anchor is well set before going ashore. Here you can land on a small stone jetty and walk up to the lighthouse.

From the harbour, Malpica looks a bit rough and rundown, but is actually a very bustling, attractive little place, with a good number of bars and restaurants. Unfortunately the harbour is completely full with local fishing boats, so you would have to squeeze in where possible. The outer harbour is often subject to heavy surge caused from the swell outside the breakwater. The inner harbour is locked off, but still dries in places at LW. The lock gates in fact really only serve to dampen the surge, which they do highly effectively. All in all, berthing at Malpica is far from ideal, but it is the place to try *percebes* (goose barnacles). Mussels can best be tasted in the restaurant O Burato, just above the harbour next to the Casa do Pescador.

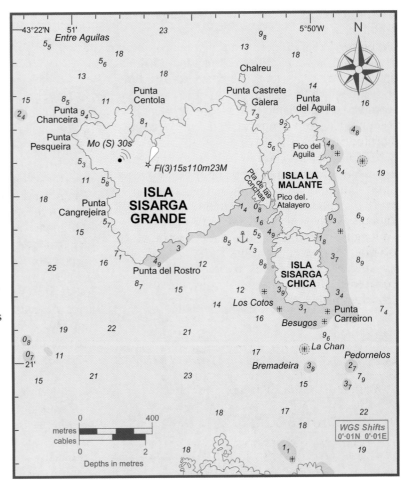

RIA DE CORME Y LAGE

Harbour entrances: Corme – 43°15'.67N/08°57'.74W; **Lage** – 43°13'.40N/08°59'.72W

The Ria de Corme Y Lage is a wide ria open to the west, which offers two sheltering ports, one to the north of the bay and the other to the south. It is part of the beautiful but wild Costa da Morte (coast of death), extending between Isla Sisargas and Finisterre, and even today many ships founder on the rocks and cliffs of this wind and wave-battered coast. This ria, although small in comparison to the Rias Bajas, is the first of the really beautiful estuaries cutting deep into western Galicia.

LOCATION/POSITION

It is situated on the very north-west tip of Spain.

APPROACH AND ENTRANCE

Approach waypoints: **Corme** - 43°15'.32N/08°58'.22W; 045°; 0.5M to harbour entrance. **Lage** - 43°13'.90N/08°59'.72; 180°; 0.5M to harbour entrance.

The ria is easily approached from the sea, although you should keep at least a mile off each of the headlands of Punta del Roncudo (north) and Punta de Lage (south), as these have off-lying rocks on which the sea breaks. In heavy swell, you would be wise to avoid the five-metre patch, Bajo de la Averia, a mile south-west of Corme pier.
Corme: come into the bay on a north-easterly course once the breakwater head is abeam. There are no off-lying dangers here and the approach is quite straightforward so long as you keep a safe distance of about half a mile from the shores.
Lage: again a simple approach and entrance, now on a southerly course, heading for the pier-head or the middle of the bay, which is clear of any hazards.

Casa d'Arco, at Corme

BERTHING

Both Corme and Lage are crowded fishing harbours, but with a bit of luck you may find a berth alongside the piers or next to a fishing trawler. If the latter, make sure you establish with the crew what time they are planning on leaving as, at times, this can be in the middle of the night. Depending on wind directions, use either Corme if the wind has any north in it, or Lage if it's blowing from a southerly direction. If you can't find a space in one of the harbours, you can always anchor off in either bay. Bear in mind, however, that this can be tricky in Corme, as it is littered with small craft moorings and the area to the north-east is taken over by *viveiros* (mussel-rafts).

FACILITIES

Corme: has a four-ton crane and slipway but no other facilities.
Lage: has a 16-ton crane and diesel on the pier, but for commercial craft only.

PROVISIONING

There are shops in both Corme and Lage, with the latter offering more in the way of supermarkets within easy walk from the harbour. (The Charter supermarket is just off the small square, close to the harbour).

A RUN ASHORE

These are pleasant little towns, each with its own ambience.
Corme: this is a very busy holiday town in summer and, although the place itself is rather ugly with many high, modern buildings, the surrounding countryside is exceedingly beautiful.

A walk from the harbour out towards the lighthouse on Punta del Roncundo offers superb views of the ria, but may prove too far for some. The many crosses along the rocks are there to remind us of the sailors and the fishermen who

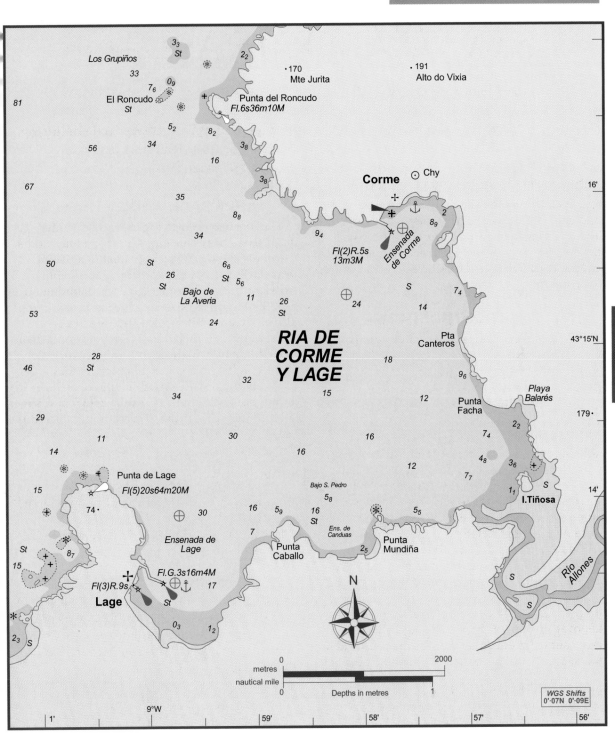

Los Grupiños

3₃ St

33

7₆ 0₉

El Roncudo
St

81

56

34

5₂

8₂

3₈

16

3₈

3₈

35

8₈

34

9₄

22

•170
Mte Jurita

•191
Alto do Vixia

Punta del Roncudo
Fl.6s36m10M

Corme ⊙ Chy

16'

Fl(2)R.5s
13m3M

Ensenada de Corme

2

8₉

S

7₄

67

50

26

St

6₆

St 5₆

Bajo de
La Averia

11

26
St

24

24

14

Pta
Canteros

43°15'N

53

RIA DE
CORME
Y LAGE

18

9₆

179•

28
St

46

32

15

12

Punta
Facha

7₄

Playa
Balarés

2₂

29

11

30

16

16

12

4₈

3₆

77

1₁

S

I.Tiñosa

14'

14

St

15

Punta de Lage
Fl(5)20s64m20M

30

16

5₉

16
St

Bajo S. Pedro
5₈

5₅

74•

St

8₇

15

Ensenada de
Lage

7

Punta
Caballo

Ens. de
Canduas

2₅

Punta
Mundiña

S

Río
Allones

Fl.G.3s16m4M

Fl(3)R.9s

Lage

St

17

0₃

1₂

N

S

S

S

2₃ S

0   2000

metres

nautical mile

0   Depths in metres   1

9°W

1'

59'

58'

57'

56'

WGS Shifts
0'-07N 0'-09E

Chapter 4

have sadly lost their lives along this savage coast.
Lage: this is the larger of the two harbours. It
has an attractive beach virtually in the town,
behind the port, and is fast developing into
another busy tourist centre. Besides the
numerous bars and restaurants, there is a
pleasant waterfront promenade, the typical
Paseo Maritim, and a 14th century church
overlooking the harbour.

EATING OUT

There is no shortage of small restaurants and
bars in both places. Corme is noted for its
percebes (goose barnacles), which are a rather
expensive delicacy. In Lage, the Restaurant Plaza,
offering superb views of the bay and harbour,
comes highly recommended. Alternatively,
you could try the Casa d'Arco, which is situated
right next door.

CAMARIÑAS

Camariñas entrance – 43°07'.53N / 09°10'.52W

Camariñas has for some time been a favourite port of call for visiting yachts, which is easy to see why. The town has a relaxed atmosphere and offers a large and well-sheltered harbour, providing berths on two floating pontoons along with all the services and facilities of a friendly yacht club.

The scenery in the Ria de Camariñas is undeniably spectacular: this must surely be one of the more beautiful rias. On the other side of this ria is the commercial fishing harbour of Mugia, which is part of a quiet and charming little town.

LOCATION/POSITION

The Ria de Camariñas is immediately south of Cabo Villano.

APPROACH AND ENTRANCE

Approach waypoint: 43°06'.97N / 09°11'.12W; 038°; 0.7M to harbour entrance.

Cabo Villano can be easily identified. When approaching from the north, stay well off the coast, as there are unmarked rocks and shoals up to 1.5 miles offshore, over which seas break in heavy weather. The unmarked bank, Las Quebrantes, 1.5 miles south-west of Cabo Villano, is a real danger, with as little as 0.5 metres of

The Ria de Camariñas

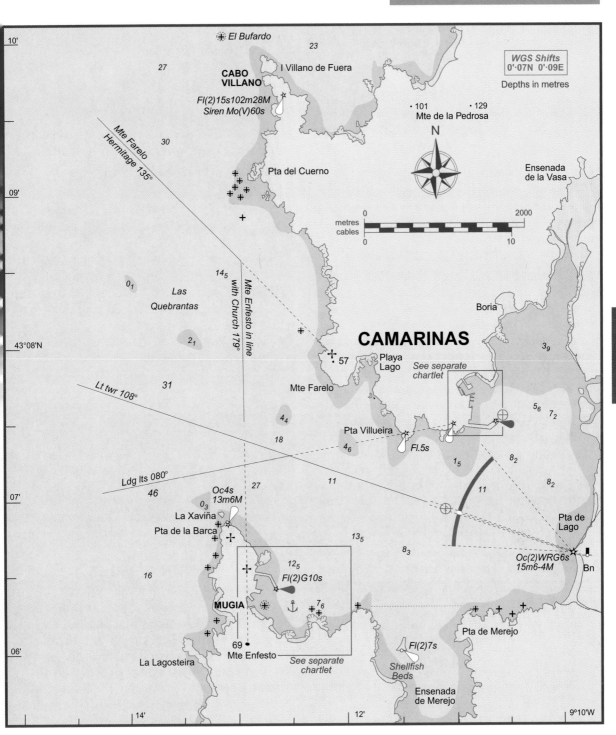

water over it. Another shoal extending half a mile north-north-west from Punta de la Barca, on the south side of the entrance, is the Bajo Peneirón, which only has 0.3 metres of water.

The ria should be approached carefully on an easterly course, staying in the middle by keeping Punta de Lago on a bearing of 108°. This landmark has a sector light (Oc(2)WRG 6s), which shows red over Las Quebrantes, white on the safe approach bearing and green to the south of it. If approaching from the south, use the 080° leading marks on Punta Villueira initially, then follow the 108° course.

Once inside the ria, there are no more dangers. For Camariñas, continue until the breakwater bears due north, to avoid the shallow water to the west of Punta Villueira, then head for the end of the mole. The visitors' pontoons are easily spotted on rounding the breakwater.

BERTHING

Camariñas' yacht club has pontoons for visiting yachts in depths of around four metres. Mooring is Mediterranean-style, with fixed mooring lines picked up from the pontoon. To ensure you get a berth, it is best to book in advance and aim to arrive at about midday when several boats are leaving and the yacht club staff are on hand to tell you where to moor up.

FACILITIES

Water and electricity are available on the pontoons, with showers and toilets in the yacht club. Small quantities of diesel (15 – 25 litres) can be pre-booked through the club, which will then be delivered by truck. Alternatively, you could try negotiating with the crew of one of the tankers moored in the fishing harbour, although in this case a knowledge of Spanish is essential. Other facilities include a bar and cafeteria incorporated into the clubhouse as well as a crane and hard-standing area, where repairs are possible. To get to the internet café in the town, take the road turning right immediately behind the Familia supermarket, where it can then be found past the pharmacy on the right-hand side of the side-street.

PROVISIONING

All types of shops and supermarkets in Camariñas, with two of the latter close to the port.

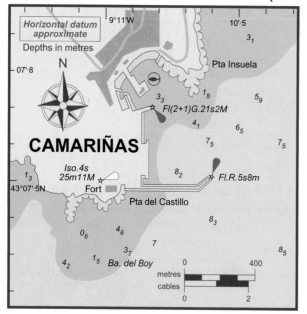

Camariñas is a colourful and comfortable port with good facilities for visiting yachts

A RUN ASHORE

As mentioned previously, Camariñas has a friendly feel and offers spectacular surrounding scenery. Perhaps the absence of beaches is an asset here, as the town doesn't change as dramatically in summer as some others do along this coast. As this town is renowned for lace-making, you shouldn't miss the opportunity of visiting the local museum, where you can watch the skilful *palilleiras* (lace-makers) at work.

EATING OUT

Camariñas has many bars and restaurants, but one of the best is the restaurant in La Marina, where they serve excellent food (particularly seafood) for very reasonable prices. (Only open in summer, credit cards are accepted). The Club Nautico also comes highly recommended, offering top quality food at good value for money.

Cabo Villano guards the northern entrance to the Ria de Camariñas

DAYTIME ANCHORAGES NEARBY

Several anchorages north-east of Camariñas are certainly worth visiting for their scenery and tranquillity. On the south side of the ria is Mugia – purely a fishing harbour, although you may be able to tie up alongside the pier or next to a fishing vessel. Otherwise it is possible to anchor in the bay south-east of Mugia harbour. Note, however, that Mugia has no dedicated facilities for yachts.

The town is known for the 17th century church, Nuestra Señora de la Barca, which is close to the village on a promontory high over the sea. Apart from the ship models to lure sailors here, there are fantastic views over the coast to Cabo Villano.

USEFUL INFORMATION

Yacht club (Club Nautico de Camariñas)
Tel: 981 73 71 30

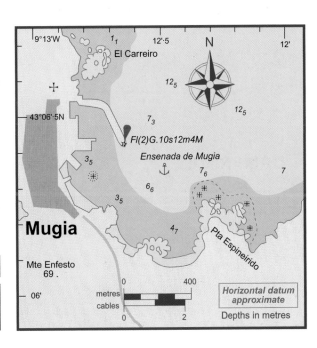

Cabo Finisterre

Finisterre harbour entrance – 42°54'.65N / 09°15'.12W

Finisterre, thought by the Romans to be the end of the world (*Finis Terrae*), is now a bustling, overcrowded tourist town in summer and as such, is not as attractive as you may hope. The small harbour is tucked away just inside the famous cape, although many yachtsmen prefer to carry on sailing past, knowing full well that the crowded fishing harbour doesn't specifically cater for yachts and finding space to moor behind the breakwater can be tricky. The lighthouse is about a two-mile walk from the harbour.

LOCATION/POSITION
The town lies on the eastern side of this famous landmark, nearly two miles north of its tip.

APPROACH AND ENTRANCE
Approach waypoint: 42°53'.65N / 09°15'.20W; 000°; 1M to harbour entrance.

Keep your distance from Finisterre's west side, although once around the tip, the water is fairly steep-to and there are no more rocks inside the promontory. Note the traffic separation scheme off Finisterre (marked on the Admiralty Charts).

BERTHING
The small harbour of Finisterre is often crowded, therefore securing a berth alongside the pier can be virtually impossible. Also, most of the area behind the breakwater is taken over with moorings, so again, finding a suitable place in which to anchor may be tricky. There should be space to the north of the moorings, which is not

The western side of Finisterre is guarded by the Centolo de Finisterre

too far from the village. If all else fails, you can always anchor a little further north of the harbour, in Ensenada de Llagosteira, although neither this anchorage nor the harbour are sheltered in north-easterly winds.

PROVISIONING

Finisterre is very much a seasonal holiday town, with a prolific number of bars, restaurants and banks. Shops are less abundant, although your day-to-day needs can of course be met.

A RUN ASHORE

Finisterre is a busy town with an active fishing harbour. The famous cape is a pleasant two-mile walk along the eastern side of the promontory, although you may have mixed reactions on arrival – the lighthouse is surrounded by souvenir-stands and tatty café-bars.

A statue of a man carrying a suitcase at Finisterre harbour symbolises the many Galicians who have emigrated over the centuries.

EATING OUT

Of the many restaurants in Finisterre, two stand out: O Centolo (by the harbour, near the statue of the emigrant) serves excellent seafood while, opposite, O Tearron is equally good and has a

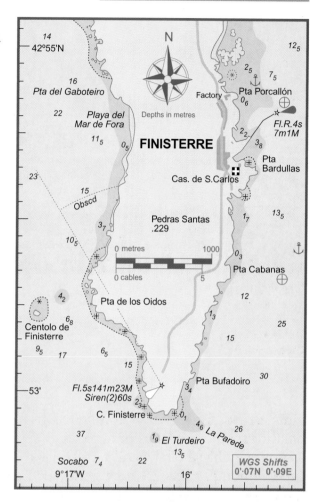

Playa de Llagosteira is just north of Finisterre harbour

Cabo Finisterre, and its equally famous lighthouse

The emigrant monument in Finisterre village

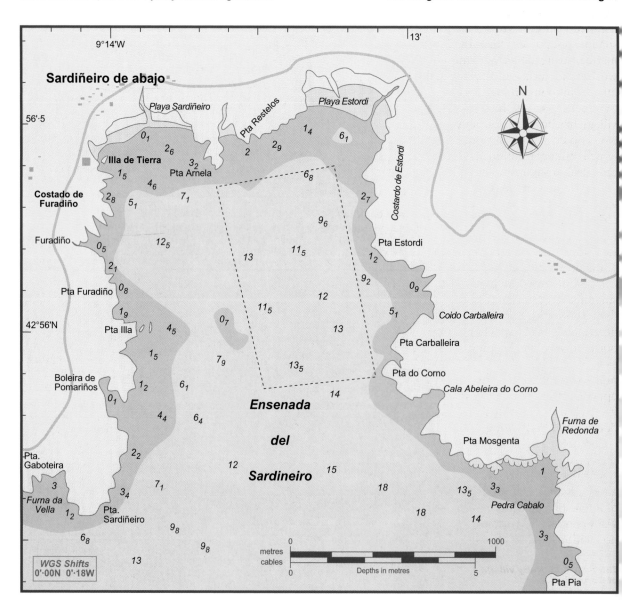

9°14'W

13'

Sardiñeiro de abajo

N

56'·5

Playa Sardiñeiro

Pta Restelos

Playa Estordi

0_1

1_4 6_1

2_6

Illa de Tierra 3_2

Pta Arnela

2 2_9

6_8

1_5

Costado de Furadiño

4_6

7_1

2_7

Costardo de Estordi

2_8 5_1

9_6

Furadiño

0_5

12_5

13 11_5

Pta Estordi

1_2

2_1

9_2

Pta Furadiño

0_8

0_9

42°56'N

1_9

Coido Carballeira

Pta Illa

4_5

11_5

12

5_1

Pta Carballeira

1_5

0_7

13

Pta do Corno

7_9

13_5

Cala Abeleira do Corno

Boleira de Pomariños

1_2 6_1

14

0_1

Furna de Redonda

4_4 6_4

Ensenada

Pta Mosgenta

2_2

del

1

Pta. Gaboteira

7_1

12

Sardineiro

15

18

13_5 3_3

3

3_4

18

Pedra Cabalo

Furna da Vella 1_2

Pta. Sardiñeiro

9_8

14

3_3

6_8

9_8

13

metres
cables

Depths in metres

1000

0   5

0_5

Pta Pia

WGS Shifts
0'·00N 0'·18W

slightly more attractive terrace. The bars along the harbour-front are lively and crowded during the summer season.

OTHER ANCHORAGES NEARBY

Ensenada de Sardiñeiro, about two miles north of Finisterre harbour, is a bay with two pleasant, sandy beaches (Sardiñeiro to the west and Estordi to the east of the bay). Anchor off the beaches on sand, but bear in mind that this bay is open to the south. Also beware of a shallow spot of less than a metre of water, slightly to the west of the middle of the bay, off a small point fronted by two rocks. Ashore, the village has beach restaurants, bars and even a small store which, rather ambitiously, calls itself a supermarket.

The Ria de Corcubion, leading north up to the twin towns of Corcubion (on the west side) and Cée (on the east side) is on the other side of the promontory. Corcubion incorporates a small fishing harbour, but there is no space for yachts here, so it is best to anchor north of the mole, keeping clear, if possible, of the numerous moorings. The opposite side of the ria, with its shipyards and industry, doesn't look so inviting.

Corcubion has a picturesque old quarter, which is well worth seeing, although there is little else of interest for maritime visitors here and certainly no facilities for yachts.

The quay and pretty village of Corcubion

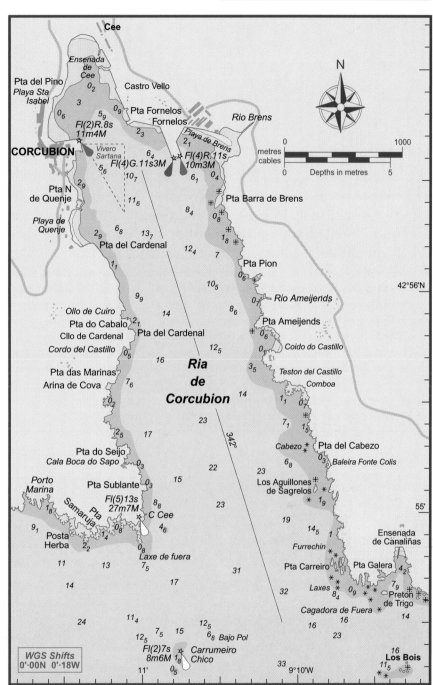

WEST GALICIA
THE RIAS BAJAS

The four large rias on the west coast of Galicia are, from north to south, Ria de Muros, Ria de Arosa, Ria de Pontevedra and finally Ria de Vigo. Each of them has its own individual character and all offer at least one convenient marina (Portosin in Ria de Muros, Santa Eugenia de Riveira

and Villagarcia in Ria de Arosa, Sangenjo in Ria de Pontevedra and Bayona and Vigo in Ria de Vigo).

Generally speaking, the west coast of Galicia is much more developed as a holiday destination than the Rias Altas in the north, which remain more remote and romantic than the Rias Bajas. Up to a point, the same can be said for the Rias de Corme y Lage and de Camariñas on the north-west coast, although these are more like large bays rather than the long fjord-like rias to the north and south.

The Rias Bajas are famous for their seafood, with mussels being cultivated on a very large scale using *viveiros* (mussel-rafts). These often occupy entire bays inside the rias that might otherwise be quite good for anchoring. Nevertheless, as the majority of us like our seafood, growing mussels in this way is an efficient method of ensuring a plentiful supply. The mussels grow on ropes dangling down from the rafts and are harvested by boats with crane-like grabs. The rafts' anchor chains run down almost vertically

Ria de Arosa

to enable the harvest-boats to come alongside, which also makes it possible to sail through them. Although this may be necessary in some harbour or bay approaches, given a choice, it is simpler to stay outside the *viveiro* areas.

Small, fast and often ill-lit, fishing boats can be a hazard here (as they can practically everywhere off the coast of the Iberian peninsula), but another type of maritime traffic may be even more dangerous – illegal drug running has been a massive problem recently, especially in some of the Rias Bajas. However the authorities have now clamped down heavily, so high-speed, unlit motorboats at night and the James-Bond-like scenes of coastguard patrols or helicopters chasing fast powerboats should be a thing of the past.

Bear in mind that yachts passing the area are sometimes checked by customs, but this is to try to keep drug smuggling into Europe under some sort of control, so it's best to cooperate with them and, needless-to-say, it's advisable not to carry any illegal drugs on board.

RIA DE MUROS

Ria de Muros is widely regarded as the prettiest of the Rias Bajas. As you approach the outer part of the ria and the town of Muros, you can't fail to be impressed by the hilly vista. Further inland, the town of Noya (Noia), which is best visited by land from the marina at Portosin, is also worth seeing.

The approach from the sea is straightforward and, once inside, there are no notable dangers apart from various isolated rocks close to the shore. However, along the inshore coastal route from Finisterre harbour or the bay of Corcubion, there are shoals and reefs off Punta Remedios and Punta Insua, the most hazardous of which is the Bajo de los Meixidos, so keep about five miles offshore. A little bit further on are the rocky islets of Los Bruyos, but these are usually visible.

Coming from the south – or if bound southward to Ria de Arosa – there is a shoal, La Baya, about a mile off Punta Castro. Further south are more shoals and reefs to negotiate: Banco de las Basoñas, Banco da Corrubedo, off the bay of Corrubedo, and finally Banco del Praquero, off the Punta Falcoeiro. To be on the safe side, you should keep a good offing of at least three miles and plot or check your position regularly.

RIA DE AROSA

The largest of all Galician rias, Ria de Arosa offers some spectacular cruising ground,

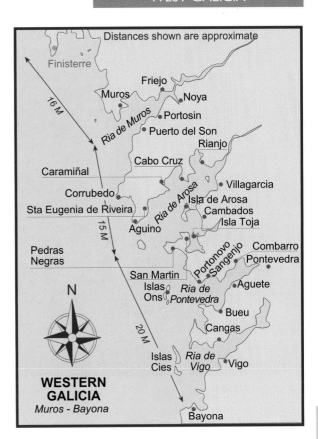

incorporating several beautiful places. The inner part of the ria is rather built up with sprawling towns and villages and is extremely popular both with fellow yachtsmen and land-tourists.

Ria de Arosa is unlike the others rias in that it has extensive areas of shallows as well as large patches of drying rock, which at low tide resemble parts of Brittany. There is something for almost everyone here: modern, convenient marinas; large and often interesting towns; small fishing villages and attractive anchorages off popular holiday islands and beaches. The only thing you might have a little difficulty in finding is a secluded anchorage, unless sailing well out of season.

The approach to the Ria de Arosa from seaward is straightforward if you stick to the main channel from the south-west, the Canal Principal, which is deep and has no hidden dangers.

However, if you are coming from the north, there is a choice of inshore passages that save a considerable distance, but which require careful pilotage after precise identification of the hazards both on the chart and in the sea. Good visibility and fair weather are prerequisites, especially for a first attempt.

The first choice is to pass outside the isolated offshore rocks – La Marosa, Tomas, Los Cobos,

Chapter 5

Ria de Pondevedra

Banco del Pragueiro and Canteiro – which lie off the Ensenada de Corrubedo, to continue south of Isla Sagres, taking care to avoid Meixon de Vigo to the south, and then to carry on into the Paso del Carreiro, which is marked by a beacon (lit).

However, given that the off-lying rocks must be identified and avoided, in fair weather you can just as easily set a course inside them, using the Canal de Sagres to approach the Paso del Carreiro. You need to approach Canal de Sagres carefully, in order to avoid the rocks to the north. Although the channel is only a cable wide, it is deep (5 – 10 metres) and straight. A large scale chart is essential, not to mention both skill and enthusiasm for demanding pilotage. Finally, remember that breaking swell is a good way of locating any off-lying rocks.

RIA DE PONTEVEDRA

Entering the Ria de Pontevedra is straightforward and, as this ria is home to the Spanish naval port of Marin, the few shallows and off-lying rocks are clearly marked. The main ship route is south of Isla Ons, but for yachts the Paso de Fagilda, between Bajo Picamillo and Punta Fagilda, saves many miles and is deep enough to be a safe channel in all but the worst of north-westerly gales.

Once in the Ria de Arosa, you can choose from the rather crowded bay of Porto Novo, the attractive town and marina of Sangenjo, the traditional fishing village of Combarro and the hospitable yacht club and small marina at Aguete. Aguete is the most convenient place for visiting the historic town of Pontevedra, from where it is about a six-mile taxi ride. Setting off from Sangenjo is equally feasible, although the journey is a little longer. For details of what Pontevedra has to offer, see under Aguete.

RIA DE VIGO

The last of the Spanish rias is the Ria de Vigo. It may be the least scenic, but is notable for other reasons. Firstly, there are two towns of interest, Bayona and Vigo, as well as the remarkably beautiful Islas Cíes in the approach. Secondly, this ria can lay claim to literary fame – according to Jules Verne, the legendary Captain Nemo came here in his fabulous submarine *Nautilus* in 1868 (as depicted in *20,000 Leagues Under The Sea*). Even earlier than that, in 1702, a Spanish-French fleet laden with gold from South America was sunk here by the British Navy. This vast hoard of treasure not only attracted Nemo to the Ria de Vigo, but also various other treasure hunters after him. It is alleged, however, that Nemo did run off with the gold, as nobody has ever been successful in finding any since. A street in London is named

Ria de Muros

Vigo, in remembrance of the battle.

The approach from sea is again straightforward, with large cargo ships being the main hazard as they make for the commercial harbour at Vigo. They also drop anchor in the entrance, in the lee of the Islas Cíes.

The main channel, Canal del Sur, passes south of the Islas Cíes and is deep, well-marked and lit. Coasting from the north, bound for either the ria or Bayona, you can pass through the Canal del Norte north of the Islas Cíes, which again is deep so long as you keep a reasonable distance offshore. There are some rocks and shallows off the north-western tip of Islas Cíes, but they are not an obstruction to the above course.

Finally, there is a 'backdoor' entrance to the Ensenada de Bayona on the south side of the Ria de Vigo approach, which is favoured by the locals. It passes through a narrow but deep channel between the innermost of two small rocky islets (Las Estelas) off Monte Ferro (for details see under Bayona). The simplest approach to Bayona, and hence the one to use in heavy weather, is outside the Islas Cíes and Las Estelas, a route both well-lit and hazard-free.

Once past Cabo Silleiro, which should be given a wide berth, the coast south of Ria de Vigo is clean, although you should generally keep a couple of miles offshore.

Ria de Vigo

RIA DE MUROS

The south shore of Ria de Muros, from seaward

Ria entrance 0.7M S of Punta Queixal light – 42°43'.73N / 09°04'.6W

Ria de Muros is the northernmost of the really large Rias Bajas. Although it is picturesque, the landscape, especially around the inner part of the ria, is rather built-up, with many villages and detached houses scattered around the countryside. Apart from the recognised harbours, there are a number of bays and beaches off which you can anchor. The entrance to the ria, described in the introduction to this chapter, is pretty straightforward.

LOCATION/POSITION

Ria de Muros is approximately 16M south-east of Finisterre.

APPROACH AND ENTRANCE

Approach waypoint: 42°46'.27N/09°01'.93W; 038°; 3.2M to waypoint off Cabo Reburdiño.

From the north, keep a good distance off to avoid the shoals of Bajo de los Meixidos and Ximiela, as well as the rocks and islets of Los Bruyos (all of which are around two miles off the coast and are unmarked – see chart). Or, if you choose to coast inside these features (a typical fine-weather option on passage between the ria and Finisterre), be aware of the assorted rocks which lie up to half a mile off the coast between Punta Queixal and Punta Remedios.

Similarly, from the south, you should keep a good offing in order to avoid the unmarked shoals and rocks of Banco las Basoñas and La Baya.

Muros, which is tucked into the north-west corner of the ria, is well sheltered from ocean weather. After passing Punta Queixal, its lighthouse and off-lying rock, and then the Ensenada San Francisco, the lighthouse at Cabo Reburdiño comes into view. Muros is tucked away in the bay behind it, and in the final approach you can pass fairly close to Cabo Reburdiño.

BERTHING

Muros is primarily a working fishing harbour, but there might be a chance of finding a berth alongside the pier (the usual long warps and fender-boards will be needed), or short-term alongside a fishing boat. On approach, and from some charts, there would appear to be a small marina in the northern basin of the harbour, but this is usually full of local small craft, is reported to be in shallow water and has no facilities anyway. Most yachts anchor (using a tripline) to the north of the harbour, between the mole and the shallows of the next bay, landing either at the adjacent slipway or using the pier.

FACILITIES IN THE HARBOUR

Muros has no dedicated facilities for yachts, although it does have a fishing boat chandlery. There is the usual crane for lifting out fishing boats, and diesel - Gasoleo A is available in the inner basin. Mechanics can be found around the harbour for any repairs that you need carried out.

TRANSPORT

Buses run from Muros to La Coruña and Santiago.

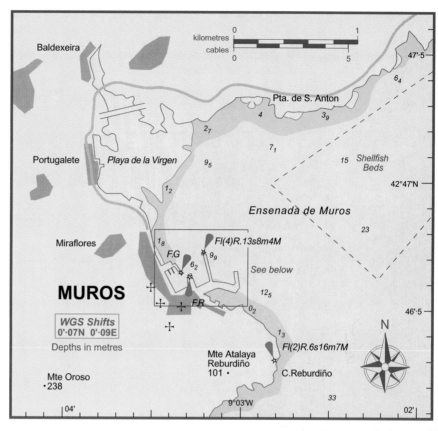

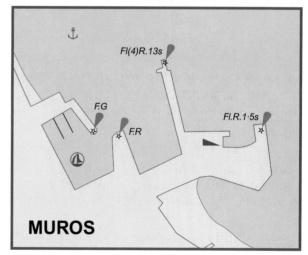

Muros anchorage, looking south towards the port

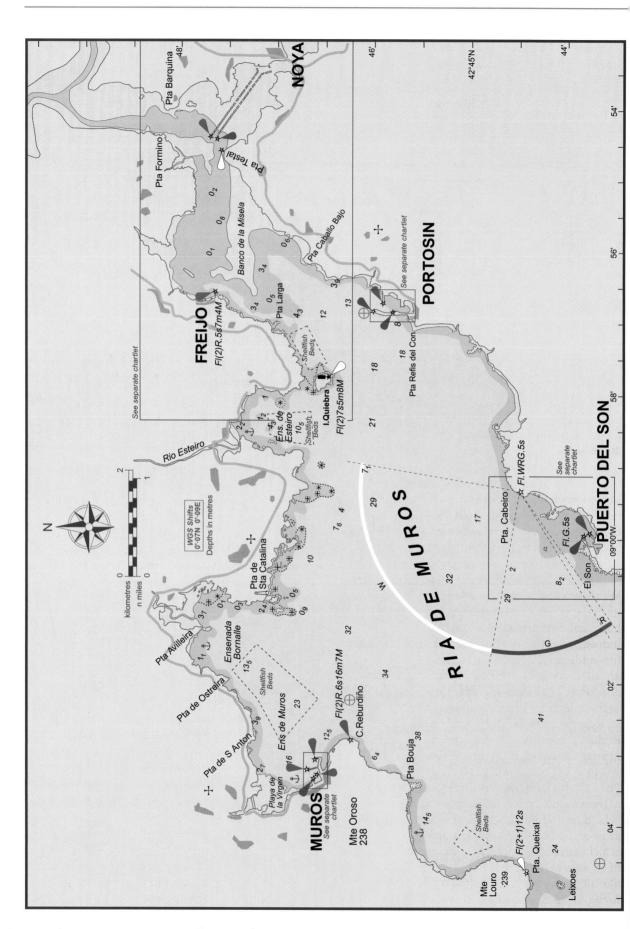

Muros harbour

PROVISIONING

Muros has a a supermarket along the road to the north, just on the outskirts of the town, as well as the usual small corner shops for everyday items. There is also a large hardware shop.

A RUN ASHORE

Muros is a lovely old town which, with its lively waterfront promenade and historical centre, is well worth a visit. Indeed, you shouldn't miss the chance to wander underneath the shaded arcades, along the winding, cobbled alleyways or across romantic squares.

The Iglesia San Pedro is of Gothic style, but was built on the remains of a Roman predecessor. If you have any form of transport, it might well be worth going to the old tide-mill of Pozo Cachon, on the road to Serres.

The Fiesta Nuestra Señora do Carme is held on 16 July to honour the patron saint of the fishermen and seafarers. It is a cheerful affair, involving town folk of all ages in a variety of activities and, like all fiestas in Spain, is accompanied by fireworks and general explosive activity.

The pier at the tiny fishing harbour of Freijo

EATING OUT

There are various restaurants and bars in Muros, although none are really outstanding. You could try the cosy restaurant Don Bodegos at the west side of the harbour (Porto da Vila), but check your bill carefully when paying. Alternatively the Hotel Muradana on the waterfront and the Hospedaje La Vianda, a few houses further along the road, both have restaurants, the latter being budget-priced.

NORTH SHORE ANCHORAGES NEARBY

The Ensenada de San Francisco, a pleasant bay not far from Muros, is well sheltered from the west to the north. You can anchor off the beach on sand, before going ashore to the shops and bars in the village or along the seafront.

The Ensenada de Esteiro is a quiet spot opposite Portosin, well sheltered from all except southerly winds. At the head of the bay is an unassuming country village with a tiny, drying harbour. Pick your spot

using the echo-sounder, noting that there is a 1.2 metre shallow more or less in the middle of the bay, with greater depth all around. Holding is fair on sand and weed.

Nearby, the Isla Quiebra offers a more remote anchorage, tucked in behind the island and its off-lying rocks to the east. The amount of space here may depend on the exact location of the nearby *viveiros* (mussel-rafts).

Freijo, a mile or so further up the ria, is another quiet country village, where there is nothing very much besides a handful of bars and houses along with a tiny fishing harbour (just a pier, really) and a small amount of boatbuilding activity.

Some of the mysteries of mussel farming revealed

Muros is a most attractive town. Its colonnaded granite buildings are in communion with the sea

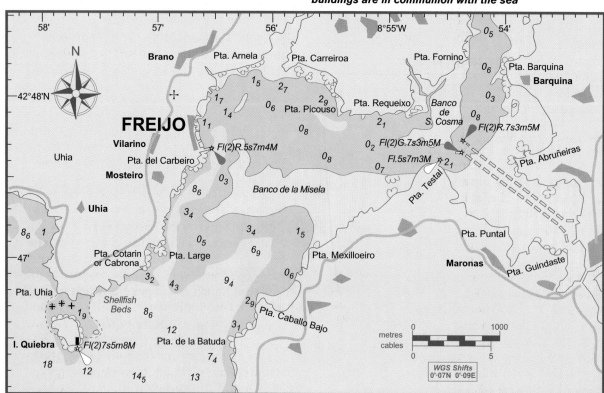

The inner harbour at Muros

It also boasts one supermarket, situated on the waterfront towards the boatyard.

Freijo is well past Isla Quiebra: in this inner part of the ria proceed with care, using a large scale chart to find the unmarked channel to Freijo. Make sure you stay very close to the north shore, as there is a large shoal extending right across the ria from the opposite bank (Banco de la Misela), and take care to avoid the shallow rock patch off Punta Larga. At Freijo, anchor

The town square and town hall

USEFUL INFORMATION

Habour office at Muros Tel: 981 82 61 40

off the mole, somewhere clear of moorings.

Finally, you can also find a spot in which to anchor just off the entrance to the ancient port of Noya. Although the channel leading to Noya is enclosed between two training walls, it has completely silted up and is now very shallow, drying out at low tide. You could venture up here by dinghy, but it seems to be easier and more practical to get to Noya from the convenient marina of Portosin (see the section on Portosin for details). As far as the anchorage is concerned, there is one area between the end of the pier at Punta Testal and the head of the starboard training wall leading to Noya. To find your way here, firstly you need to be on the top half of the flood tide and secondly you need to have a large scale chart, an echo-sounder and good pilotage skills. The water is quite shallow all around here, and the channel, which is not necessarily continuous from Freijo to the entrance of Noya, is unmarked.

Chapter 5

PORTOSIN

Portosin marina entrance – 42°46'.11N / 08°56'.78W

Portosin is situated about half way up the Ria de Muros, on the south side. Apart from the convenience of a purpose-built marina, the small town of Portosin itself holds little of particular interest. However, the yacht club, which is an integral part of the marina complex, is well equipped, very hospitable and is happy to supply travel and tourist information.

Portosin may be regarded more as a pit stop for any necessary supplies or repairs or if you want access to nearby significant places, most notably Santiago de Compostela. The marina is a secure spot to leave your yacht for a few days, and has conscientious staff who really do look after their customers' property.

LOCATION/POSITION

Portosin is approximately half way up the Ria de Muros, on the south side.

APPROACH AND ENTRANCE

Approach waypoint: 42°43'.73N / 09°04'.66W; 068°; 6.3M to marina entrance.

Ria de Muros is easy to enter (for details, see under Muros), as is the marina itself. Continue up the ria past Muros, staying more or less in the middle, until Isla Quiebra (to the north, opposite the marina) and the marina itself are identified. Enter from the north.

BERTHING

Floating pontoons with finger berths for all yachts up to about 20 metres in length. Larger yachts

Good shelter and facilities at Portosin

should consult the marina before entering. Be warned that weekends during the summer season can get rather busy here, so if you want to be guaranteed of a place, make sure you book in advance. There may also be space for very large yachts alongside the inner side of the outer mole in the fishing harbour.

FACILITIES IN THE MARINA

All facilities for yachts are available, including water and electricity on the pontoons, diesel - Gasoleo A from the marina pump and petrol from the town filling station (inquire at office). There are showers and toilets in the clubhouse as well as a launderette within the marina compound. Club Nautico Portosin has a rather grand clubhouse with an excellent bar and restaurant on the top floor, offering not only good food but also great views across the ria. Other amenities include a tennis court and a television lounge. As far as boat-lifting and storage are concerned, they have a 32-ton travelift and a large hard-standing area. A workshop and mechanic are on site for any possible repairs.

TRANSPORT

Buses run from the village to Noya and several other towns.

PROVISIONING

The marina is a short walk from the town (approximately 10 minutes), which has a limited assortment of shops, including one or two small supermarkets.

A RUN ASHORE

The marina is a good place to leave the boat if visiting Santiago de Compostela inland (it is the same distance from Santiago as Villagarcia, in the next ria), but check with the yacht club for the bus times from Portosin to Noya, from where buses go quite frequently to Santiago.

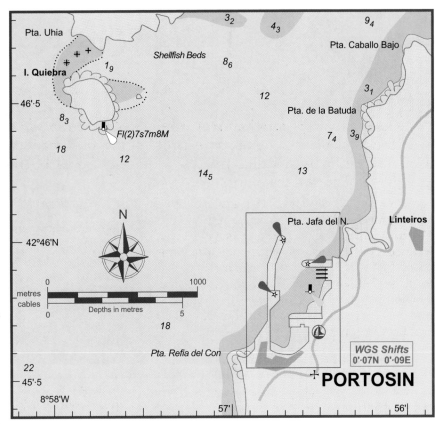

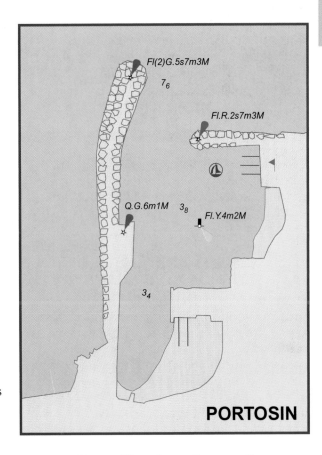

PORTOSIN

The view across Ria de Muros from the marina at Portosin to Isla de Quiebra

Noya (spelt also as Noia) is a wonderful mediaeval town full of palaces, squares and churches. It used to be a busy harbour but has now silted up completely and, although you could perhaps take the dinghy up there for a day trip from an anchorage or from the marina at Portosin (just under six miles away), going by taxi or bus is probably more practical.

EATING OUT

The clubhouse restaurant can be recommended, or in Noya, try the restaurant of the Hotel Ceboleiro (Calle Galicia 15), which offers good quality regional cooking. There are several other enticing-looking restaurants in Portosin and its surrounding areas, although it's worth making a reservation on weekends.

OTHER HARBOURS AND ANCHORAGES NEARBY

Puerto del Son (El Son) is a small fishing harbour sheltered behind a long, new breakwater. When approaching, you need to keep close in to the pier-head, as there is a visible rock off to the north-east of it. If you're lucky, there may be enough space to anchor in the outer harbour or even a vacant berth alongside the pier, but usually you would have to anchor outside, taking care to avoid the rocks and shoals in the bay. This

village is of no specific interest to sailors, nor are there any facilities in the harbour apart from the usual shops, bars and cafés along with the restaurant, the Marisqueira, situated near the outer mole.

Portosin has a boatyard and hoist facilities

Corrubedo is another little fishing village outside the ria, towards the south. Thanks to its scenic location and the wide, sandy beach backed by the largest dune in Galicia, this place is attempting to take on a new role as a summer holiday town. The tiny harbour, surrounded by several bars as well as a few shops and a bank, is nothing more than a short breakwater. The rest of the area behind this breakwater is strewn with rocks, so don't attempt to anchor here. Instead, you could try either in the bay south-west of the pier, which is sheltered from north-westerly to northerly winds, or off the long beach east of the village. The approach here is quite difficult, however, involving accurate pilotage between some unmarked rocks and reefs, so only come here during daylight hours in fine, settled conditions.

SANTA EUGENIA DE RIVEIRA

Santa Eugenia de Riveira harbour entrance – 42°33'.68N / 08°58'.94W

Santa Eugenia de Riveira is one of the larger towns along Ria de Arosa. Although not particularly spectacular, it has an important commercial harbour along with a well-equipped marina that is only a 20-minute walk from the town centre.

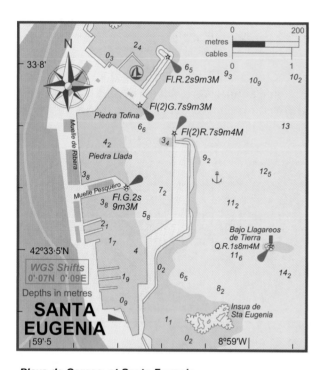

LOCATION/POSITION

It is located on the north side of the Ria de Arosa.

APPROACH AND ENTRANCE

Approach waypoint: 42°32'.35N/08°58'.30W; 340°; 1.4M to harbour entrance.

Approach Ria de Arosa through the Canal Principal. Once past Isla Salvora, continue on a course slightly east of north, passing the red buoy Sina del Castro to your port, and later on leaving Isla Rua (an island with a lighthouse) to starboard. When sailing into the bay, head first for the green beacon, Bajo Camuco, and then for the marina breakwater, which is north of the main commercial harbour, before finally entering from a north-easterly direction.

BERTHING

Moor to the floating pontoons. There are some berths with fingers, but most have

Playa de Coroso, at Santa Eugenia

Mediterranean-style mooring lines which are picked up at the pontoons, then led aft or forward, depending on whether you moor bow or stern-to.

MARINA FACILITIES

Water and electricity are available on the pontoons, while showers and toilets can be found ashore in the clubhouse. This is also where you will find the office (only Spanish spoken during our visit), a bar and a diving shop. Mechanics are available, but there is currently no haul-out facility here.

TRANSPORT

Buses, hire cars and taxis in town.

PROVISIONING

Shops of all descriptions are based in the town, along with supermarkets and other services.

A RUN ASHORE

Riveira is not particularly attractive, although it is a lively town. The bars along the fishing harbour and in the bustling quarter around the Maria Carmen church may appeal to some. You could take a bus from here to the nature reserve and sand dune near Corrubedo, especially if the weather rules out anchoring there.

EATING OUT

There are numerous restaurants, but none that are really outstanding.

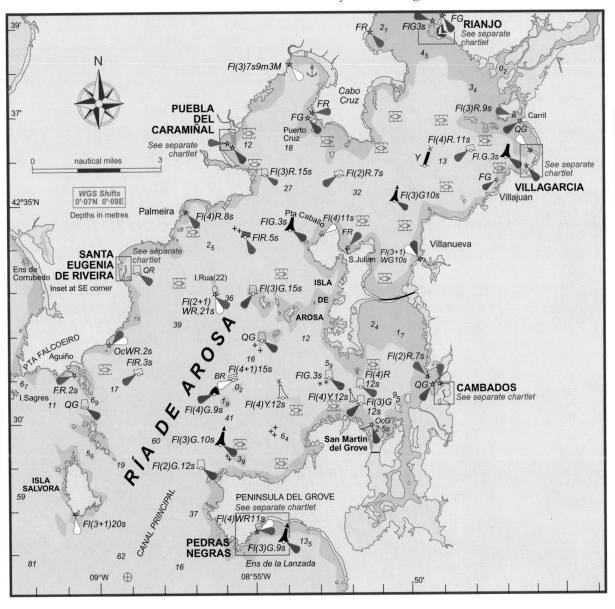

HARBOURS AND ANCHORAGES NEARBY

Aguiño is purely a fishing harbour attached to a rather nondescript village. The approach is not easy either from inside or outside the ria. Coming from the east, you would pass through the narrow Paso del Carreiro, with submerged rocks on both sides, then head north for the harbour breakwater on a course slightly east of north to avoid the rocks and shoals of Las Centolleiras. From the sea, you would use the Canal del Norte, taking an exact bearing from a large scale chart to avoid the submerged rocks on both sides of that approach and steering about 30° towards the pier-head of Aguiño. Another option is the Canal de Sagres, just north of the islands of Sagres, but again this is a narrow passage between rocks.

In reality, you would probably think twice before going to all this trouble to visit Aguiño, where the harbour is entirely devoted to fishing boats. If you do come here, you can only anchor to the north-east of the pier-head, taking care not to get too close to the rocks further north and east and not to get entangled in the moorings. When all is said and done, however, you might be tempted to sample the gastronomic delights of one of the *pulperias* along the harbour, where the speciality is octopus.

Palmeira is another fishing harbour, a few miles north-east of Riveira. It's a very quiet and unassuming place, but again with a rock-strewn approach, little space to anchor and mussel-rafts galore, just to add to the obstructions. In short, it doesn't come highly recommended. In Riveira itself, if you don't feel inclined to use the marina, you could always anchor off the beach to the north-east or, to be closer to town, immediately north or even north-west of the marina, between it and the beach.

USEFUL INFORMATION

Club Nautico de Riveira Tel: 981 87 38 01

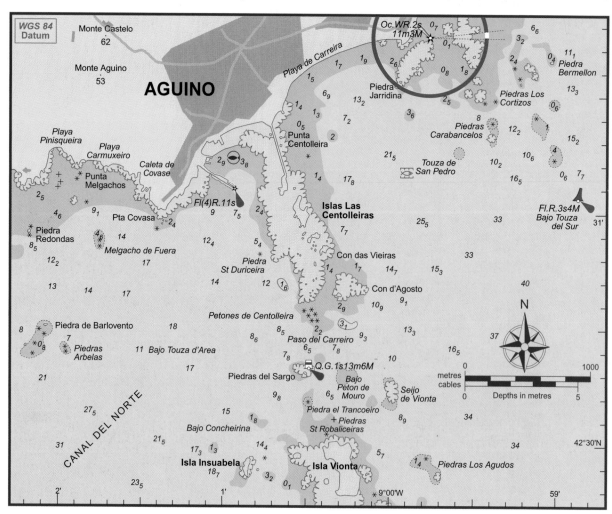

PUEBLA DEL CARAMIÑAL

Puebla del Caramiñal harbour – 42°36'.30N / 08°55'.71W

Puebla del Caramiñal, or A Pobra do Caramiñal, is a very pleasant, medium-sized town – just big enough to offer good shopping, bars, night-life and other urban pleasures, but still small enough to get your bearings quickly. Besides a large commercial harbour, there is also a friendly local yacht club, which has two floating pontoons where visitors are welcome to moor up.

LOCATION/POSITION

Located north-east of Santa Eugenia de Riveira, past Punta de Cabio, on the north shore of the Ria de Arosa.

APPROACH AND ENTRANCE

Approach waypoint: 42°35'.95N / 08°54'.43W; 290°; 1M to harbour entrance.

If coming up the ria from the sea, leave Isla Rua to port in order to miss the rocks of Lobeira Grande. You also need to pass the next red buoy on your port-hand side, so as not to hit the Sinal del Maño rock. From here, round Punta del Cabio, again leaving both the buoy and the light to port. Finally, head for the commercial harbour, before turning to cross its entrance

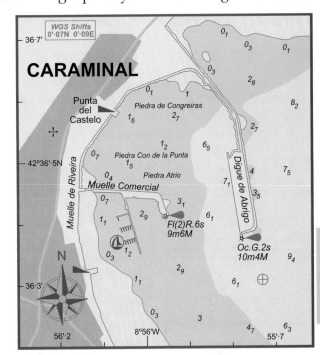

The harbour at Caramiñal

A popular sandy beach near Puebla del Caramiñal

Pontoon berths at Caramiñal

towards the clearly-visible club pontoons, keeping, of course, a sharp look-out for any commercial traffic.

BERTHING

Berthing is to the floating pontoons, bow or stern-to, with Mediterranean style mooring lines that are picked up from the pontoon and led aft (or forward) on board.

MARINA FACILITIES

Water and electricity are on the pontoons and diesel can be arranged through the helpful (Spanish speaking) harbour master, who will order a truck to deliver it. Bar and showers are in the clubhouse close by, mechanics are on hand for any repairs and hauling out is possible with a 40-ton travelift.

TRANSPORT

Buses and taxis in town.

PROVISIONING

All shops, including supermarkets, are conveniently not too far away.

A RUN ASHORE

The town has a pleasant historic centre, to the left of the small park as you come ashore. This is a good place to just wander around, with many inviting bars along the way. Among the town's main historic buildings are the mansion house, Casa Grande de Aguiar, dating back to the 16th century and rebuilt in the 18th century, and the Bermudéz Tower, which houses the Valle-Inclán museum.
There are many festivals held here throughout the year, the most notable one being the feast of the Nazareno, which takes place in September.

To get to the internet café, continue straight on across the road when coming from the harbour (past the restaurant O Lagar), go uphill beyond the taxi-rank on the left-hand side, then take the next turning to the right.

EATING OUT

The restaurant O Lagar, situated just across the road as you come into town from the harbour, is a pleasant, cosy place. The cheap and cheerful bar, La Cantina, is always good for

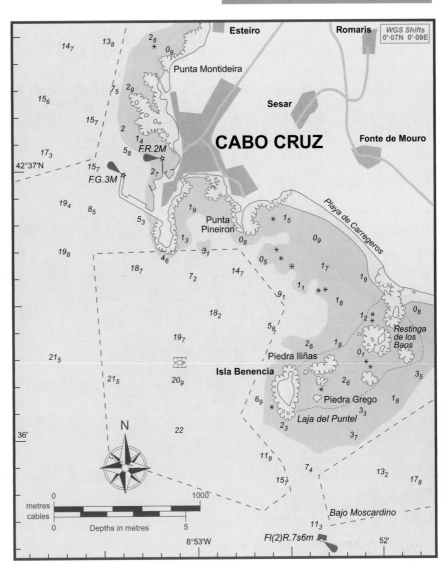

a quick (or a prolonged) and inexpensive lunch. It can be found in the pedestrianised part of the old quarter.

HARBOURS AND ANCHORAGES NEARBY

Puerto de Cruz is a rather bland fishing harbour near the point of Cabo Cruz, literally just across the bay from Caramiñal. The bay and harbour are full of fishing craft and mussel-rafts, and the village is not particularly remarkable. There is a small bay on the other side of this cape in which you could anchor, but it is surrounded by a rather delapidated village.

The next anchorage to the east, off the beach Playa de Carregeros, is a bit more scenic. You can drop anchor here in one to three metres on sand, but take care as there are isolated rocks.

RIANJO

Rianjo harbour

Rianjo – 42°38′.99N / 08°49′.61W

Rianjo, or Rianxo, is another fishing village of little touristic value. To Galicians, the town is best known as the birthplace and part-time home of the writer and politician Alfonso Castelao, who helped to keep the Galician language and culture alive during the dark years of the Franco dictatorship.

He died in the 1950s in Buenos Aires.

Inside the harbour is a pontoon for yachts, although this is often fully occupied with local craft. Plans to build a new marina have been heralded for some years now, but there is still no sign of any activity in this respect.

LOCATION/POSITION

Rianjo is located at the inner end of the Ria de Arosa, still on the north shore.

APPROACH AND ENTRANCE

Approach waypoint: 42°38′.00N/08°49′.61W; 000°; 1M to harbour entrance.

The approach up the ria from the south-west is straightforward as far as Rianjo.

BERTHING

To the floating pontoon (with fingers on some berths, mooring lines on others) in the south part of the fishing harbour, if space can be found there. If not, anchor south of the harbour, off the clubhouse of the local Club Nautico or, depending on the weather, in the bay north of the harbour.

FACILITIES

Water and electricity on the pontoon, showers and toilets ashore in the small building of the Club Nautico, which is reputedly friendly and helpful.

The planned marina will, in due course, make this port more useful to visiting yachts

TRANSPORT

There are buses and taxis in town.

PROVISIONING

Shops, supermarkets and a local market in the town, which is a fair walk from the Club Nautico.

A RUN ASHORE

Rianjo is an important historic centre, famous for its archaeological findings, the most notable of

which is the gold Leiro helmet. Among the town's significant monuments are the parish church at Santa Coloma and the Guadeloupe chapel.

Two of the interesting festivities held here each year are the sardine festival in June and the Fiesta de Santa Maria de Guadeloupe in September.

EATING OUT

Bars and restaurants can be found in town, while the clubhouse incorporates a cafeteria and bar.

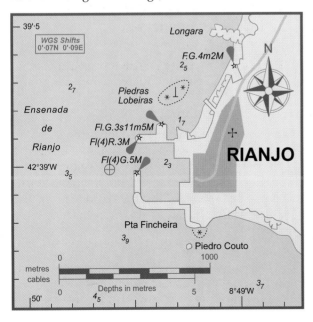

Rianjo is a busy harbour for inshore fishing boats

USEFUL INFORMATION

Club Nautico de Rianjo: Tel: 981 86 06 20

VILLAGARCIA

Villagarcia marina entrance – 42°36'.16N / 08°46'.22W

Villagarcia is a medium-sized town which is officially past its former glory, as many derelict villas and *palacios* show. However, it is now bustling again with activity, but not all of which is entirely *bona fide* – a few years ago Villagarcia was a centre of drug-smuggling in western Galicia.

This has since been reduced drastically by a big anti-smuggling campaign, and to the casual visitor, the town is as friendly and harmless as any other in this part of the world.

The clean and pleasant marina is close to the centre and offers yachtsmen all the facilities they need.

LOCATION/POSITION

Villagarcia is situated in the inner part of Ria de Arosa, past Isla de Arosa, on the south bank.

APPROACH AND ENTRANCE

Approach waypoint: 42°36'.16N/08°47'.58W; 090°; 1M to marina entrance.

The approach is simple, keeping to the buoyage past Isla de Arosa and entering Villagarcia from the west. The marina is at the north end of the commercial harbour.

BERTHING

On floating pontoons with Mediterranean-style mooring lines. Yachts up to 25 metres in length can be accommodated in this 450-berth marina.

Villagarcia harbour. The sheltered marina has over 400 berths

Fishing boats moored near Villagarcia in the Ria de Arosa

The pleasant marina building caters for most requirements

FACILITIES IN THE MARINA

Water and electricity are available on the pontoons. Toilets, showers and washing machines can be found ashore in the two-storey wooden building, which also houses the office and, on the first floor, a very good restaurant and bar. Among the facilities are a 70-ton travelift, a hard-standing area and repair services. Diesel and petrol can be obtained here (inquire at office).

A *libreria* (book shop) in town sells charts (inquire at office for directions) and there is also a chandlery.

TRANSPORT

Buses run to Santiago (see under 'A run ashore') and Vigo. Alternatively you can either go by taxi or hire a car.

PROVISIONING

A supermarket is situated just across the road from the marina, with more shops and a local market in town.

A RUN ASHORE

Santiago de Compostela is less than an hour away by bus, so the marina at Villagarcia is one of the better places to leave the boat and visit this pilgrim town (for more details, see under 'Major Attractions' on page 13 of the introduction).

EATING OUT

There is a wide choice of bars and also some restaurants in town, but you really don't need to venture that far – the restaurant on the top deck of the wooden marina building is perfectly adequate.

The secure marina is a good base for visiting Santiago

The picturesque harbour at Carril

HARBOURS AND ANCHORAGES NEARBY

Carril is a charming little village with a tiny small-craft harbour, just a proverbial stone's throw further to the north-east and still within sight of the cranes and high-rise buildings of Villagarcia. It sits in a scenic location on the south-west side of a narrow, shallow pass between the wooded island of Isla Cortegada and the mainland. The harbour is far too small for yachts, but you can moor alongside the outside of the new mole, if space permits or, alternatively, anchor off, taking care of the depths and the tide, which is sometimes strong in this narrow channel. There are many delightful bars and restaurants along the waterfront in Carril: Loliña, with its overgrown terrace, is a good one to try, as is the restaurant Casa Bovela, which is extremely popular with the locals.

The Isla de Arosa (Illa de Arousa) is a favoured summer holiday destination and can become quite crowded. There are two main anchorages on either side of the narrow part in the middle,

Isla de Arosa

A view of Villagarcia de Arosa

which is the main village of the island, San Julian, offering all the usual amenities such as shops, bars, restaurants, banks and a post office. The north-east bay, Porto O Xufre, also has a long pier for fishing boats, at the end of which is a fuel station selling diesel - Gasoleo A and petrol to yachts, as well as a large chandlery (beside the fuel-station). The approach from the north into Porto O Xufre is easy and clear of dangers, as is the bay, apart from some isolated rocks very close into the shore. This bay, however, is congested with moorings, so finding a space to anchor might not be so easy and using a trip-line is definitely a good idea in a place like this. If space permits, you can go alongside the fishing pier for a brief stay only.

A more idyllic anchorage exists on the north coast off the Playa Arena de la Secada. Again, the approach from the north is easy: anchor off the beach past the mussel-rafts. Holding is poor to average, due to thick weed. There is a bar ashore, and the village is within walking distance (although it is not particularly a short walk).

The bay south of San Julian is difficult to enter due to many unmarked rocks. Like its neighbour on the other side of the isthmus, it is crowded with moorings. On the whole, you may consider that there is little to be gained from coming here, bearing in mind the numerous rocks. If you do attempt to visit, however, you will need a large-

scale chart, good visibility and a high-level of pilotage skills.

Finally, you could also anchor off the beach on the east side of the island, north of the mainland bridge. Watch out for a cable here (see chart), but otherwise the bottom is sand and weed with some rocky patches, and the approach from the north is clear.

Just south of Villagarcia is the small fishing harbour of Vilajuan, but this is purely a working harbour and with the new yacht marina so close by, yachts are not really welcome here. Much the same applies to the large commercial harbour of Vilanova (Villanueva), about three miles south-east of Villagarcia, opposite the north end of Isla de Arosa. It has no space or facilities for yachts and few attractions for visitors either.

USEFUL INFORMATION

Marina Villagarcia Tel: 986 51 11 75

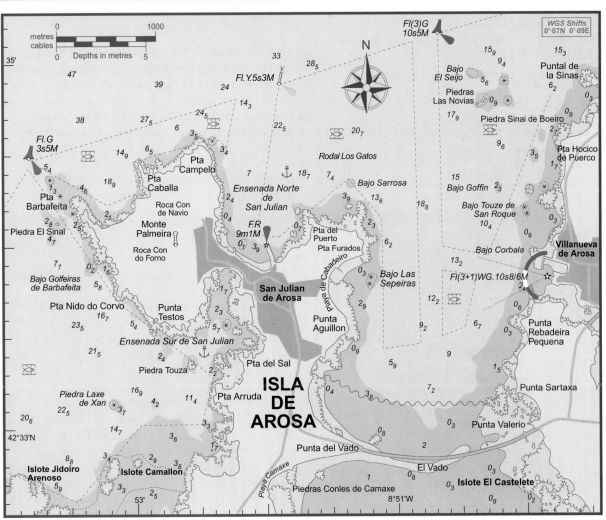

CAMBADOS

Cambados (Santo Tomé) harbour – 42°30'.86N / 08°49'.14W

Cambados, with its old centre, is one of the more interesting towns on the Ria de Arosa. You can guarantee that you will be enchanted by its charm, especially when you reach the Plaza Fefiñas, where there are two enticing cafés with beautiful, shady terraces. However, there are no facilities here for berthing a larger cruising yacht, so you would have to anchor quite far off unless you have a shoal draught boat capable of taking the ground in the old harbour. As Cambados is well worth a visit, either plan to leave your yacht at another more suitable harbour or anchorage, or anchor off the town for a day visit, moving to a more sheltered location (such as Isla Toja) for the night.

LOCATION/POSITION

Cambados is tucked away in the bay formed behind the Isla de Arosa in the north and the peninsula of O'Grove to the south, on the southern shore of the Ria de Arosa.

APPROACH AND ENTRANCE

Approach waypoint: 42°30'.86N/08°50'.50W; 090°; 1M to Santo Tomé harbour entrance.

Give Isla de Arosa a good offing if coming from the north, as rocks and shoals extend quite far south, marked by the Lobeira de Cambados tower, which must be left to port. The inner approach to Cambados, indeed the whole of the south part of the ria, is very congested with *viveiros* (mussel-rafts), but there is a fairway between them. The shoal patch of Orido (1.5 metres) is marked by an unlit buoy. After that, head for the Ensenada de Cambada, south of the large fishing harbour, and then to the harbour entrance of Santo Tomé.

BERTHING

A fairly large harbour, Santo Tomé, has floating pontoons for small craft in its southern corner, but depths here are less than a metre at LWS – indeed the chart shows it as drying. With a shoal draught boat, you can easily find space to anchor inside this harbour or even dry out alongside, and the

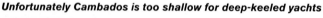
Unfortunately Cambados is too shallow for deep-keeled yachts

fuel berth is conveniently situated on the outer pier. Otherwise, you will have to anchor in the bay outside of the harbour, south of the new fishing harbour, in depths of between two and three metres, using the pontoons as a dinghy landing place.

The large fishing harbour to the north is for commercial fishing craft only, with no suitable berths for yachts, although you might be able to anchor or even get the use of a vacant mooring in the south-east corner. The drawbacks are its distance from the town – at least half a mile, if not more – as well as the continuous activity of the small fishing skiffs, which enter and leave the harbour at high speed, and larger fishing trawlers, which are continually on the move.

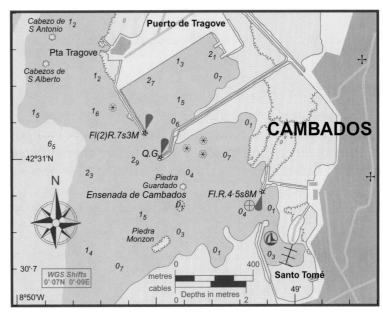

FACILITIES IN THE HARBOUR

A fuel station, on the pier-head to starboard as you enter Santo Tomé, sells petrol and diesel. Gasoleo A may be available to yachts here. Depth alongside the fuel facility is limited, so it can only be regarded as a HW option for keel boats.

TRANSPORT

A bus service to Pontevedra, with onward connections along the coast.

PROVISIONING

This busy town has all the usual shops and facilities. A supermarket can be found a few yards up a street opposite the root of the north pier of the old harbour, and the tourist information office is in a wooden building by the main square.

A RUN ASHORE

As mentioned above, the Plaza Fefiñas and its associated side streets are well worth exploring. There are many bars, cafés and restaurants, plus a large number of wine bars and shops selling the local Albariño wines, beautifully presented in souvenir packs. Albariño is generally considered to be Galicia's best wine and commands premium prices as a result, although when bought near its source, it is not that expensive. A clean-tasting, light wine, it is

The fuel berth is on the head of the south pier. Watch the depth

ideal with seafood – you could loosely describe it as Spain's equivalent to Muscadet, but the best thing to do is to judge for yourself. A good time to do this would be during the Fiesta del Albariño, which is always held on the first weekend in August.

When walking through the old town, you will soon notice that there are many old *palacios*, called *Pazo* locally. These, of course, hint at the town's more glorious past when, for example, the impressive Pazo Fefiñas was built by the Spanish ambassador to Russiac court, Don José Pardo de Figueroa, in the 17th century. Another good example is the Pazo Bazan, again from the 17th century, which once belonged to the writer Countess Emilia Pado-Bazan. Nowadays, anyone can stay here: the Pazo was converted into the local Parador in the 1960s.

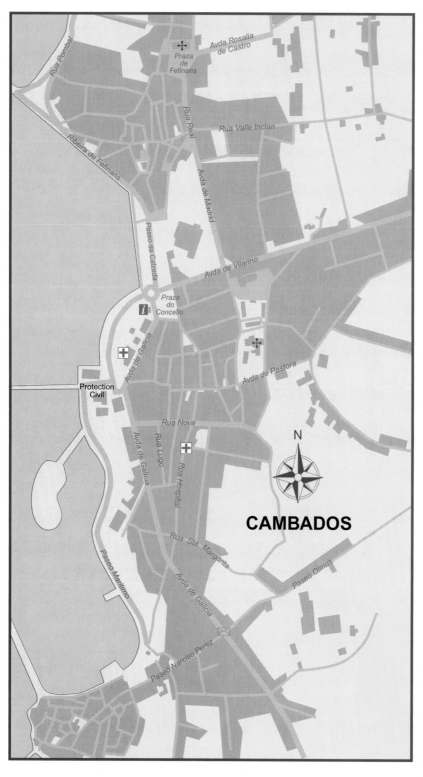

CAMBADOS

OTHER ANCHORAGES NEARBY

Isla Toja (Illa da Toxa): if you feel the urge to see where some of the richest Spaniards are hiding away in summer, and where even Franco liked to spend his summer holidays, then this island is the place to go. A room for a night in the local Grand Hotel is the most expensive option possible in all of northern Spain. The island has some pretty scenery, nearly all of it kept in perfect trim by a team of gardeners, and an unusual chapel, which is covered in shells from the ground right up to the tip of the bell-tower (close to the Grand Hotel).

To get here from the sea, take a direct line from the Cambados north (fishing) harbour to the north-east corner of Isla Toja. The UK charts indicate that the water is quite shallow, but there is actually at least five metres all the way. If in doubt, watch or follow one of the many day-tripper boats that ply to and fro. As they have submarine observation facilities, they are probably as deep-draughted as a sailing yacht.

You can anchor off the east shore of the island, either near the private pontoons north of the Grand Hotel, or in the channel just off the Grand Hotel. Beware though of the shallow spit between these two spots. You will be lying in a moderate tidal stream, which fills and empties the large bay to the south, so be prepared to be spun around abit when the tide turns. The bottom is quite good holding, mainly on sand, and you can land at a slipway just south of the pontoons. There is nowhere to eat on Isla Toja

EATING OUT

The Parador, not far from the harbour or anchorage, is always a sure bet for a treat (Parador de Cambados, Principe 1, Tel: 986 54 22 50). There are also at least two other noteworthy restaurants such as Ribadomar (Terra Santa 17,

The southern end of Cambados old harbour

(other than the Grand Hotel), but a 10-minute walk will take you to the bridge linking the island with San Martin where, right at the other end of the bridge, is Posada del Mar, an excellent and moderately priced seafood restaurant. It is popular, so either book ahead (Tel: 986 73 01 06) or get there early.

O Grove (San Martin del Grove), another lively holiday town, is the main hub of this busy and very popular peninsula. It is about a half-an-hour walk from the above anchorage and offers an array of shops and other services, plus a market close to the harbour, at the root of the main pier. However, this harbour, besides being rather shallow, is distinctly fishing oriented and has no facilities for yachts. There is a floating pontoon for small boats only, so you must anchor off, taking care of the moorings and the many *viveiros* (mussel-rafts) which litter practically the entire approach and anchorage.

Porto Melojo (Meloxo): this is a bay on the north-west side of the Peninsula del Grove, sheltered by a short mole with a red light at the end. As it is the centre of the mussel farming industry, it is predominantly full of fishing boat moorings, but you may be fortunate enough to find a spot in which to anchor. Fuel for yachts is available from the quay to starboard as you round the pier-head. For a good, simple meal, you could try the little bar O Porto, located in the sleepy village at the end of the bay.

Cambados has pleasant tree-lined avenues and a Parador, all close to the harbour. Wine enthusiasts will find a number of outlets for the excellent local wine, Albariño

USEFUL INFORMATION

Tourist office, Cambados Tel: 986 52 07 86

Chapter 5

PORTO PEDRAS NEGRAS

Porto Pedras Negras entrance – 42°27'.50N / 08°54'.94W

Porto Pedras Negras is a modern marina that is situated beside the equally new and man-made holiday village of San Vicente do Mar. The area around the marina is subsequently crowded with holiday homes in a somewhat suburban style.

LOCATION/POSITION

Just south of the approach to the Ria de Arosa, on the south-west side of the Peninsula del Grove.

APPROACH AND ENTRANCE

Approach waypoint: 42°26'.86N/08°53'.91W; 310°; 1M to marina entrance.

Approach and entrance are straightforward, although you need to avoid two areas of drying rock and a shallow patch on the way in. Enter the bay Ensenada de la Lanzada, where the rocks half-a-mile south of the marina are marked by a south cardinal mark (Lobeiras de Fuera), which

should be left to port. The other rocks, the Sinal de Balea, are marked by a starboard buoy, while the shallow patch in between has a port-hand mark. All the marks are lit.

Further in is a starboard-hand post to identify the approach, from where you can head straight for the marina entrance, keeping close to the port breakwater head.

BERTHING

On two floating pontoons with fingers. The marina is usually full, but they do keep a few spaces for visitors.

The approach and entrance to the new marina are well marked and lit

MARINA FACILITIES

Water and electricity on the pontoons. Showers and toilets are in a building ashore, which also houses a small chandlery-cum-dive-shop. Other amenities include diesel and petrol, a travelift and hard-standing area. The Club de Mar has a bar/restaurant.

PROVISIONING

There is one small shop in the village.

A RUN ASHORE

The holiday village is pretty non-descript, but you can find attractive beaches along the Ensenada de Lanzada.

EATING OUT

Besides the Club de Mar, there's a pub and cafeteria in the village, plus a pizzeria a little further west of the village.

DAYTIME ANCHORAGES NEARBY

In settled weather it is possible to anchor off the beach, Playa de la Lanzada, which offers protection from northerly to easterly winds. Otherwise, however, there are no alternatives, as this bay faces the open Atlantic.

PEDRAS NEGRAS MARINA

WGS Shifts 0'·07N 0'·09E
Depths in metres

USEFUL INFORMATION

Marina office Tel: 986 73 84 30

Pedras Negras is located on the ocean facing the south-western coast of the Peninsula del Grove

ISLA ONS

The Isla Ons, viewed from the north

Almacén jetty – 42°22′.7N / 08°55′.7W

Isla Ons is a rugged and beautiful island with only a few permanent inhabitants. It attracts many visitors in the summer, who are brought in by ferry from Portonovo, Sangenjo and Bueu. There are two anchorages off the east coast, one off the main jetty at Almacén, the other off a small beach a mile further north,

Vessels are warned off these rugged shores by the lighthouse, 127m above sea level

Besides the gull, the island is also home to the wild dove and pelican, depending on the time of year

but both are somewhat exposed and not ideal. A day stop is therefore often more advisable than an overnight stay.

LOCATION/POSITION

The Isla Ons lies in the approach to the Ria de Pontevedra.

APPROACH

Approach waypoint: Canal de los Camoucos 42°24'.00N / 08°54'.75W; 208°; 1.5M to Almacén jetty.

The approach from the sea is the same as for the Ria de Pontevedra (see also under Sangenjo). There are no dangers off the east coast of the island, apart from some rocks very close inshore. Both anchorages can be reached directly from the east.

ANCHORAGE

Anchor off the main jetty at Almacén, where the depth is over 10 metres, on rocks and weed. Alternatively, you could pick up one of the visitors' buoys off the pier. A more hospitable spot to drop anchor is off the Playa de Melide, just under a mile to the north, which offers a little more shelter and an anchorage in under five metres of water, on sand, rocks and weed.

A RUN ASHORE

Walks around the island are highly recommended. There are some wonderful picnic spots ashore or else you can visit the tabernas at Almacén.

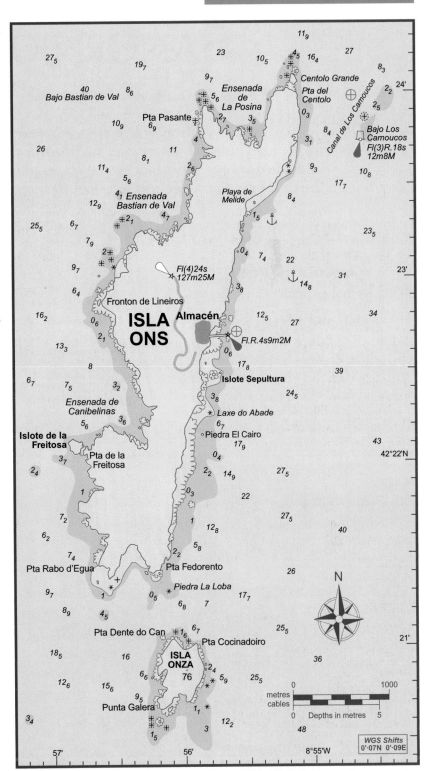

Chapter 5

FERRY TIMETABLE – Departure times from Sangenjo and Portonovo to Isla Ons

Sangenjo	Portonovo	Isla Ons	Sangenjo	Portonovo	Isla Ons
10.00	10.15	11.00	12.45	13.00	16.30 (a Portonovo)
10.45	11.00	11.45			
11.15	11.30	13.00	16.15	16.30	17.30
12.00	12.15	13.45	18.30	18.45	19.30

Ferry timetable as available – November 2002

SANGENJO

Sangenjo marina entrance – 42°23'.86N / 08°47'.88W

Sangenjo (Sanxenxo) is a lively place, which can get rather crowded with summer visitors. As with so many Spanish towns, the skyline from afar looks ugly and uninviting, with high-rise apartment blocks that could have been imported straight from the Costa del Sol. Once you step ashore, however, the town reveals a certain charm, particularly in the small streets just above the harbour. It has the added benefit of a large and comfortable marina.

LOCATION/POSITION

On the north shore of the Rio de Pontevedra.

APPROACH AND ENTRANCE

Approach waypoint: 42°22'.71N/08°49'.76W; 050°; 1.8M to marina entrance.

The approach to the Ria de Pontevedra from the sea is straightforward, passing either north or south of Isla Ons, which lies directly in the approach to Pontevedra. The ria is wide and deep, with no off-lying dangers, and, since it leads to the Spanish naval base at Marin, is distinctly well marked. There are, however, some isolated rocks and shoals close inshore, so keep a safe distance of about half a mile off. You need to approach Sangenjo bay from the south and enter the marina from the east, noting the starboard-hand mark to the north of the entrance, which warns of a rocky area opposite the end of the breakwater.

BERTHING

The marina has finger pontoons, alongside which yachts of up to 45 metres in length can moor up in a minimum depth of five metres.

Sangenjo is described locally as the 'capital of Galician tourism' and is a totally modern town

The recently extended marina may now have room for visitors

MARINA FACILITIES

There is a full range of facilities in the marina, with the exception of a launderette. Water and electricity are supplied on the pontoons, with showers ashore. Diesel is available (currently from the containers from the inside south mole, but this is only provisional). Services include a 65-ton travelift and a five-ton mobile crane, with a hard-standing area, where repairs can be carried out.

TRANSPORT

Buses (to Pontevedra and elsewhere), taxis and hire-cars.

PROVISIONING

A good supermarket is conveniently placed just across the road from the harbour, with another one on the road up the hill, plus several other shops.

A RUN ASHORE

The town has a certain charm about it: sitting in the sun, preferably outside the taberna by the waterfront, watching the world go by, is a great way to pass the time. Sangenjo is also a good base from which to visit Pontevedra by bus. (For details of Pontevedra, see under Aguete).

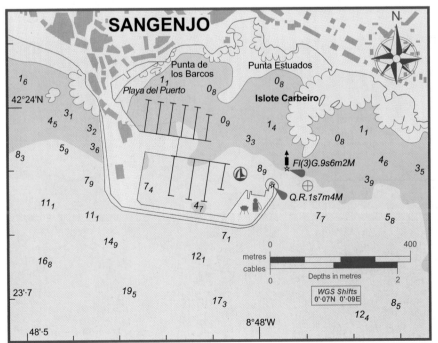

The marina offers a full range of facilities to yachts

The attractive, but crowded harbour at Portonovo

EATING OUT

Sangenjo is the only place for miles around that can boast a restaurant with a Michelin star. This is La Taberna de Rotilio (Avenida del Puerto, Tel: 986 72 02 00, closed Sunday nights, credit cards accepted). Another good and decidedly cheaper option here is Meson Don Camillo (Calle Poetas Galegos 9, Tel: 986 69 11 24). For a restaurant that is closer to hand, try the Taberna del Nautica, housed in the Club Nautico at the harbour, or the cosy restaurant Meson a Galeta, opposite the harbour on the waterfront, which specialises in shellfish and tapas and has outside seating.

HARBOURS AND ANCHORAGES NEARBY

Portonovo, located about a mile to the west of Sangenjo, is a small fishing harbour with some local, private yacht moorings. Alas, it has no space for visiting yachts, and the bay is so full of moorings that you would probably only look for an anchorage here as a last resort. It is certainly better to go to Sangenjo instead and, if you don't want to moor in the marina, you could always anchor off the Playa de Silgar, in the bay between the two harbours. The bottom here is predominantly sand, with some weed and rocky patches.

Combarro is a small fishing village near the head of the Ria de Pontevedra. The tourist guides fall over each other in praise of this unspoilt gem which, it has to be said, is undeniably pretty.

Its narrow streets and archways, along with ancient houses made from rough stones and typical Galician *horreos* (grain stores), situated mainly along the waterfront, all contribute to its charm. Sadly, however, this small place is dominated more and more by sprawling, ugly buildings all around, not to mention the noise from the main road just behind it and the vista of the heavily industrialised town of Marin on the opposite side of the ria.

There is a small harbour sheltered by a mole, behind which you can anchor almost anywhere, but check the depth carefully as this part of the ria gets quite shallow. You should also take the depth into account when approaching the village, passing south and east of Isla Tambo, before heading more or less north for the village, making sure that you keep to the middle of the bay. Depths here are four metres, shallowing to two metres or less off the village itself.

The old part of Combarro is east of the harbour, along a very shallow bay which you can visit by dinghy if you don't fancy the walk. Alternatively, you can land by dinghy on the small stone pier, taking you straight into the heart of the old village, with the added benefit of there being a cosy taberna to welcome you as you step ashore.

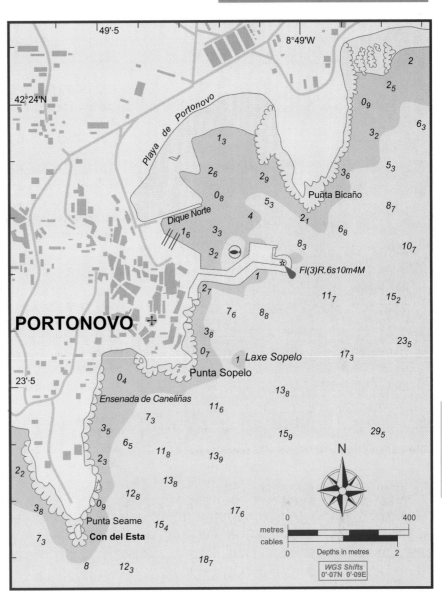

The quay at Portonovo

USEFUL INFORMATION

Marina Sangenjo
Tel: 986 720517; Fax: 986 72 05 78
General tourist information www.sanxenxo.com
Tourist office, Pontevedra Tel: 986 85 08 14

Aguete bay and marina

AGUETE

Aguete marina entrance – 42°22'.65N / 08°44'.04W

This small and sheltered marina is about half way up the Ria de Pontevedra, on the south shore. It is situated in a pleasant bay, where there is a good beach and a popular residential area. The village is not far from the marina, although there is a rather steep climb to get to it.

LOCATION/POSITION

On the south shore of the Ria de Pontevedra, about half way up.

APPROACH AND ENTRANCE

Approach waypoint: 42°23'.00N/08°44'.52W; 135°; 0.5M to marina entrance.

The approach from the ria is relatively easy, so long as you keep a safe distance from the shore. Enter the marina on a course which is slightly west of south.

BERTHING

Alongside berthing for visitors on long pontoons with no fingers. The outermost pontoon is a floating breakwater and is not normally used for berthing. There are numerous private mooring buoys in the bay.

Some swell and surge can curl around the mole into the harbour in strong westerly and northerly winds, making the berths slightly uncomfortable.

MARINA FACILITIES

Diesel - Gasoleo A is available, and there are shower facilities at modest charges in the clubhouse.

TRANSPORT

Taxis can be ordered from the clubhouse.

PROVISIONING

The village shops, uphill about half a mile away, provide everyday requirements, although it is preferable to choose another place to stock up with heavy items.

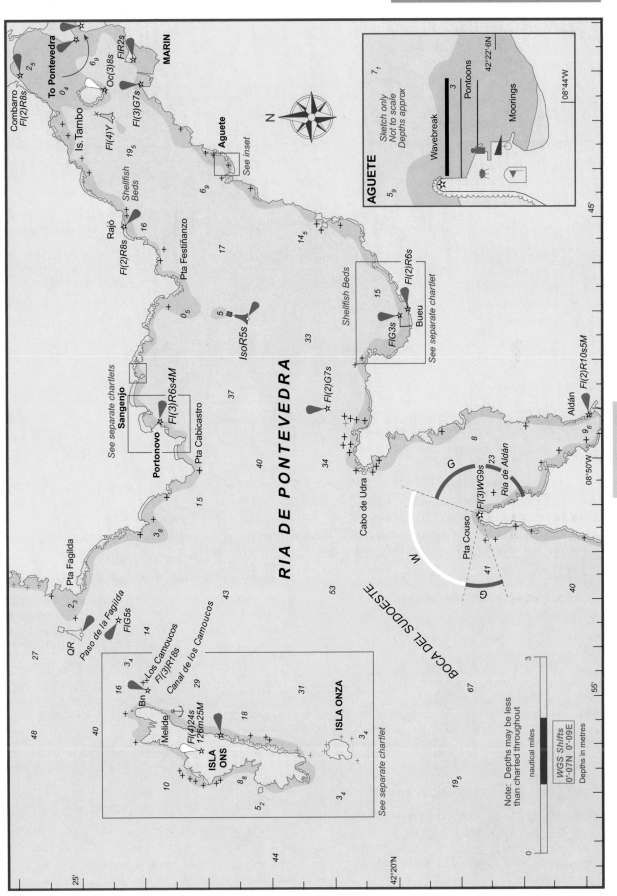

AGUETE

Sketch only
Not to scale
Depths approx

Wavebreak
Pontoons
Moorings

7_1

3

5_9

42°22'·6N

08°44'W

45'

N

To Pontevedra

MARIN

Combarro
Fl(2)R8s

2_5

0_4

Oc(3)8s

FlR2s

6_9

Is.Tambo

Fl(4)Y

Fl(3)G7s

Aguete

See inset

19_5

6_9

Shellfish
Beds

Rajó
Fl(2)R8s

16

Pta Festiñanzo

17

14_5

Shellfish Beds

15

Fl(2)R6s

Bueu

FlG3s

See separate chartlet

0_5

5

IsoR5s

33

Fl(2)G7s

34

RIA DE PONTEVEDRA

See separate chartlets

Sangenjo

Portonovo

Fl(3)R6s4M

Pta Cabicastro

37

40

15

Cabo de Udra

8

Aldán

Fl(2)R10s5M

9_6

08°50'W

G

23

Fl(3)WG9s

Ria de Aldán

Pta Couso

W

41

G

40

Pta Fagilda

2_3

QR

Paso de la Fagilda
FlG5s

14

3_4

3_8

53

BOCA DEL SUDOESTE

67

55'

16

Bn ×Los Camoucos
Fl(3)R18s

Canal de los Camoucos

29

31

ISLA ONZA

3_4

43

Melide

Fl(4)24s
126m25M

18

3_4

ISLA
ONS

8_8

10

5_2

3_4

19_5

See separate chartlet

48

40

27

Note: Depths may be less
than charted throughout

WGS Shifts
0'·07N 0'·09E

Depths in metres

nautical miles

3

0

44

42°20N

25'

Chapter 5

The outer structure is a floating breakwater and the yachts moor up to the inner pontoons

A RUN ASHORE

Near the marina is a café-bar, while the Real Club de Mar is very hospitable, offering spectacular views across the ria. It is a 30-minute taxi ride to Pontevedra, making Aguete a practical and secure stopping place for visiting this historic city.

The marina, viewed from the hospitable clubhouse

The shallow river entrance to the port of Pontevedra

A TRIP TO PONTEVEDRA

The mediaeval centre of Pontevedra has been lovingly restored and is full of interesting sights and historic buildings. Pontevedra used to be an important harbour until it silted up in the 19th century. The ancient town dates back to Roman times, but its heyday was in the middle ages. When wandering around, don't miss the Plaza de la Leña, where you will also find the provincial museum which spreads over five different buildings. The Plaza de la Leña, often referred to as one of the most beautiful squares in Spain, has remained outwardly unchanged for over 200 years. The museum has some remarkable exhibits, among these a Celtic treasure, paintings of some old Spanish masters and a replica of the admiral's cabin on board the *Numancia*, the ship of Méndez Nuñez in the Spanish war against Chile and Peru. If you want to stay overnight, which you could do if you leave the boat in the secure marinas of Aguete or Sangenjo, then try the Parador: Parador de Pontevedra (Calle Baron 19, Tel: 986 85 58 00).

There are numerous inviting tapas bars in the area surrounding the Plaza de la Leña, especially in the Calle Figueroa and Calle Pasanteria. Noteworthy and of superior quality are the Restaurant Roman (Calle Augusto Garcia Sanches 12, Tel: 986 84 35 60) and Doña Antonia (Calle Soportales de la Herreria 4, Tel: 986 84 72 74).

EATING OUT IN AGUETE

The marina has a hospitable clubhouse, which offers simple and excellent food.

HARBOURS AND ANCHORAGES NEARBY

Bueu is located further down the ria, on the south side, but is purely a fishing village with a working harbour. Although the usual supermarkets and restaurants can be found here, neither the town nor port have any notable

Basilica de Santa Maria la Mayor at Pontevedra

Pontevedra's Museo Provincial houses an interesting and varied collection

attraction for visiting yachts, and there's no guarantee that you'll find a space in the harbour. If you do decide to come here, you should anchor near the entrance, taking care not to obstruct the passing fishing boats. Another option would be to anchor west of the harbour, in the bay on sand and mud, in depths of around three metres.

The Ria de Aldan is more like a longish bay, which runs north to south and is open to the north. There is a small village at the very

Isla Tambo lies off the naval port of Marin, where there are no yachting facilities

southern end, but the water here is shallow. You do, however, have several options for anchoring nearby – almost anywhere in the little beach-bays along the west shore, clear of the moorings and *viveiros* (mussel-rafts), taking care to avoid the isolated rocks.

USEFUL INFORMATION

Real Club de Mar Aguete Tel: 986 70 23 73
Pontevedra tourist office Tel: 986 85 08 14

Chapter 5

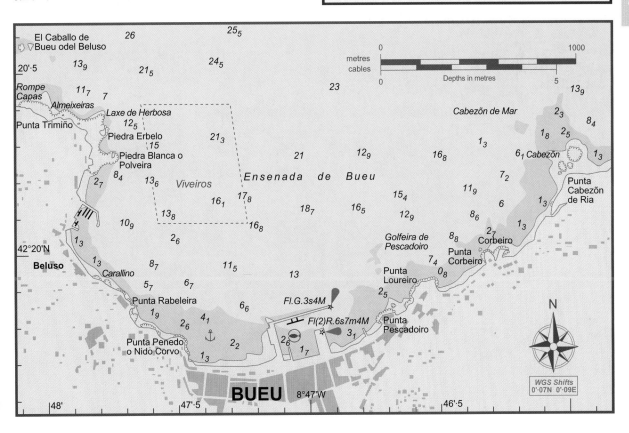

Islas Cíes

Islas Cíes, between the islands of Isla del Faro and San Martin – 42°12'.66N / 08°54'.60W

The Islas Cíes, which lie in the mouth of the Ria de Vigo, have a total surface area of 433 hectares. The group consists of three islands: San Martin in the south and the connected islands of Isla del Norte and Isla del Faro to the north. The western coasts facing the Atlantic Ocean are steep and rugged, while the eastern side, facing the rias, slope gently down to long, unspoiled beaches.

Due to the saltiness of the air and the poor soil, there is not much vegetation. Yew is the most numerous species, together with laurel-leaved cistus and gorse. Pine and eucalyptus have also been replanted here. The value of these islands lies in their wealth of seabirds, for they are the nesting ground of over 4,000 herring gulls, a smaller number of the lesser black-backed gulls and of the shag. The islands are also one of the few breeding grounds in this area for the guillemot, of which there are 20 pairs. Strictly a bird sanctuary, landing is not permitted on San Martin.

Islands are always special areas to explore for the cruising yachtsman, but popular locations like this become even more idyllic when the day trippers go home on the last ferry, leaving the place deserted.

LOCATION/POSITION

The Islas Cíes lie in the approach to the Ria de Vigo.

APPROACH AND ENTRANCE

Approach waypoint: 42°12'.33N / 08°55'.59W; 066°; 0.8M to waypoint between the islands.

You should approach from the sea as for the Ria de Vigo. It is possible to pass north or south of the islands, or even between San Martin and Isla del Faro, through a narrow but deep and clear sound. The two northern islands,

Isla del Norte and Isla del Faro are joined only by a strip of sandy beach and a foot bridge

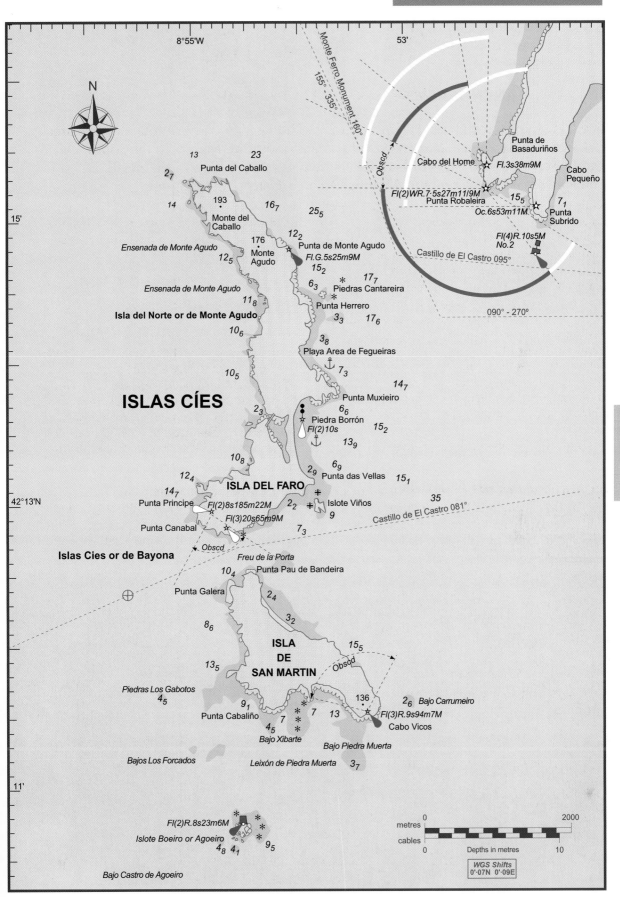

ISLAS CÍES

ISLA DEL FARO

Islas Cies or de Bayona

ISLA DE SAN MARTIN

Punta del Caballo

Monte del Caballo

Ensenada de Monte Agudo

Monte Agudo

Ensenada de Monte Agudo

Isla del Norte or de Monte Agudo

Punta de Monte Agudo
Fl.G.5s25m9M

Piedras Cantareira

Punta Herrero

Playa Area de Fegueiras

Punta Muxieiro

Piedra Borrón
Fl(2)10s

Punta das Vellas

Islote Viños

Punta Principe
Fl(2)8s185m22M

Fl(3)20s65m9M

Punta Canabal

Obscd

Freu de la Porta

Punta Pau de Bandeira

Punta Galera

Piedras Los Gabotos

Punta Cabaliño

Bajo Xibarte

Bajo Piedra Muerta

Bajos Los Forcados

Leixón de Piedra Muerta

Bajo Carrumeiro

Fl(3)R.9s94m7M

Cabo Vicos

Fl(2)R.8s23m6M

Islote Boeiro or Agoeiro

Bajo Castro de Agoeiro

Monte Ferro Monument 160°

155° - 335°

Obscd

Punta de Basaduriños

Cabo del Home
Fl.3s38m9M

Cabo Pequeño

Fl(2)WR.7·5s27m11/9M
Punta Robaleira
Oc.6s53m11M

Punta Subrido

Fl(4)R.10s5M
No.2

Castillo de El Castro 095°

090° - 270°

Castillo de El Castro 081°

Obscd

metres
cables

0   2000

0   Depths in metres   10

WGS Shifts
0'·07N 0'·09E

Chapter 5

Isla del Norte and Isla del Faro, are interconnected with a small causeway and a beach on the eastern side.

ANCHORAGES

The Islas Cíes offer some good anchorages off the eastern shores of both the northern pair of islands, or off the southern island. Holding is generally quite good in the sand, but as in many places on this coast, swell tends to creep in if conditions offshore are creating it.

Pick your anchorage according to the wind direction – the bay north of Punta Muxieiro and the anchorage off the southern Isla de San Martin give some protection from the south, while the main anchorage off the beach between the two islands of Isla del Norte and Isla del Faro – the Playa Arena das Rodas – offers protection from the north, as does the small bay south of Punta das Vellas, tucked inside Isla Viños. The latter two anchorages are designated bathing beaches, with the shallower water zoned off by the usual string of yellow buoys. The jetty at the northern end of the central bay is used by the ferry, so don't anchor too close to it. Naturally, if conditions are unsettled, it might be best to retreat to one of the havens in the rias.

The beautiful woods and beaches are typical of the area

A RUN ASHORE

The islands are a protected area, therefore barbecues or open fires on the beach are not allowed. There is a small campsite on Isla del Faro, next to which is a tiny and rather expensive supermarket. If you land at the jetty at the northern end of the central bay, you will find several notice-boards giving details of both walks

The southern island, Isla de San Martin, is a bird reserve and landing is prohibited

The main anchorage off the beach

There are many pleasant walks through the trees

Chapter 5

around the islands and locations of other places of interest, such as the lighthouse and the information centre on Isla del Faro, which is well worth a visit. The more energetic can climb Monte Agudo, on the north island. At 197 metres, it is the highest point on Islas Cíes. The Islands have been inhabited since prehistoric times and, during the Middle Ages, were occupied by Benedictine monks. You can still see today the remains of one of the two monasteries that existed all those years ago.

Besides the supermarket, there are a couple of other café-bars located on Isla del Faro, so it is possible to spend a bit of time here, enjoying the peaceful evenings, even if the days, especially at weekends, are somewhat busy.

EATING OUT

The Playa Arena das Rodas has two beach café-bars, with a couple of similar establishments at and near the campsite.

Information boards at the landing place

USEFUL INFORMATION

Vigo tourist office Tel: 986 60 17 89

The jetty is used by trip boats, so keep off

CANGAS

Cangas harbour entrance – 42°15'.69N / 08°46'.59W

Cangas is a modern town with a small old quarter, a working fishing harbour and a few yacht moorings, but is otherwise unremarkable. Many people who live here actually work in Vigo, commuting daily on the ferry, which takes about 20 minutes to cross the ria.

LOCATION/POSITION

Cangas is on the north bank of the Ria de Vigo, opposite the western outskirts of Vigo.

APPROACH AND ENTRANCE

Approach waypoint: 42°14'.40N; 08°46'.88W; 010°; 1.3M to harbour entrance.

The approach to the Ria de Vigo, past the Islas Cíes either by way of the Canal del Norte or the Canal del Sur, both of which are lit, is pretty straightforward. In calm weather and good visibility, it is also possible to pass through the narrow channel between the Isla del Faro and Isla de San Martin. The ria is deep and hazard-free, with isolated rocks and shoals inshore clearly marked with buoys. For the Ensenada de Cangas, leave the beacon tower of Bajo Boerneira to port, then aim for the head of the breakwater.

BERTHING

This is a fishing harbour with some private yacht moorings in the north part of the harbour, past the second mole as you come in. It is advisable to anchor near the yacht moorings, where the bottom is mud and the depths are around five metres.

FACILITIES IN THE HARBOUR

There is a small Club Nautico in the fishing harbour at the foot of the breakwater, where you may be able to use the showers. However, there are no other specific facilities for yachts in Cangas.

TRANSPORT

Ferries go back and forth to Vigo; buses and taxis.

Cangas harbour

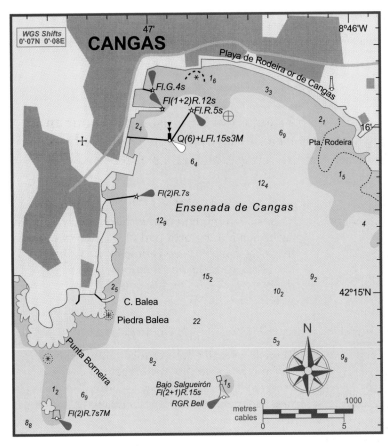

sand, weed, rocks and debris.

For Celtic fans, however, there is an international Celtic Festival in Moaña, which takes place on the local football field at the end of each June. This is when theatre groups and musicians come from Scotland, Ireland and other Celtic places, one of which of course is Galicia, for some music making and general celebration.

A few miles further on, around another little headland and about one mile below the huge bridge spanning the ria, you will find the private pontoons of the Association Nautico Deportive A Tella. These, however, are not in a particularly attractive area and are not even close to a proper village, although some shops and bars might be found along the main through-road not far inland. If you pass beneath the bridge, which has a clearance of 38 metres, you finally arrive in the Ensenada de San Simon, a round, shallow bay at the very end of the ria. This is really a suburb of Vigo and, again, has no outstanding features. There are various possible anchorages here – in theory any spot where you can find sufficient depth. One favourite place seems to be south of the little islets, Islas de San Simon, in the south-eastern corner of the bay, where the depth is about two metres. Another option is off the beach along the west shore, in a modest depth of two metres or less, although this varies according to the location chosen and generally decreases towards the north.

PROVISIONING

The town has all the shops necessary for day-to-day provisioning, but there are none really close to the harbour.

A RUN ASHORE

Cangas is a rather average town without any special attractions.

OTHER ANCHORAGES IN THE RIA DE VIGO

There are various anchorages upriver from Cangas and Vigo although, with all the shores now being built-up areas, none of them are particularly picturesque. Indeed, there are far prettier spots within the cruising ground of western Galicia, including, of course, the nearby Islas Cíes.

The village of Moaña, approximately three miles up the ria from Cangas, has a small and shallow anchorage between two moles, lacking both charm and space for visiting yachts. Alternatively, you could anchor in the adjacent bay. This is slightly more scenic, although you would not only have to negotiate the *viveiros* (mussel-rafts) moored here, but also find a space in about five metres of water. The ground is a mixture of

USEFUL INFORMATION

Cangas tourist office Tel: 986 30 50 00

VIGO

Ria de Vigo

Vigo marina entrance – 42°14'.75N / 08°43'.38W

Located on the southern shore of Ria de Vigo, Vigo is Galicia's largest conurbation as well as Spain's premier fishing port. This busy, modern city, which has a population of 300,000, certainly couldn't be considered beautiful, but if you require any of the facilities of a large European city, of either a material or cultural nature, then this is the obvious place to go.

Vigo is a major port with excellent yachting facilities

LOCATION/POSITION

Vigo harbour is located in the southernmost of Galicia's rias.

APPROACH AND ENTRANCE

Approach waypoint: 42°14'.20N / 08°47'.36W (south of Cabo Balea); 080°; 3M to marina entrance.

The approach to Ria de Vigo, past the Islas Cíes either by way of the Canal del Norte or the Canal del Sur, both of which are lit, is pretty simple. In calm weather and good visibility, it is also possible to pass through the narrow channel between the Isla del Faro and Isla de San Martin. As long as you keep in the middle, the ria is deep and hazard-free. Isolated rocks and shoals inshore are clearly marked with buoys.

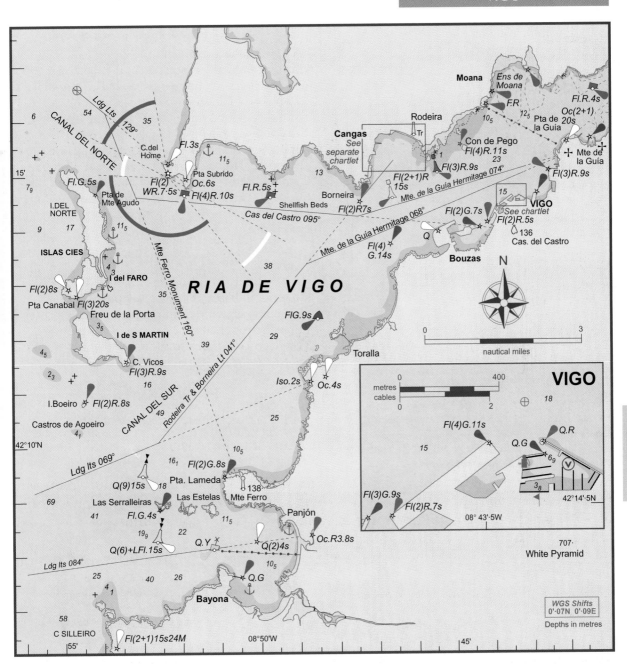

RIA DE VIGO

VIGO

BERTHING

Vigo has two yacht basins: the Real Club Nautico marina in the town centre and a smaller one in Bouzas, about a mile and half to the south-west. The latter, however, is not really suitable for visitors, having little space, few facilities and being a long way from the town centre. The Real Club Nautico marina, on the other hand, is ideal, offering all the facilities you could want and being literally on the doorstep of the attractive historical quarter of Vigo. Berthing in the club marina is to floating pontoons, with Mediterranean-style mooring lines picked up at the berths.

In the marina

MARINA FACILITIES

All facilities are available, including fuel, hauling out and mechanical services at the Real Club Nautico Vigo. Its impressive clubhouse, in the shape of a large steamer's superstructure, complete with a bridge-deck and funnel, offers all domestic amenities as well as a distinctive upmarket bar and restaurant. There is a large chandlery (Ronautica) just up the road from the harbour, opposite the Hotel Compostela in Calle Olloqui 6, which stocks a wide selection of clothes and fashionable items, as well as electronics, hardware and fittings.

Real Club Nautico Vigo

Vigo marina has more than 400 berths

TRANSPORT

Vigo's domestic airport has flights to Barcelona, Madrid, Bilbao and some other Spanish destinations (with most international connections actually from Barcelona, rather than Madrid). There are also trains to all major towns in Spain, as well as buses. Hire-cars are available in town.

PROVISIONING

Vigo has all the shops you would expect to find, so getting provisions presents no problems. A small supermarket lies just across the road

from the marina, up the street opposite the chandlery. Other shops are further uphill on the main shopping street.

A RUN ASHORE

Vigo is a noisy and fascinating town. It is regarded as the birth-place of the Movida, the cultural rebellion of younger Spaniards against the establishment. This was back in the 1980s, when young artists, writers, painters, sculptors, film-makers and theatre people kicked off a new subculture, which of course became associated with wild parties and night-life. Needless-to-say, most of these people are now establishment figures themselves, but the Movida certainly helped the new Spanish culture along in a big way.

Going further back, Vigo is also home to one of the oldest daily newspapers in Spain, *The Faro de Vigo*, which was first published in 1853 and is still going strong today. In those times, only a few thousand people lived in Vigo which, over the years, has had a particularly harsh history, beginning probably in Roman times, when the settlement was at the foot of the hill in the quarter we now know as Berbés (see page 246). In the 10th century, the town was invaded by the Moors, and only in 1170 could Fernando II reconquer it and begin settling anew. However, constant raids from norsemen and other pirates kept the people of Vigo on their toes, and in the 14th century nearly the entire population died of the plague.

When Carlos V gave the town some trading privileges in 1529 it finally started to bloom, particularly due to its trade with South America. This new affluence drew the attention of ever more freebooters and pirates, and in 1589 Francis Drake set fire to the town, burning it almost to the ground. In 1619, it was the turn of the Turks, who plundered the Ria de Vigo.

A sea battle in the Ria de Vigo in 1702 between a

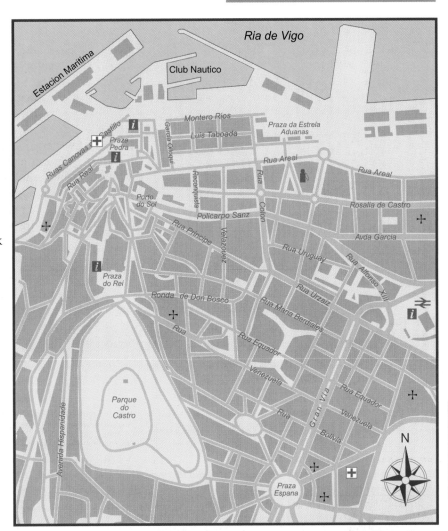

Food and drink are readily available close to the marina

Despite its turbulent history, Vigo is a thriving city with an industrious port

Spanish-French fleet of ships, which was mostly laden with gold from South America, and a British naval contingent ended with a British victory, after which they again plundered and burnt the long-

The marina is situated conveniently close to the old quarter

suffering town. Finally, Napoleon's troops added to the general destruction when they invaded Vigo in 1808, but they were soon forced back again by the inhabitants, who by this time had learned to defend themselves.

Considering this checkered history, it's miraculous that there is a large and wealthy town here at all, or even that a few historic buildings have survived. Indeed, remnants of ancient architecture can still be seen today in the old quarter of Berbés, close to the Real Club Nautico.

The main shopping road is the Calle Principe, a pedestrianised zone not far from the harbour, on the way to the Castillo del Grove. In keeping with the violent history of Vigo, this fortress has been destroyed many times in the past, so what you see today dates back only to the 17th century.

The Barrio de Berbés is the old fishermen's quarter near the harbour which, thanks to its small alleyways and numerous bars and restaurants, exudes a certain charm. It is also famous for its many shellfish stalls.

Vigo is a cosmopolitan city

Vigo's fishing port, the Barrio de Berbés, has cobbled streets and plenty of atmosphere

EATING OUT AND NIGHT-LIFE

Vigo is known for its very vibrant night-life which, up until about midnight, takes place predominantly in the bars of the Barrio de Berbés, after which the action shifts to the modern clubs and discotheques in Arenal, east of the Estacion Maritim.

For seafood lovers, the Rua de Pescaderia is the best place to go to in Vigo – it has more specialist fish and seafood restaurants than you would care to count. Why not try the largest fish restaurant in Spain, Marisqueira Bahia or, alternatively, La Espuela or the Casa Vella. Around the corner and straight uphill from the yacht club, in the Calle Laxe (also dubbed the Rua de Pulpo meaning 'road of octopus') are two good restaurants that are slightly less touristy – La Cazuela and Don Quijote.

Located on the hill, the restaurant El Castillo (Paseo de Rosalia del Castro, Tel: 986 42 11 11, closed Sunday evening and Monday, credit cards accepted) offers spectacular views but is not cheap. For good food at reasonable prices try La Oca (Purificacion Saavedra 8, Tel: 986 37 12 55, closed Saturday and Sunday, credit cards accepted), which is opposite the Mercado de Teis off Avenida de Garcia Barbon.

USEFUL INFORMATION

Tourist information: Tel: 986 43 05 77
Puerto Deportivo de RCN Vigo: Tel: 986 22 40 02
Club Nautico Liceo Maritimo de Bouzas:
Tel: 986 23 24 42; Fax: 986 23 99 55

BAYONA (BAIONA)

Bayona marine entrance – 42°07′.50N / 08°50′.30W

This is a favourite port with many cruising folk, although some think that it is somewhat over-rated. Whatever your thoughts, Bayona is undoubtedly a friendly place, sooner or later attracting almost all cruising yachts visiting the area. A popular holiday-resort for Spaniards, it is a small and interesting town, with plenty of convivial bars and restaurants filling the narrow back streets and a particularly pleasant Parador (luxury hotel) in the castle grounds overlooking the marina. Bayona has an active and helpful yacht club, which runs a marina, moorings, fuel services and limited boatyard facilities. On top of this, it hosts many racing events (some international), and its very comfortable club bar is also set within the castle.

The town is famous for the fact that, back in 1493, the badly battered caravel *Pinta* landed here, bringing the first news of the New World reaching southern Europe.

For those seeking the atmosphere or the facilities of a large and modern city, Vigo is just up the road by bus or taxi.

LOCATION/POSITION

Bayona is tucked away in a little bay just east of Cabo Silleiro in the entrance to the Ria de Vigo.

APPROACH AND ENTRANCE

Approach waypoint: 42°08′.25N / 08°50′.90W; 145°; 0.8M to marina entrance.

The approach and entry to Ria de Vigo is not difficult, either from north through the Canal del Norte to the east of the Islas Cíes, or through the Canal del Sur to the south of the islands. Coming from the north, local yachts pass through the Canal de la Porta between the peninsula of Monte Ferro and the innermost rock of La Estelas – Estelas de Tierra. Although this isn't really advisable without local knowledge, the only

Bayona is at the extreme south-west corner of the Ria de Vigo

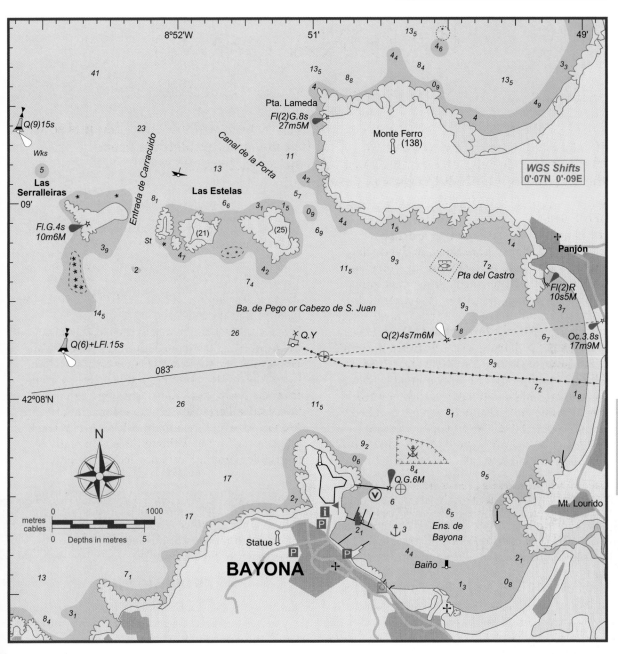

hazard is a 0.9m patch right in the middle of the channel so, by keeping closer to the island than the mainland, a safe passage can be made. However, it is undoubtedly wiser to pass west of Las Serralleiras, leaving all associated cardinal marks to port. Once inside the little bay of Bayona, you need to round the headland with the castle and the mole to reach the marina. The approach, as well as the relevant buoys and pier-head, are all lit, so entry at night presents no problems.

BERTHING

Yachts tie bow or stern to the floating pontoons with Mediterranean-style mooring ropes.

Alternatively, you can pick up one of the swing moorings, which also belong to the yacht club and for which a fee is charged. Although it is perfectly possible to anchor in the bay just off the pontoons, still keeping in the lee of the outer mole, cruising yachts are discouraged to do so by the yacht club staff and are often asked to move onto a mooring or the pontoons instead. If you do remain at anchor and therefore don't pay any fees, bear in mind that you will neither be allowed to use the club's facilities nor land with your dinghy on the pontoons; an attitude which seems understandable enough from the club's point of view, as their berthing charges are

The approach from the north is through the Canal de la Porta, between Punta Lameda and Las Estelas de Tierra

actually quite modest and they offer many amenities to their guests. During the height of the season, especially on weekends, the marina can get quite busy, so it's best to phone up in advance if you want be sure of getting a berth.

MARINA FACILITIES

The pontoons have water and electricity, while fuel (diesel and petrol) is also available in the marina. Ashore, the club has good showers, a launderette and a small office with helpful and friendly staff, who will receive and hold incoming mail for visiting yachts, although this must be pre-arranged. Upstairs on the terrace, with glorious views across the bay, a first-class bar is open to visitors from yachts staying in the harbour.

Repairs are possible, although here facilities are somewhat limited. There is no commercial boatyard as such, but the club has many employees who are able to carry out mechanical or boatbuilding repairs. Smaller yachts can be hauled out with a travelift and kept ashore. It is also safe to leave your boat here unattended for various periods of time, as the yacht club staff regularly patrol the pontoons to see that all is well.

The fuel berth on the south side of the central pier

The marina is run by the Monte Real Club de Yates

TRANSPORT

Bayona is a bit out of the way, literally being at the end of the road. Buses and taxis go to Vigo, where you can either hire a car (no hire-cars in Bayona) or get train or bus connections to all other parts of Spain.

PROVISIONING

There are a few small supermarkets in town, but if you seriously need to stock up on provisions, you would be better off going to Vigo. For normal, day-to-day shopping, however, Bayona is perfectly adequate. The shopping area is conveniently situated in the area closest to the yacht club.

A RUN ASHORE

The Parador Conde de Gondomar is situated in the castle of Monte Real on the promontory, which dates back to 1500 and was once the residence of the governor. A stroll through the gardens is rather pleasant and provides some lovely views of the sea and the islands.

When you walk through the town, take a look at the picturesque and historic buildings in the old quarter. The replica of the *Pinta*, which is

to the southerly and south-westerly winds of autumn, winter and spring. The harbour is quite shallow, especially further inside, with rocks scattered along the edges. The best depth of around five metres can be found just off the west pier. It might be possible to anchor inside, but space is very limited here because of all the fishing boat moorings.

When approaching this harbour, beware of rocks (especially to the north) and keep at least one mile off. You then enter from the south-west. The town is actually larger than it at first appears and has a certain, tired charm about it, but probably the best argument for going to A Guarda is to try out its numerous seafood restaurants.

The Rio Miño has a shallow and difficult approach and entrance, which should only be attempted in calm weather, on a rising tide and when there's no swell. Although the river is attractive, it is really only navigable for shoal draught yachts and multihulls. Once inside, there are several anchorages to choose from and you can venture quite far upriver.

Its entrance is south of the small islet, Insua Nova, which you should pass about half a mile off on the leading line on the Portuguese side. Behind the island, take a northerly course and proceed carefully up the unmarked, shifting channel towards a hotel on the Spanish side, before turning into the river. A large scale chart is needed for this trip, as well as good nerves and pilotage skills.

Chapter 5

moored on a special pontoon between the marina and the fish quay, is also well worth a visit. Due to its geographical position, there are no really interesting day trips from Bayona, save to the modern and bustling city of Vigo.

EATING OUT

Being a popular holiday resort, eating out is one of the strong points of Bayona. In the old quarter, you will find many dimly lit, romantic bars and restaurants serving Spanish food of all descriptions, ranging from lavish menus to interesting platters of tapas. If you feel like really treating yourself, book a table in the Parador's restaurant (Tel: 986 35 50 00, credit cards accepted). The restaurant El Tunel in the old quarter is a good bet for high quality seafood, as are O Moscon (Alferez Barreiro 2) and El Candil (San Juan 46).

OTHER HARBOURS AND ANCHORAGES NEARBY

A Guarda is a few miles south of Bayona, just north of the estuary of the Rio Miño, which forms the border between Spain and Portugal. A Guarda has a small harbour, which is not much more than a rocky bay protected by two moles and is open

Bayona's pleasant streets and squares are hidden behind its holiday waterfront

USEFUL INFORMATION

Real Club Nautico de Bayona Tel: 986 35 52 34
Emergency and police Tel: 091
Taxis Tel: 986 35 53 89

GLOSSARY

English	Spanish	English	Spanish	English	Spanish
Abeam	Por el través	Cold front	Frente frio	Firing range	Zona de tiro
Aft	Atrás	Commercial port	Puerto comercial	First aid	Primeros auxillos
Ahead	Avante	Companionway	Entrada cámera	Fishing harbour	Puerto de pesca
Air filter	Filtro a aire	Compass	Compás	Five	Cinco
Air mass	Massa de aire	Compass course	Rumbo de aguja	Flood	Flujo de marea
Airport	Aeropuerto	Compression	Compresión	Fog	Niebla
Anchor	Ancia	Cooling water	Agua refrigerado	Fog bank	Banco de niebla
Anchor chain	Cadena	Cruising chute	MPS	Forecast	Previsión
Anchor warp	Cabo	Current	Coriente	Foresail	Foque
Anchor winch	Molinete	Customs	Aduana	Forestay	Estay
Anchoring	Fondear	Customs office	Aduanas	Foul ground	Fondo sucio
Anticyclone	Anticiclón	Cutter stay	Estay de tringqueta	Four	Cuatro
Area	Zona	Cyclonic	Ciclonica	Fracture	Fractura
Ashore	A tierra	Dead reckoning	Estimación	Frequent	Frecuenta
Assistance	Asistencia	Deck	Cubierta	Fresh	Fresco
Astern	Atrás	Declare	Declarar	Front	Frente
Babystay	Babystay	Decrease	Disminución	Fuel filter	Filtro de combustible
Backing wind	Rolar el viento	Deep	Profundo	Fuel tank	Tanque de Combustil
Backstay	Estay de popa	Deepening	Ahondamiento	Fuse	Fusible
Bandage	Vendas	Degree	Grado	GPS	GPS
Bank	Banco	Dentist	Dentista	Gale	Temporal
Barometer	Barómetro	Depression	Depresión	Gale warning	Aviso de temporal
Battery	Baterías	Depth	Profundidad	Garage	Garage
Bearing	Maración	Deviation	Desvio	Gearbox	Transmisión
Beating	Ciñendo a rabier	Diesel	Gas-oil	Generator	Generador
Bilge	Sentina	Diesel engine	Motor a gas-oil	Genoa	Génova
Bilge keel	Quillas de balance	Dinghy	Chinchorro	Good	Bueno
Bilge pump	Bomba de achique	Direction	Direción	Gradient	Gradiente
Binoculars	Prismáticos	Dismasted	Desarbolar	Grease	Grasa
Block	Motón	Dispersing	Disipación	Grounded	Encallado
Boat	Barco	Distance	Distancia	Guest berths	Amarradero visitantes
Boathoist	Travelift	Distress	Pena	Gust, squall	Ráfaga
Boatyard	Astilleros	Distress flares	Bengalas	Hail	Granizo
Boom	Botavara	Disturbance	Perturbación	Halyard	Driza
Bow	Proa	Doctor	Médico	Handbearing	Compás de
Breakwater	Escolera	Downstream	Río abajo	compass	marcaciones
Breeze	Brisa	Dries	Descubierto	Harbour	Puerto
Bridgedeck	Bridgedeck	Drizzle	Lioviena	Harbour entrance	Entradas
Buoy	Boya	Drying port	Puerto secarse	Harbour guide	Guia del Puerto
Bureau de change	Cambio	Dynamo	Alternador	Harbour master	Capitán del puerto
Burns	Quemadura	EPIRB	Baliza	Harbourmaster's	Capitania
Bus	Autobús	East	Este	office	
Cabin	Cabina	Ebb	Marea menguante	Harness	Arnés de seguridad
Cable	Cadena	Echosounder	Sonda	Hazard	Peligro
Calm	Calma	Eight	Ocho	Haze	Calina
Can I moor	Puedo atracar	Electrical wiring	Circuito eléctrico	Head gasket	Junta de culata
here please	aqui por favor?	Emergency	Emergencias	Headache	Dolor de cabeza
Cap shrouds	Obenques altos	Engine mount	Bancada del motor	Heart attack	Ataque corazón
Capsize	Volcó	Engine oil	Aceite motor	Heavy	Abunante
Carburettor	Carburador	Engineer	Mecánico	Height	Alturas
Catwalk	Pasarela	Estimated position	Posición estimado	Helicopter	Helicóptero
Centre	Centro	Exhaust pipe	Tubos de escape	High	Alta presión
Centreboard	Orza	Exhaustion	Agotamiento	High water	Altamer
Certificate	Documentos	Extending	Extension	Holding tank	Tanque aguas negras
of registry	de matrícuia	Extensive	General	Hospital	Hospital
Chandlery	Efectos navales	Falling	Bajando	How far is it to..?	A que distancia esta
Channel	Canal	Fathom	Braza	How much	
Charging	Cargador	Feet	Pie	does that cost?	Cuanto cuesta ...?
Chart	Carta náutica	Fender	Defensa	Hull	Carena
Check in	Registrar	Ferry	Ferry	Illness	Enfermo
Chemist	Farmacia	Ferry terminal	Terminal marítimo	Inboard engine	Motor intraborda
Clouds	Nube	Fever	Fiebre	Increasing	Aumentar
Coastguard	Guarda costas	Filling	Relleno	Inflatable	Bote Hinchable
Cockpit	Bañera	Fin keel	Quilla de aleta	Injectors	Inyectores
Cold	Frio	Fire extinguisher	Extintor	Injury	Lesión

English	Spanish	English	Spanish	English	Spanish
Insurance	Seguro	Please take	Por favor cojan	Stanchion	Candelero
Insurance certificate	Certificado deseguro	my line	mi cabo	Starboard	Estribor
Is there	Hay bastante	Police	Policía	Starter	Arranque
enough water?	agua?	Poor	Mal	Staysail	Trinquete
Isobar	Isobara	Port	Babor	Steamer	Buque de vapor
Isolated	Aislado	Post office	Correos	Stern	Popa
Jackstay	Violín	Pratique	Prático	Stern gland	Bocina
Jetty	Malecón	Precipitation	Precipitación	Storm	Temporal
Jumper	Violín	Pressure	Presión	Storm jib	Tormentin
Keel	Quilla	Prohibited	Prohibido	Storm trysail	Vela de capa
Landing place	Embarcadero	Prohibited area	Zona de prohibida	Sun	Sol
Latitude	Latitud	Propeller	Hélice	Supermarket	Supermercado
Leading lights	Luz de enfilación	Propeller bracket	Arbotante	Superstructure	Superestructura
Leeway	Hacia sotavento	Pulpit	Púlpito	Surveyor	Inspector
Let go aft	Suelta los cabos	Pulse	Pulso	Swell	Mar de fondo
	del amarre de popa	Pushpit	Balcón de popa	Swing bridge	Puente giratorio
Let go forward	Suelta los cabos	RDF	Radio-gonió	Taxi	Taxis
	del amarre de proa	Radar	Radar	Ten	Diez
Lifeboat	Lancha de salvamento	Radio receiver	Receptor de radio	Tender	Anexo (bote)
Lifejacket	Chaleco salvavidas	Radio transmitter	Radio-transmisor	Three	Tres
Liferaft	Balsa salvavidas	Railing	Guardamencebos	Throttle	Acelerador
Lighthouse	Faro	Railway station	Estación de ferrocanil	Thunder	Tormenta
Lightning	Relampago	Rain	lluvia	Thunderstorm	Tronada
List of lights	Listude de Luces	Reaching	Viento a través	Tide	Marea
Local	Local	Register	Lista de tripulantes/rol	Tide tables	Anuario de mareas
Lock	Esclusa	Regulator	Regulador	Tiller	Caña
Log	Corredera	Rest	Reposo	Toe rail	Regala
Long keel	Quilla corrida	Ridge	Cresta	Topsides	Obra muerta
Longitude	Longitud	Rigging	Jarcia	Tow line	Cabo
Low	Baja presión	Rising	Subiendo	Trough	Seno
Low water	Bajamar	River outlet	Embocadura	True course	Rumbo
Lower shrouds	Obenques bajos	Rope	Cabo	Two	Duo
Main engine	Motor	Rough	Bravo o alborotado	Unconscious	Inconsciente
Mainsail	Mayor	Rudder	Pala de Timón	Underwater	Debajo del agua
Make fast aft	Asegurar los amarres	Running	Viento a favor	Underwater hull	Obra viva
	de popa	Running backstay	Burde volanto	Upstream	Río arriba
Make fast forward	Asegurar los amarres	Sail batten	Sables	Upwind	Vienta en contra
	de proa	Sailing	Navegar a velas	VHF	VHF
Man overboard	Hombre al agua	Sailmaker	Velero	Variable	Variable
Marina	Marina	Scattered	Difuso	Variation	Variación
Mast	Mast	Sea	Mar	Veering	Dextrogiro
Mast crane	Grúa	Seacock	Grifos de fondo	Village	Pueblo
Metre	Metro	Seasickness	Mareo	Warm front	Frente calido
Minute	Minuto	Seaway	Alta mar	Water pump	Bomba de agua
Mist	Nablina	Seaworthy	Marinero	Water tank	Tanque de agua
Mizzen	Mesana	Seven	Siete	Waypoint	Waypoint
Moderate	Moderado	Shackle	Grillete	Weather	Tiempo
Moderating	Medianente	Shaft	Eje	Weather report	Previsión
Mooring	Fondeadero	Sheet	Escota		meteorologica
Motoring	Navegar a motor	Ship	Buque	West	Oeste
Moving	Movimiento	Ship's log	Cuaderno de	Wheel	Rueda
Nautical almanac	Almanaque náutico		bitácora	Where can I get...?	Donde puedo
Nautical mile	Milla marina	Ship's papers	Documentos		conseguir ...?
Navigate	Navegar		del barco	Where can I moor?	Dondo puedo
Neap tide	Marea muerta	Shock	Choque		atracar?
Nine	Nueve	Shops	Tiendas	Winch	Winche
North	Norte	Shower	Aguacero	Wind	Viento
Occluded	Okklusie	Shrouds	Obenques	Working jib	Foque
One	Uno	Sinking	Hundiendo	Wound	Herida
Outboard engine	Motor fuera borda	Six	Seis	Wreck	Naufrago
Passport	Pasaporte	Sleep	Sueño	Yacht	Yate
Permitted	Permitido	Slight	Leicht	Yacht club	Club náutico
Petrol	Gasolina	Slip	Varadero	Yacht harbour	Puerto deportive
Petrol engine	Motor a gasolina	Slow	Lent		
Pier	Muelle	Snow	Nieve		
Pilot	Práctico	South	Sud, Sur		
Pilotage book	Derrotero	Spark plug	Bujia		
Please direct	Por favor,	Spinnaker	Spi		
me to ...?	digame a ...?	Spinnaker boom	Tangon		
		Spring tide	Marea viva		

INDEX

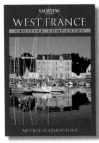
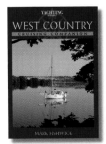
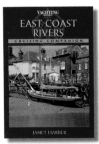
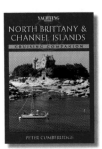